50 THINGS THEY DON'T WANT YOU TO KNOW

50

THINGS

THEY

DON'T WANT YOU TO

KNOW

JEROME HUDSON

BROADSIDE BOOKS
An Imprint of HarperCollins*Publishers*

HarperCollins books may be purchased for educational, business, or sales promotional use. For information, please email the Special Markets Department at SPsales@harpercollins.com.

Broadside Books™ and the Broadside logo are trademarks of HarperCollins Publishers.

FIRST EDITION

Library of Congress Cataloging-in-Publication Data has been applied for.

ISBN 978-0-06-293252-5 (pbk.)

19 20 21 22 23   LSC   10 9 8 7 6 5 4 3 2 1

To George and Annie

CONTENTS

CONTENTS

CONTENTS

50 THINGS THEY DON'T WANT YOU TO KNOW

INTRODUCTION

Americans are bombarded with an informational avalanche every day. News clips come whizzing at us at Mach speed on social media. Voters, hustling to stay informed, readily attempt to drink from this fire hose of headlines. The average person sees and shares one hundred articles a day.

The political left's response to our ever-expanding ocean of information has been to gin up hysteria over Russian bots and ring alarm bells about so-called *fake news*. The real problem, of course, is far deeper and much more complex: Establishment media, marketers, and advertisers have conditioned us to choose emotion over logic, feelings over facts. Why? Sensationalism sparks more clicks. Emotionalism ignites more shares. And in the process, sharing, liking, and commenting on emotion-laden content has morphed into a virtue-signaling shortcut to critical thought. This is a dangerous downward spiral that only serves the elites who profit from it.

The result of all this has been a devolution of the national dialogue on many of the most axial issues of our time.

50 Things They Don't Want You to Know rips back the curtain and, using data and facts, uncovers startling, hidden truths. This book bypasses the ideological guards keeping these facts from becoming mainstream: the professorial radicals running the intellectual meat grinders that are our country's college campuses; the legacy media machine that minimizes, misinforms, and flat-out ignores these truths; the lawmakers, who lecture and lie about these facts—all while the sphere of societal damage widens.

This book examines the true tragedy of our deeply mismanaged immigration system, from the rampant sexual assault of women and girls being trafficked, to the migrants being beaten and slaughtered while attempting to survive the dangerous 1,000-mile journey from Central America to the U.S. border. This system is condoned by craven politicians and applauded by mega-corporations that get filthy rich, thanks to a never-ending supply of cheap labor. It's this human misery the mainstream media and elitist politicians choose to ignore. The same media outlets incite massive moral panic over border enforcement tactics. The same politicians compare those enforcement methods to actions carried out by Nazi soldiers during the Holocaust. What these people fail to tell you is that more than half of the Border Patrol agents carrying out these so-called Gestapo tactics are Latino. President Obama deported more illegal immigrants than all presidents of the twentieth century combined. Separating family members who illegally crossed the U.S. border also expanded with Obama's blessing. He was the first U.S. president to place hundreds of unaccompanied children in steel cages. But the Democrats' fake rage, on display every day, exploded just two years ago. Indeed, how can a country run by President Trump, whom media and Hollywood elites smear as an anti-immigrant xenophobe, also lead the world year after year in accepting refugees? Both cannot be true.

This book blows up and disproves some of the political left's most treasured tenets. The truth is, you are far more likely to die from falling or influenza than you are in a mass shooting. The United States has dramatically decreased its carbon footprint for decades in the absence of a massive federal mandate or a grandiose U.N. decree. Border walls work, keeping people safe in countries around the world, and American taxpayers provide those walls to the tune of billions of dollars a year. Meanwhile, the rate of U.S. federal arrests related to immigration rose from 46 percent in 2006 to 58 percent in 2016.

This book questions how a culture constantly discussing how America systematically marginalizes and mercilessly oppresses black people, constantly *fails* to ask where that so-called oppression ends and self-sabotage begins. For years, woke white media elites have delighted in showcasing Black Lives Matter's message about the value of black life in America. But those same woke white liberals never ask how one in three black pregnancies ending in abortion fits into the equation. Woke white activists smear law enforcement after a white cop tragically kills a black boy but are silent when black killers send hundreds of black bodies to the morgue every day. Democratic politicians openly campaign for stricter gun laws but can't explain how those laws will put an end to the gang- and drug-related maimings carried out on a daily basis right under their noses.

This book confronts the fact that after decades of affirmative action, black and Hispanic students are more underrepresented at America's top colleges and universities than ever before. It also uncovers and celebrates the incredible educational triumphs blacks achieved in America fifty years before the civil rights movement began. The first public high school for black Americans graduated students who went to Harvard and other Ivy League institutions as early as 1903. That seven in ten blacks in America were literate just one generation removed from slavery leaves in tatters the political

left's gospel that blacks needed racial preferences to overcome inequality and racism and achieve any level of mainstream academic
or socioeconomic success.

Immigration, race, national defense, health care, education
policy—you name it—on each issue we see elites weaponizing emotion at the expense of facts and data that don't yield the politically
correct conclusions they desire. This must stop.

I didn't write this book because I figured out how to stop these
elites from selling us lies. I wrote this book because I remember
when I realized I was being lied to. It was about a year before
America elected its first black president. It was then that I had begun to pass through the three stages of political awakening that
so many young people go through. The first stage found me fever-
ishly quenching my thirst for knowledge and news. I read hundreds
of books about history, economics, philosophy, and culture from
authors on the ideological Left and Right. The news I read and
watched came mostly from the dinosaur, alphabet media. I trusted
America's mainstream press blindly. Like many people, I swallowed
whole their carefully crafted narratives without objection. But I
came to realize that the legacy media were telling me something
far less than the whole story. That was stage two. So, I sought and
started reading much more partisan media outlets. Then came the
third step of political awakening, when I realized that *my side* was
also not telling me the whole truth. I was bewildered and ambivalent, and the establishment media's affinity for reporting half-truths
forced me to find all kinds of new sources like Breitbart News. The
network, much like its late founder, Andrew Breitbart, reveled in
blowing up everybody's agenda—on the left and right.

But perhaps no moment of clarity presented itself more flagrantly about how wrong I was to trust the mainstream media than when veteran news broadcaster Charlie Rose of PBS interviewed legendary NBC News anchorman Tom Brokaw in October 2008. It was five days before voters went to the polls. The two men, sitting across from each other, openly admitted to each other how neither could honestly say they knew what Barack Obama's true beliefs were on the pivotal political issues facing the nation.

Rose: I don't know what Barack Obama's worldview is.
Brokaw: No, I don't, either.
Rose: I don't know how he really sees where China is.
Brokaw: We don't know a lot about Barack Obama and the universe of his thinking about foreign policy.
Rose: I don't really know. And do we know anything about the people who are advising him?
Brokaw: Yeah, it's an interesting question.
Rose: He is principally known through his autobiography and through very aspirational [*sic*] speeches.
Brokaw: Two of them! I don't know what books he's read.
Rose: What do we know about the heroes of Barack Obama?
Brokaw: There's a lot about him we don't know.

How could these two men—with eighty-four years of journalism between them—find themselves baffled and clueless about one of the most fascinating figures in the history of American politics? And Tom Brokaw had spent more than eighteen months covering Obama's historic candidacy. In a weird way, Brokaw and Rose grappling with their tragic failings as journalists gave me cover to confront my own vulnerabilities as my sphere of social influence had increased tenfold. I had made a psychological dislocation from the culturally driven, media-enforced expectations for how I should think about an array of issues. There were accepted orthodoxies that, if adhered to, promise the kind of social validation any twenty-year-old college student seeks. My campus looked then like what most college campuses look like today: islands of closed-mindedness where young people are not encouraged to think critically but are instead programmed to be skeptical of those who do. I chose, however, a harder path. As a black man in America, I rejected my expected role as victim. I rejected what felt increasingly like a carefully choreographed, phony political discourse. This made me a pariah. Friends affectionally referred to me as the "Conservative Kanye West." This was years before my hairline had begun to recede and more than a decade before the multi-platinum, Grammy-winning rapper-producer-couturier became a fiery cultural critic supporting the Second Amendment and lambasting the China trade deficit from the Trump Oval Office. I spent the next decade braving an increasingly contorted public conversation around race, gender, and politics. Being true to my deeply held beliefs, seeing and comporting myself as an individual first and foremost, left me often alienated and alone. Thankfully, my family and friends were mostly a healthy mix of supportive and affirming, if at times perplexed. Their confusion about my naked refusal to reduce myself to empty melodramatics on issues of race (which was and still is *en vogue*) challenged me in those solitary moments when I found myself agonizing over questions about my identity and my place in politics.

This book has been years in the making. While it is not an autobiographical work, it is shot through with my most unabashed beliefs. My criticism of the failure of twentieth-century public policies is fueled by the refusal of people in positions of power in the twenty-first century to acknowledge their tragic results. Andrew Breitbart famously said, "Politics is downstream from culture." In other words, popular culture drives politics, not the other way around.

As entertainment editor at Breitbart News, I spend most days holding a giant mirror over Hollywood, where self-righteous, often narcissistic, leftist celebrities fire off angry tweets and sappy Instagram sermons to their millions of followers, wailing on about how hard life in their privileged bubble is in the Trump era. These virtue-signaling elites, with their massive social influence, have one thing in common with their mainstream media counterparts—something that Andrew Breitbart warned about: contempt for the American people. Many of these Hollywood elites endorse a politics of victimhood for people who look like me, no matter how condescending that assumption is. They push harmful policies, donate massive amounts of money to morally corrupt politicians, and together demand you cut your carbon footprint while they fly around on private jets, purchase more homes than they could ever live in, and collect more cars than they'll live long enough to drive. These elites, from the awards stage to the campaign stump, preach down to average Americans on a daily basis.

This book confronts the beliefs that these elites hold dear, challenges the prevailing wisdom, and cuts through the fog of a censorious political correctness that's crippling our culture and shutting down serious debate. It provides people with answers and solutions to the issues shaping and influencing our shared political space. These fifty facts will spark millions of conversations that will begin to finally undo decades of damage from disinformation and liberal myth-making.

1

FROM 2012 TO 2016, MORE BLACK WOMEN IN NEW YORK CITY HAD ABORTIONS THAN GAVE BIRTH

Black babies represented 42 percent of all abortions in New York in 2013, though blacks are merely 25 percent of the population.[1] A report from the city Department of Health and Mental Hygiene shows that between 2012 and 2016, expectant black mothers terminated 136,426 pregnancies while only 118,127 gave birth to their babies.[2] Few statistical disparities illustrate the shrunken scope of African American life more than the staggering number of black pregnancies ended by abortion.

BLACK LIVE BIRTHS TOTAL IN NEW YORK CITY 2012–2016

Mother's Ethnic Group	2012	2013	2014	2015	2016
Live Births, Total	123,231	120,457	122,084	121,673	120,367
Puerto Rican	8,673	7,960	7,897	7,561	7,159
Other Hispanic	27,969	27,621	27,753	27,994	26,915
Asian and Pacific Islander	21,149	19,767	20,746	20,535	21,566
Non-Hispanic White	39,112	39,573	40,443	40,607	40,633
Non-Hispanic Black	24,758	24,108	23,680	23,116	22,465
Other or Unknown	1,570	1,428	1,565	1,860	1,629

Source: https://www1.nyc.gov/assets/doh/downloads/pdf/vs/2016sum.pdf

BLACK ABORTIONS TOTAL IN NEW YORK CITY 2012–2016

Ethnic Group					
Hispanic	22,917	21,555	20,371	18,139	16,718
Asian and Pacific Islander	4,493	4,615	4,547	4,012	3,490
Non-Hispanic white	9,704	9,422	9,401	9,652	9,139
Non-Hispanic black	31,328	29,007	27,367	25,515	23,209
Other	2,555	2,591	2,477	2,155	1,711

Source: https://www1.nyc.gov/assets/doh/downloads/pdf/vs/2016sum.pdf

Black women account for more than 36 percent of all abortions nationally.[3]

In Michigan, black women make up about 14 percent of the female population. They accounted for over 50 percent of all abortions reported in the state in 2017. In Mississippi, 72 percent of abortions are obtained by black women. In Washington, DC, the number is over 60 percent. In Georgia, it's 59.4 percent, and in Alabama it's a whopping 58.4 percent. These figures are no accident. According to a study released by Protecting Black Life, an outreach of Life Issues Institute, "79 percent of Planned Parenthood's surgical abortion facilities are strategically located within walking distance of African and or Hispanic communities."[4]

A total of 638,169 women ages 15–44 and from forty-nine reporting areas underwent abortions in 2015, as reported to the Centers for Disease Control and Prevention (CDC). Among the thirty areas that reported race and ethnicity data for that year—roughly 338,800 abortions—"Non-Hispanic white women and non-Hispanic black women accounted for the largest percentages of all abortions (36.9 percent and 36.0 percent, respectively), and Hispanic women and non-Hispanic women in the other race category accounted for smaller percentages (18.5 percent and 8.7 percent, respectively)."[5]

While the election of America's first black president precipitated an incessant debate around race and racism in the United States, largely missing from that discussion was the issue of racial disparities in abortion rates. Indeed, the loudest voices on the American left entered the 2010s ceaselessly spouting pseudoscientific drivel about how our deeply racist country systematically "otherizes" black people. This obsession with race has persisted and, ironically, came into full bloom in a twenty-first-century America that had thrust a black man with an African surname into the Oval Office. Despite this, there was a daily bludgeoning of left-wing activists and New York City news anchors lecturing America about why black lives matter. Equally intense acrimony was missing when it came to the oft-ignored news that thousands more black babies were being aborted each year than born alive. As author Jason Riley notes, it's not as if the American left, in its entirety, from its academic elites to its press corps and its judiciaries, hasn't spent decades decrying racial disparities for blacks when it comes to bank loans, or as if courts haven't litigated racial disparities in college admissions, or as if the media haven't promoted the fallacy of racial disparities in police shootings. After years of wall-to-wall coverage of city streets filling with protesters pleading about the value of black life, why was there a dearth of influential African Americans on TV or posted up in front of abortion clinics, speaking up for the black unborn?

This comes as no surprise if you know the eugenic origins of Planned Parenthood. Margaret Sanger, the woman who founded the organization that went on to become Planned Parenthood Federation of America, spent decades promoting the idea that "racial betterment" could be achieved by "stopping not only the reproduction of the unfit but upon stopping all reproduction when there are not economic means of providing proper care for those who are born in health." Former White House hopeful Ben Carson singled out Sanger for systematically targeting blacks and Latinos. He claimed in August 2015 that abortion had become the number-one cause of death for black Americans, and suggested that such an alarming reality was the long-intended result of Sanger's "Negro Program," which in the 1940s produced a pamphlet called "Better Health for 13,000,000," by which civic and religious leaders were encouraged to seduce other blacks into "the program of family planning for Negroes."[6]

Abortion rates decreased to historic lows in 2015. The decline represented a decades-long national downtrend. However, while the number of women having abortions steadily decreased, Planned Parenthood continued to perform the procedure at an increasingly higher clip. "Despite a nearly 20 percent decline in the number of abortions in the country between 2000 and 2011, the number of abortions Planned Parenthood performed during that time increased from 197,070 to 333,964, thereby more than doubling its share of the abortion market from 15 percent in 2000 to 32 percent in 2011, the latest year for which national data are available," a Heritage Foundation study found.[7] The debate over shutting off the tax-subsidy spigot to the nation's largest abortion provider has raged for decades. Defunding campaigns in Congress have intensified in recent years as Planned Parenthood has come under fire for one embarrassing scandal or another. In 2011, Planned Parenthood offices across the country welcomed people pretending to be a pimp and an underage girl. The undercover duo taped the organization's employees offering advice on how to obtain illegal abortions so the couple could get back into the sex trade as quickly as possible without running afoul of the law. The fallout from the videos going viral online created enough political pressure that, in February 2011, a vote to end federal funding of Planned Parenthood passed in the U.S. House of Representatives, which had a Democratic majority. The taxpayer funding, however, continued. Two months later, the Senate voted down Republican-backed measures to strip Planned Parenthood's federal funding.

A few years later, a string of videos released by the Center for Medical Progress saw several senior medical advisers for Planned Parenthood seemingly negotiating the price of selling aborted baby body parts to actors playing entrepreneurs from a biomedical startup. The videos sparked congressional investigations into illegal profiteering from the sales of aborted baby body parts. A United States Senate investigation concluded that Planned Parenthood's partners paid the abortion giant's affiliates for the aborted body parts "and then sold the fetal tissue to their respective customers at substantially higher prices than their documented costs."[8] The sale or purchase of human fetal tissue is a felony punishable by up to ten years in prison or a fine of up to $500,000. In December 2016, Senator Chuck Grassley (R-IA) referred Planned Parenthood to the FBI and the Justice Department for investigation and possible prosecution. A year later, the DOJ opened an investigation into Planned Parenthood's practices related to human fetal tissue.

Abortion became a primetime topic during the 2016 presidential election, and two scenes were front and center: Planned Parenthood employees cackling about providing cheap abortions to underage prostitutes and callously conversing about the market value for aborted baby tissue.

Despite its sordid history and a horde of humiliating headlines, Planned Parenthood remained a billion-dollar business, according to its annual reports. While closing some fifty facilities in 2017, the organization's revenues skyrocketed. Planned Parenthood fetched $1.46 billion from 2016 to 2017, an increase of more than $100 million from 2015 to 2016. While it saw slightly less taxpayer dollars, private donations were up nearly $90 million. The organization aborted fewer babies from 2016 to 2017 (321,384) compared with the previous year (328,348). But between 2017 and 2018, Planned Parenthood performed more abortions and brought in more money. The group performed 11,373 more abortions in 2017–2018 than in 2016–2017, and it also took in $1.67 billion in revenue, breaking the record set just a year prior. Between 2017 and 2018 it increased its tax funding by $20 million, taking in $563.8 million through Medicaid reimbursements and government family-planning grants. Private donations also jumped $98 million between 2017 and 2018, with $630.8 million coming from "private contributions and bequests."[9]

While aborting hundreds of thousands of babies every year, the group continued to argue in its annual reports that abortion accounts for just three percent of its services. The "3 percent" talking point, however, had long been debunked, even by left-leaning news outlets like *Slate*—whose senior editor called the figure the "most meaningless abortion statistic ever"—and the *Washington Post*.[10] The outlets note that Planned Parenthood inflates its total number of services by counting services rather than patients. For example, one patient coming through its doors for an abortion may also leave with a pack of pregnancy tests and a prescription for birth control. This one patient is counted as three separate services. "The 3 percent figure that Planned Parenthood uses is misleading, comparing abortion services to every other service that it provides," the *Washington Post* reported in 2015. That year the same paper published one positive article about abortion every twenty-four days. Mere months before Planned Parenthood produced data showing that it had aborted nearly a half-million babies, the organization's newly minted president, Leana Wen, admitted that abortion is Planned Parenthood's "core mission." The statement begs: How can a procedure at the "core" of the organization's "mission" represent just three percent of its services?

Decades after the birth-control pill became ubiquitous throughout society, abortion has taken on the role of another form of contraception, one that is appallingly pervasive to the point of infanticide. Under the ever-expanding definition of a "woman's right to choose," abortion even morphed into a talking point for prosperity. At an August 2018 Rise Up for Roe abortion rights event, Chelsea Clinton said that trillions in economic growth were created after *Roe v. Wade* "became the law of the land in January of 1973."[11]

Seemingly in acknowledgment that *Roe* might soon be overturned, states started passing laws that allowed abortions up until moments before birth. Vermont passed a law enshrining the "fundamental right" to an abortion, which could be decided eight months and thirty days into gestation. New York governor Andrew Cuomo signed a similar bill into law, allowing late-term third-trimester abortions, a procedure that 87 percent of the country believes should be outlawed. Babies who survive a botched abortion are denied their constitutional rights and are to be left to suffer and die—a vicious fate that puts New York on par with North Korea. The New York state assembly exploded in applause when the bill passed. One World Trade Center in New York City—the hallowed ground where Muslim extremists murdered thousands of Americans—was lit pink at Cuomo's request to celebrate his state's new abortion law.

Another abortion poll said that "pro-choice" Americans overwhelmingly oppose late-term abortion, with 68 percent of pro-choice Americans opposing abortion the day before a child is born, and 66 percent of pro-choice Americans strongly opposing abortion in the third trimester.[12] The American left, however, is hellbent on making abortions fashionable, from "Shout Your Abortion" campaigns to fifty-foot billboards urging women to be unapologetic about having an abortion to Planned Parenthood's chatbot, Roo, which teaches sexual health to teenagers. The harsh reality is that too many women are callously choosing to terminate unwanted pregnancies. There have been more than 60 million lives ended in the womb since the Supreme Court legalized abortion in all fifty states. But more Americans from all political leanings are starting to support additional restrictions on abortion. One survey showed 49 percent of millennials say they support a ban on abortions after twenty weeks. Three Republican women in Congress—two in the House and one in the Senate—introduced bills in January 2019 to eliminate taxpayer funding for Planned Parenthood. And a growing number of voters are souring on the idea that they must subsidize a procedure they abhor.

2

THE U.S. GOVERNMENT AWARDED IOO MILLION IN TAX DOLLARS FOR CONTRACTS TO THE ABORTED-BABY-TISSUE INDUSTRY

Scientists in the United States have used cells from fetal tissue for research since the 1920s. The Heritage Foundation notes that in 1988 President Ronald Reagan suspended the use of federal funds for research that used tissue from elective abortions. President Bill Clinton, however, lifted that moratorium in 1993.

According to the House Subcommittee on Healthcare, Benefits, and Administrative Rules, in 2018, the National Institutes of Health (NIH) is estimated to provide about $100 million in taxpayer funding for research grants that involve the use of fetal tissue.[1] This amount represents another tie that American taxpayers have to the abortion industry. In addition, biomedical procurement companies that purchase aborted fetal tissue for resale to researchers have conducted business with little oversight.

While supporters of the use of fetal tissue for research claim it has led to advancements such as the polio vaccine, the Heritage

Foundation observes that this assertion overlooks the difference between historic fetal cell lines—for which new abortions are not needed—and fresh fetal tissue from new elective abortions. Additionally, transplants of fetal tissue have not been successful in treating many disorders, including anemia, diabetes, and Parkinson's disease.

Ethical alternatives to fetal tissue from elective abortions include adult stem cells, placenta and umbilical cord tissue, amniotic fluid, and postmortem tissue. National pro-life leaders have urged the Department of Health and Human Services (HHS) to end its use of fetal tissue from elective abortions.

In August 2018, a CNSNews.com report revealed the Food and Drug Administration (FDA) had contracted with Advanced Bioscience Resources (ABR)—a biomedical procurement company that had already been referred for federal criminal investigation—to provide "fresh" aborted baby tissue to engineer humanized mice for drug experimentation.[2] A General Services Administration contract noted the FDA, an agency of HHS, paid ABR $15,900 for the fetal tissue. The report of the new contract came after several years of congressional investigations into the abortion industry's alleged complicit relationship with biomedical companies, such as ABR, that purchase the body parts of aborted babies.

In December 2016, at the conclusion of one of those investigations, Senate Judiciary Committee Chairman Chuck Grassley wrote a letter to then attorney general Loretta Lynch and then FBI director James Comey.[3] He was referring "the paid fetal tissue practices of the following organizations . . . to the FBI and the Department of Justice for investigation and potential prosecution," and named ABR as one of the organizations.

"I don't take lightly making a criminal referral," Grassley said in a statement at the time. "But, the seeming disregard for the law by these entities has been fueled by decades of utter failure by the Justice Department to enforce it. And, unless there is a renewed commitment by everyone involved against commercializing the trade in aborted fetal body parts for profit, then the problem is likely to continue." In September 2018, HHS canceled its contract with ABR, citing the concerns of pro-life leaders. Additionally, HHS launched an audit of its human fetal tissue acquisitions and said it would be continuing to review alternatives to the use of fetal tissue from elective abortions. Still, national pro-life leaders said canceling the contract with ABR is only a first step and does not adequately sever the relationship between American taxpayers and the abortion industry.

"Canceling a single contract and conducting a review is a small step forward, but overall is completely inadequate," said Marjorie Dannenfelser, president of the Susan B. Anthony List. "[HHS Secretary Alex] Azar should instead devote tax dollars to ethical alternatives that—unlike experimentation on fetal tissue—produce successful therapies for patients." Shaking whole government agencies out of a century-old contracting practice is no small feat. Francis S. Collins, MD, PhD, who served as director of the NIH under Obama, said following the controversy over the contract that human fetal tissue from elective abortions "will continue to be the mainstay" for federal research.[4] "There is strong evidence that scientific benefits can come from fetal tissue research, which can be done with an ethical framework," Collins contended. "There are certain areas where it's hard to imagine that we would know what we know without the access to fetal tissue." Collins downplayed the recent decision of HHS—which administers the NIH—to audit federal purchases of aborted fetal tissue. He said the audit is being done simply "to assure the skeptics about the value of fetal tissue research [and] that this is being done according to all the appropriate regulations, guidelines, and oversight."

Collins's comments came following the NIH's announcement—in keeping with the HHS announcement—that it would spend up to $20 million on alternatives to the use of fetal tissue from elective abortions for research.[5] The agency said that in the near future it would be seeking grant applications for the development of "models that closely mimic and can be used to faithfully model human embryonic development or other aspects of human biology, for example, the human immune system, that do not rely on the use of human fetal tissue obtained from elective abortions." However, in his comments to reporters, Collins said that even if alternatives are found, "you're going to have to compare it to the current standard, which is using fetal tissue."

Collins provided his comments just as a House Oversight subcommittee was holding what turned out to be a highly combative hearing to explore alternatives to the use of fetal tissue for research. Scientists at the hearing offered views in total opposition to those of Collins. Tara Sander Lee of the Charlotte Lozier Institute testified that human fetal tissue was never needed for research because of viable alternatives such as adult stem cells. "We do not need fetal body parts from aborted babies to achieve future scientific and medical advancements," Lee said in her prepared testimony.[6] "Very little research is being done that currently relies on abortion-derived fetal tissues.

"After over 100 years of research, no therapies have been discovered or developed that require aborted fetal tissue," she continued. "History has shown us that we never needed fetal tissue." Cell and developmental biologist David Prentice testified, "There is no scientific necessity for the continued taxpayer funding of fresh fetal tissue, organs, and body parts from induced abortion.[7]

"Ample scientific alternatives exist, and modern alternatives have overtaken any need for fresh fetal tissue," he continued. "Moreover, the practice of using fetal tissue from induced abortion raises significant ethical problems, not least of which is the nebulous interpretation of the term 'valuable consideration' or compensation for expenses in the harvest and processing of fetal organs and tissues."

The abortion industry, however, has thrived on this continued source of taxpayer funding. Collins's comments—obviously out of step with Sander Lee and Prentice—irked pro-life leaders and drew strong reactions. "Dr. Francis Collins seems to have forgotten that he no longer works for President Obama and is now working for a pro-life president," Family Research Council President Tony Perkins asserted. "His advocacy for using aborted baby parts in research is more reflective of the previous administration rather than the Trump administration, which has consistently advanced the sanctity of human life."

Dannenfelser called for the Trump HHS to "correct" Collins for his statements that are "out of step" with the pro-life Trump administration and the base of the Republican Party. "Francis Collins's remarks to *Science* magazine this week put him at odds with HHS and the whole Trump administration in the audit process and begs the question of whether anything can truly change while he's in charge at NIH," she said. Kristan Hawkins, president of Students for Life of America, called upon the Trump administration to replace Collins in light of his "continued support of inhumane fetal tissue research."

"We should no longer allow abortion vendors to profit from selling the body parts of infants who did not survive a visit to Planned Parenthood," she said. "A civil society does not traffic in human remains."

3

BLACK AND HISPANIC STUDENTS ARE MORE UNDERREPRESENTED AT AMERICA'S TOP COLLEGES AND UNIVERSITIES THAN BEFORE AFFIRMATIVE ACTION

Faced with the ugly reality that minorities were being barred from admission to colleges because of the color of their skin, civic leaders cooked up a policy that ensured their acceptance based on the color of their skin. Decades later, affirmative action has failed. Schools factoring race and ethnicity into their decision to accept a college-aspiring minority student has hurt more than it has helped.

"Even after decades of affirmative action, black and Hispanic students are more underrepresented at the nation's top colleges and universities than they were thirty-five years ago," a 2017 *New York Times* analysis said.[1] "The share of black freshmen at elite schools is virtually unchanged since 1980. Black students are just 6 percent of freshmen but 15 percent of college-age Americans."

Affirmative action, first introduced by President Kennedy and continually advanced through a slew of Supreme Court rulings and a litany of legal opinions, intended to boost the enrollment of applicants from non-white households who had been hindered by unrelenting racial adversity.

Of course, there was a point when those numbers were zero. In the U.S. Supreme Court's 1896 decision in *Plessy v. Ferguson*, segregated facilities for blacks and whites were deemed constitutional as long as they were equal. The country quietly struggled for fifty years with the dubious, if not devious, rationale that separating black pupils from their white peers established anything close to equal. It took Supreme Court Chief Justice Earl Warren's decree in the 1954 *Brown v. Board of Education* decision to determine that "separate, but equal" was "inherently unequal" because a segregated education "generates a feeling of inferiority."[2] Warren, however, was only half right. Integration in our schools was not necessary because a black child's ability to learn was not predicated on his sitting next to a white student. (Dunbar High School, among the country's first black public schools, in Washington, DC, outscored two out of three white high schools in the city as early as 1899.) No, integrated schools reflect the same sublime democratic ideals held by any integrated society and the idea was certainly a necessary step in repairing our frayed union.

Ending segregation in America was a hard, long-fought achievement. But a Pandora's box of reforms followed Kennedy's executive order, which led to affirmative action, forced-busing laws, and school assignment policies—all of which had catastrophic results. Busing ultimately left many school districts more segregated than ever. "White flight" saw large numbers of white families de facto segregating their children, either by sending them to private schools or moving to suburban neighborhoods. Underclass kids, both black and white, were left to languish in shoddy inner-city schools. Hordes of unruly neighborhood pupils populated the halls where high-quality education had once flourished.

A large part of the logic behind government-forced integration, as Justice Warren's opinion suggested, made majority-black classrooms synonymous with "inferior." But at a time when most blacks had every reason to feel inferior to whites, many performed to the contrary. At the turn of the century, former slaves showed a Herculean hunger to learn how to read and write. In just a few decades after gaining their freedom, black literacy rates skyrocketed from around 20 percent to roughly 70 percent.[3] This occurred in the era of Jim Crow, the Ku Klux Klan's terrorism, lynchings, and horrifying racial strife for black Americans. Scholar and Stanford Fellow Thomas Sowell has long observed the successes of Dunbar, which was founded in 1870 as the Preparatory High School for Negro Youth and later known as the M Street School.

Some students at the M Street School began going to some of the leading colleges in the country in the late nineteenth century. The first of its graduates to go to Harvard did so in 1903. Over the years from 1892 to 1954, thirty-four of the graduates from the M Street School and Dunbar went on to Amherst.

Of these, 74 percent graduated from Amherst

and **28** percent of these graduates were **Phi Beta Kappas. Other graduates from M Street High School and Dunbar became Phi Beta Kappas at Harvard, Yale, Dartmouth and other elite institutions.**

Graduates of this same high school pioneered as the first black in many places. These included the first black man to graduate from Annapolis, the first black woman to receive a PhD from an American institution, the first black federal judge, the first black general, the first black Cabinet member and, among other notables, a doctor who became internationally renowned for his pioneering work in developing the use of blood plasma.

"When Chief Justice Earl Warren declared in the landmark 1954 case of *Brown v. Board of Education* that racially separate schools were 'inherently unequal,' Dunbar High School was a living refutation of that assumption," Sowell wrote.[4] "And it was within walking distance of the Supreme Court" which, ironically, had "essentially declared its existence impossible."

Fast forward a few decades to a landscape where underperforming public schools routinely failed to prepare black and Hispanic students for the rigorous challenges awaiting them in many of the college classrooms they enter. Hundreds of thousands, and perhaps millions, of non-white students were welcomed to top schools that placed more weight on the hue of their skin than their academic merit. This phenomenon, played out over the course of many years, saw students being "mismatched" or accepted into schools for which they were not prepared to compete with peers who were more qualified.

Indeed, *Mismatch* was the title of a 2012 bestseller by Richard Sander and Stuart Taylor Jr. Taylor contends that in an effort to fulfill the misguided goal of producing racial parity on college campuses, "selective institutions use very large racial preferences to bring in thousands of underqualified black students without telling them that they are not close to being academically competitive with most of their classmates.

"These supposed beneficiaries of racial preferences in many cases cannot keep up with the pace of instruction; get bad grades for the first time in their lives; flee from challenging to soft, easy courses that brand them as weak students in the eyes of classmates and employers; learn less than they would if they were at colleges for which they were well qualified; abandon aspirations to become scientists, physicians, engineers, or scholars; become discouraged and lose intellectual self-confidence; self-segregate with other academically overmatched black students; and, in some cases, bitterly complain that they are being discriminated against, when the problem is precisely the opposite," [5] Taylor writes.

A remarkable amount of energy has been dedicated to trying to understand and fix the problem racial preferences were supposed to solve. In trying and failing to re-create a racial microcosm of America writ large on our campuses, scores of scholarly studies and celebrated editorials have blamed an array of obstacles, from poverty to racism and discrimination. But far too little time and energy is spent focusing on why black and Hispanic students are so ill prepared to perform at elite schools, despite the wealth of evidence piling up with each passing year.

The *New York Times* analysis, for instance, was extensive and cited enrollment trends from 1980 to 2015 from 100 schools ranging from public flagship universities to the Ivy League. The paper notes that "blacks and Hispanics have gained ground at less selective colleges and universities but not at the highly selective institutions" and that while "affirmative action increases the numbers of black and Hispanic students at many colleges and universities . . .[b]lack students make up 9 percent of the freshmen at Ivy League schools but 15 percent of college-age Americans, roughly the same gap as in 1980."

The *New York Times* cites "experts" who say the gap between black and Hispanic enrollment versus the much higher white and Asian acceptance rate is the fault of "equity issues that begin earlier" on for minorities. "Elementary and secondary schools with large numbers of black and Hispanic students are less likely to have experienced teachers, advanced courses, high-quality instructional materials and adequate facilities, according to the United States Department of Education's Office for Civil Rights," the *New York Times* argues.

"There's such a distinct disadvantage to begin with," David Hawkins, an executive director at the National Association for College Admission Counseling, told the paper. "A cascading set of obstacles all seem to contribute to a diminished representation of minority students in highly selective colleges."

Leave it to the *New York Times* to fail to mention the most obvious "distinct disadvantage" handicapping minority students, particularly blacks: a fractured family setting.

The line of white and black liberal academics, social scientists, and lawmakers who have either ignored or downplayed the role out-of-wedlock childrearing plays in black academic underperformance could stretch from here to the moon and back. Progressives have long recoiled from having the difficult and uncomfortable conversation about how forty years of racial preferences have failed to fill the hole left by the marred state of the black family. There has been a painfully precipitous moral decline in America since the 1960s. Consequently, no subgroup has been impacted more by that decade's fling with loosened morals and a widened welfare state than the black family. In the decades since, the notion of family has changed dramatically. Marriages have been declining. Divorce rates exploded. Crime and illegitimacy flourish. But the liberal elite apparently considers all these calamities a series of social non sequiturs.

In his 1965 report, "The Negro Family: The Case for National Action," future senator Daniel Patrick Moynihan expressed alarm that women headed approximately a quarter of black households.[6] Today that number has risen sharply to 70 percent. Inside these black homes, fathers are too often absent or present only part-time. Children in these homes spend significantly more hours watching television, playing video games, and staring at their smartphones than do whites, Northwestern University researchers found. That translates to less time studying, reading, and doing homework. "In the past decade, the gap between minority and white youth's daily media use has doubled for blacks and quadrupled for Hispanics," said Northwestern professor Ellen Wartella, who co-authored the paper.[7] Called "Stark Differences in Media Use Between Minority, White Youth," Wartella's study was the first national project to focus exclusively on children's media use by race and ethnicity. There's an economic disadvantage that is equally detrimental. We all know that two incomes are better than one and that children are less likely to fall into poverty when they see the unwavering commitment of their mothers and fathers to work. These children struggle to wade the often rough waters of education with one hand tied behind their back. Fewer financial resources make tutoring almost impossible. Often trapped in poor neighborhoods and forced to attend poorly run schools, the prospects for these children are bleak. But despite these glaring facts, a lot of smart people with large platforms and tons of influence continue to ignore how the social maladies poor students face have a destructive effect on their education. Those same smart people, instead, argue that, as Justice Warren did, minority students need only sit in class next to white students to succeed. As the thinking goes, according to writer Coleman Hughes, "Blacks are more likely to be poorer than whites; therefore, we must integrate schools so that black kids can reap the benefits of going to school with kids from wealthier families. But this argument only works in a world where 'black' is a synonym for 'poor.' To the contrary, most black Americans aren't poor, and most poor Americans aren't black. The same is true of Hispanics. If poverty is the real issue, then why not talk about it directly, instead of using race as a proxy?"[8]

The latest National Assessment of Educational Progress (NAEP) data, which analyzes reading and math comprehension scores for America's fourth- and eighth-grade students, continues to show a wide achievement gap between white and minority students.[9] Even when affluence among black households is factored in, lagging academic performance persists at alarming rates. As Brookings scholars Richard Reeves and Dimitrios Halikias wrote in 2017, "It is unlikely that the racial achievement gap can be explained away by class differences across race."[10]

"Income alone does not explain the racial scoring gap," The *Journal of Blacks in Higher Education* reported in 2002.[11] "Whites from families with incomes below $10,000 had a mean SAT score that was 46 points higher than blacks whose families had incomes of between $80,000 and $100,000," the pro-affirmative-action article noted. "Blacks from families with incomes of more than $100,000 had a mean SAT score that was 142 points below the mean score for whites from families at the same income level."

Of course, minority students don't suffer from an innate inability to learn, perform, and test competitively compared to whites. In 2016, a chain of public charter schools that overwhelmingly serves poor black and Latino students, Success Academy in New York City, outperformed state averages on standardized tests. Chicago's Urban Prep Academy has spent years sending all its mostly minority graduates to four-year colleges and universities. Louisiana, a state routinely ranked near the bottom for education in the country, is home to T. M. Landry College Prep, a small private school sending 100 percent of its mostly minority graduates to universities around the country. The Jalen Rose Leadership Academy in Detroit, named after the Hall of Fame former basketball star and NBA TV analyst, also boasts a 100 percent college acceptance rate for its largely non-white pupils. These are but a few examples that bust the myth that minority students can't compete on a high level, study hard, test well, graduate, and go on to perform proficiently at four-year schools.

I'm certainly not the first critic to contend that shattered families and a decaying culture—not economics—is the anvil holding down those black Americans trying to scratch and claw their way into the mainstream. But what about that second and third generation of blacks born two and three decades after race was first used to raise the rate of minority students sent to college? For black beneficiaries, affirmative action makes them "something of a separate species for whom normal standards and values do not automatically apply," Stanford Fellow and author Shelby Steele observes.[12] The policy of racial preferences imbues demoralization and what Steele calls "implied self-doubt" for the black college student. The result is a tragic one: chronic dropout rates for mismatched students. When their place on campus is unearned and merely conferred on to them by way of some form of preferential treatment, a revolving door of failure is usually the result. This cuts across racial and economic lines. So-called legacy students, often white undergraduates who gain admittance to elite universities because their parents are alumni (or wrote a big check to the school), drop out at a similarly alarming rate as their black and Hispanic counterparts, as noted by University of San Diego law professor and U.S. Civil Rights Commissioner Gail Heriot.

Diversity and equality are desired in our society, but the glaring double standard of affirmative action proves how progressive policies promote problems. Democrat-induced discrimination, especially in the Deep South, disfigured our republic. Until the civil rights era, a moral disconnect ruled the day. But the onslaught of racial preferences failed in a noble effort to reconcile America's egalitarian idealism and its discriminatory reality. Affirmative action and all its tentacles—quotas, minority-based point systems, group-based pref-erences, loosened testing and admissions standards—are an affront to our most sacred democratic principle: that all men are equal in the eyes of the law. For too long, our laws and court rulings have contorted this value. And the belief that career opportunities and educational successes should be the reward of individuals' merit and unwavering work ethic has eroded over time.

Tragically—for blacks, women, and other "oppressed" minorities—affirmative action indirectly communicated a demoralizing message of inferiority that reinforces the same separatism it set out to solve. It is pure illogic to think that you can fight fire with fire and get anything but scorched earth. Reverse discrimination cannot cure discrimination. Or as Chief Supreme Court Justice John Roberts put it: "The way to stop discrimination on the basis of race is to stop discriminating on the basis of race."

Today, two mutually exclusive Americas cannot exist. We are either an affirmative action America, where some among us are held to a lower standard based on skin color, or we are all equal under the law, free to fail or succeed no matter what group we happen to be born into. Both cannot be true.

4

AMERICA'S MOST DEADLY AND DANGEROUS CITIES ARE RUN BY DEMOCRATS

There is a miasma of human misery, where violent criminality suffocates whole communities in cities governed for decades under Democratic Party rule. Baltimore, Chicago, and Houston accounted for more than half the spike in the 8 percent rise in the U.S. murder rate in 2016. Houston, which hasn't elected a Republican mayor in nearly four decades, saw 269 murders in 2017.[1] The tally ticked up by ten a year later. In Baltimore, of the 343 people murdered in 2017, more than 90 percent were black males, and nearly 65 percent were between the ages of 18 and 34.[2] The year 2018 was the fourth year in a row where the city's murder rate reached the dreadful 300 mark.[3] The growing murder rate boosted Baltimore to number three on the list of America's most dangerous cities, with 300 murders among its 618,385 residents. The city also has the fifth highest murder rate in the country. With its 345 slayings in 2017, the city earned an odious murder rate of 56 per 100,000 people.

Though crime dropped in most major metropolitan areas in 2017, homicides increased in Philadelphia—also known as Killadelphia—where the last Republican mayor was born during the Rutherford B. Hayes administration. Philadelphia's first homicide of 2019 took place just twelve minutes after the clock struck midnight on New Year's Day. A bullet fatally struck a man in the head. In 2018, Philadelphia saw 351 homicides, its highest number since 2007, according to the Philadelphia Police Department's website.[4] In 2018, bloodshed in the City of Brotherly Love resulted in more homicides than in New York City, which recorded 287 killings that year—and has five times the population.

In Detroit, of 312 homicide victims in 2016, 279 were African American; 246 of those black victims—88 percent—were male,

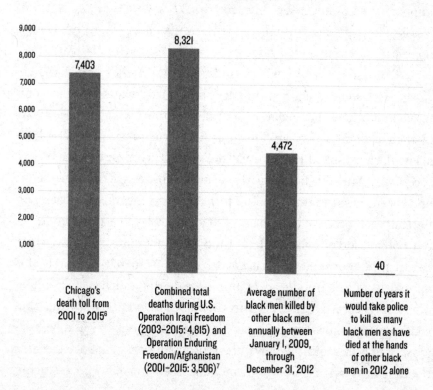

DEATH BY NUMBERS

7,403	8,321	4,472	40
Chicago's death toll from 2001 to 2015[6]	Combined total deaths during U.S. Operation Iraqi Freedom (2003–2015: 4,815) and Operation Enduring Freedom/Afghanistan (2001–2015: 3,506)[7]	Average number of black men killed by other black men annually between January 1, 2009, through December 31, 2012	Number of years it would take police to kill as many black men as have died at the hands of other black men in 2012 alone

according to figures from the Wayne County Medical Examiner's Office.[5]

Sure, Chicago is not exceptionally afflicted by violent crime compared to other large cities controlled by Democratic politicians. St. Louis and New Orleans are also deeply blue cities annually ravaged by a similar war-zone level of violence in their most segregated communities. But the culture-deep fatalism that drives the suffering in cities like Chicago is astounding, even when you remove social factors like poverty. Poor communities are no novelty for hundreds of cities across America, but you'd be hard-pressed to duplicate the sort of social nightmare that plays out every week in Chicago. Are impoverished young black men in New York City and Los Angeles less prone to violence than their counterparts in Chicago? There's no reason to think so.

Of course, poverty, prison, and gang life do not define the essence of existence for the millions of black Americans who have embraced ambition and social achievement and are enjoying the fruits of mainstream American life. It is also true that we blacks have spent decades avoiding turning the spotlight on ourselves. We've too often blamed what's clearly a mass self-destruction on racism and faceless societal woes. We're overwhelmingly responsible for putting each other in body bags—sending each other to the morgue, our bodies riddled with bullets—and we're not supposed to ask how is racism responsible for that havoc? Aside from self-sabotage, this annual litany of mindless maimings is on us and has one salient political feature: Democrats run the governments in the cities that routinely fail to protect their people. In the barbershops and hair salons, the pulpits and the pews, the truth about this violence remains the best-kept secret in our culture. The questions have been staring us in the face for decades. How many of black America's wounds are self-inflicted? Have those who cling to the core pillars of personal responsibility and self-reliance not created for their families a flourishing that will fulfill future generations? What have decades of punditry, political grandstanding, and civil rights posturing done to lift legions of poor people out of their plight? Propped-up performance artists praised for their activism have spurred their social influence and lined their pockets, sure. But these performers have also proved utterly impotent and useless in fixing the cultural cancer that continues to vex black America.

Those of us asking the hard questions had believed that along with a black president would come at least tough talk about the serious social maladies marring our communities. After all, he was from Chicago. And it was no secret that Democrat-run inner cities had long devolved into black-on-black killing fields just as the explosion of black social and economic dynamism began to take form. And Barack Obama, an Ivy League–educated community organizer, sprang out of that dynamism. Instead, the sad result of his presidency was a twisted irony. At a time when 95 percent of the thousands of black bodies sent to morgues every year were sent there by black killers, the ascendant wisdom from far-left voices, including the president's, pegged police as the prevailing problem plaguing black people. While it was painfully obvious to so many that Democratic politicians had spent decades turning black communities into islands of death, dogged black elites and many white media members—like those who make up the majority of the *New York Times*' editorial board—were anointing sanctimonious grievance groups like Black Lives Matter as moral arbiters of truth.

When black men slaughter one another with terrifying regularity,

American media elites and celebrity Democratic TV pundits repeatedly beat the public over the head with the vicious lie that black
America was under an unrelenting siege by trigger-happy white
cops. Never mind that "white police officers killing unarmed black
men represented less than 4 percent of fatal police shootings" in 2015,
according to a *Washington Post* study.[8] Black Lives Matter, whose
members marched and chanted such morally depraved anti-police
drivel as "pigs in a blanket, fry them like bacon," were held up as
civil rights heroes. The group chanted for "dead cops" and agitated
for fewer police officers, especially in minority neighborhoods. They
also called for a "national policy specifically aimed at redressing
the systemic pattern of anti-black law enforcement violence in the
United States."[9] Facts were replaced with trendy catchphrases and
feel-good virtual signaling by Hollywood stars and celebrity news-
casters. The truth had become far less interesting.

Tragic deaths of young black men at the hands of police pur-
portedly pushed some law enforcement to pull back for fear of out-
sized public scrutiny. This phenomenon was dubbed the Ferguson
Effect in the wake of Michael Brown's death at the hands of Officer
Darren Wilson in 2014. The Eric Holder–headed Justice Department
concluded that killing was justifiable but the incident nevertheless
spawned the senseless mantra of "Hands up! Don't Shoot!" The ensuing police pullback apparently accounted for inexplicable rises
and declines in police action and subsequent violence in many major American cities. One such spike in violence and drop in arrests
occurred in Chicago after officials there released dashcam video
showing an officer shooting a seventeen-year-old black boy sixteen
times.

"There have been 175 homicides and approximately 675 nonfatal shooting incidents from December 1 through March 31, according to our analysis of city data," wrote Rob Arthur and Jeff Asher in an article for statistics news outlet FiveThirtyEight.[10] "The 69 percent drop in the nonfatal shooting arrest rate and the 48 percent drop in the homicide arrest rate since the video's release also cannot be explained by temperature or bad luck.

"Even though crime statistics can see a good amount of variation from year to year and from month to month, this spike in gun violence is statistically significant, and the falling arrest numbers suggest real changes in the process of policing in Chicago since the video's release," Arthur and Asher wrote. "The spike in murders began just after the release of dash-cam video showing the victim walking away from police before being riddled with bullets. The revelation, which contradicted official accounts, sparked public outrage, particularly among African-Americans."

Again, how does historical and systemic racism explain why hordes of young black men poured into the streets, brutalizing other black men at alarmingly high rates after footage of a white cop slaying a black teen went viral? If ever there were cause for a Come-to-Jesus moment between police and communities of color, it should have been triggered by that miscarriage of justice. Instead, the exact opposite happened. The black-on-black carnage increased, often in the same communities from which Black Lives Matter wanted to toss police.

FBI data analyzed by the Washington-based Violence Policy Center concluded that there were 7,014 black homicide victims in the United States in 2015.[11] Most of their killers were black. That is more than twice as many black Americans killed by other blacks in one year than were lynched in America from 1882 to 1968, according to data from the Tuskegee Institute.

We have for far too long become inured to the ceaseless slaughter in Democrat-run cities. Fifty years ago, it was white, hood-clad killers who stalked black neighborhoods looking for blood. Today, those killers look like us. Who needs the Ku Klux Klan when we are proving a much more proficient exterminator of our own people?

5

THE OBAMA ADMINISTRATION KNEW THAT UP TO TWO-THIRDS OF AMERICANS MIGHT NOT BE ABLE TO KEEP THEIR HEALTH CARE PLANS UNDER OBAMACARE

President Barack Obama failed to uphold two key promises that would come with the passage of the Affordable Care Act (ACA, also called Obamacare). Obama said: (1) "If you like your health care plan, you can keep it," and (2) The Affordable Care Act will reduce premiums by "as much as $2,500 per family."

Many Americans can attest that, contrary to Obama's claim, health insurance premiums have continued to skyrocket under Obamacare.

A 2017 study commissioned by the Department of Health and Human Services (HHS) found that premiums have more than doubled since 2013, the year that Obamacare officially went into effect.[1]

The HHS found that individual insurance premiums doubled from $2,784 in 2013 to $5,712 on the federal Obamacare exchange in 2017. This amounts to an increase of $2,928, or a 105 percent increase in insurance premiums.

AVERAGE MONTHLY PREMIUMS IN THE INDIVIDUAL MARKET FOR HEALTHCARE.GOV STATES

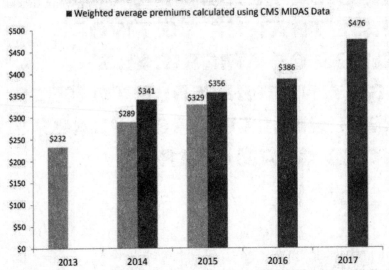

■ Premiums calculated using MLR data
■ Weighted average premiums calculated using CMS MIDAS Data

Note: Earned premiums are equal to premium revenue collected by issuers. Individual market calculations are based on Medical Loss Ratio (MLR) data from 2013 to 2015. These data represent the entire individual market – including on- and off-exchange plans, as well as ACA-compliant and non-ACA-compliant plans. Healthcare.gov calculations are based on enrollee plan selections during the annual Open Enrollment Periods from 2014 to 2017. These data do not take into account premium tax credits.

Source: ASPE analysis of CMS MLR data, 2013–2015, and CMS MIDAS data, 2014–2017

Three states—Alaska, Alabama, and Oklahoma—saw premiums double from 2013 to 2017.

Obama promised during the 2008 presidential election that he would cut the cost of a family's health insurance premiums by $2,500 per year. "I will sign a universal health care bill into law by the end of my first term as president that will cover every American and cut the cost of a typical family's premium by up to $2,500 a year," Obama said during a speech in 2007.[2]

The HHS study shows that the opposite happened—Obamacare doubled rather than cutting premiums by $2,500 per year. Fact-checking organization PolitiFact reached out to David Cutler, an Obama advisor who had calculated the $2,500 figure, about Obama's promise to cut health insurance premiums. In response to PolitiFact, Cutler backtracked and suggested that the $2,500 figure also includes out-of-pocket costs, employer-provided insurance costs, and taxes to pay for public insurance programs. Cutler said that Obama made "occasional misstatements" regarding the cost of premiums. PolitiFact rated Obama's campaign pledge to cut health insurance premiums by $2,500 per family as a "promise broken."[3]

Obama also claimed over thirty-seven times that "If you like your health care plan, you can keep it." PolitiFact rated this claim their 2013 "Lie of the Year."[4]

To reassure reluctant Americans about the Affordable Care Act, then–Health and Human Services (HHS) Secretary Kathleen Sebelius announced a rule in 2010. It grandfathered many health insurance plans so they did not have to comply with many of Obamacare's onerous insurance regulations, such as coverage of essential health benefits, guaranteed issue, and community rating. However, this rule did not save many Americans' health insurance plans.

By 2014, millions of Americans found out that, despite Obama's campaign promises, many of them would lose their health insurance plans.

Obama's lie about Americans keeping their health-care plans

inflamed so much controversy that the president made a public apology in a 2013 interview with *Meet the Press*'s Chuck Todd.

"We weren't as clear as we needed to be in terms of the changes that were taking place, and I want to do everything we can to make sure that people are finding themselves in a good position, a better position, than they were before this law happened," Obama admitted.[5] "And I am sorry that they are finding themselves in this situation based on assurances they got from me."

Despite Obama's pledge, an NBC investigation found that the Obama administration knew that millions of Americans would lose their health insurance plan.

A 2013 NBC News investigation found that the Obama administration knew from the beginning that roughly half of Americans would not be able to keep their original, pre-Obamacare, plans once the legislation become law.[6]

Deep within Obamacare regulations published in July 2010, the administration wrote that, due to normal turnover in the individual health-insurance market, "40 to 67 percent" of Americans would not be able to keep their pre-Obamacare health insurance policy. The regulations also stated that because many rules have changed since the turnover date, the same number of Americans will lose their grandfathered, pre-ACA plans.

Robert Laszewski, a health-care consultant, said in 2013 that this proves that roughly half to two-thirds of Americans would not be able to keep their pre-Obamacare plan. "This says that when they made the promise, they knew half the people in this market outright couldn't keep what they had, and then they wrote the rules so that others couldn't make it either," Laszewski said.[7]

After Obamacare became law, millions of Americans lost their health insurance plans and subsequently had to purchase a more expensive Obamacare-compliant plan, often on the individual market. However, under Obamacare, individual health insurance premiums continued to climb ever higher.[8]

Average individual health insurance premiums doubled since 2013, the year before many of Obamacare's insurance mandates took effect.

What part of Obamacare raised health insurance premiums to record-breaking highs?

HHS commissioned consulting giant McKinsey and Co. to analyze what exactly led to the rise in health-insurance premiums. McKinsey found that Obamacare regulations related to pre-existing conditions, which includes guaranteed issue and community ratings, were primarily responsible for Obamacare's increasing premiums.

Guaranteed issue requires that health insurers issue a health insurance plan to any American who applies for one, regardless of health status or cost. Community rating requires that insurers charge the same premium figure to citizens regardless of health status, gender, location, use of health services, and so on.

Senators Mike Lee (R-UT) and Ted Cruz (R-TX) proposed an amendment, known as the Consumer Freedom Amendment, to the Senate Obamacare repeal proposal, which McKinsey found could have lowered premiums substantially by altering Obamacare's health-insurance regulations.

Lee and Cruz's amendment would have allowed health insurers to offer plans that do not comply with Obamacare regulations as long as they offer plans that do follow the Obamacare rules.

McKinsey found that the Cruz amendment could have lowered the premiums for Obamacare-compliant plans for a forty-year-old by as much as 30 percent; premiums for non-Obamacare–compliant plans could be as much as 77 percent lower. Former senator Jim DeMint (R-SC) said that the Cruz amendment could have served as a promising solution to Obamacare's crushing premiums. "What Senator Cruz and his allies would allow in his amendment would allow a private market to co-exist with a heavily regulated and subsidized federal insurance market," he said. "This is not ideal by any means, but it would, perhaps, allow innovation, lower costs, a variety of product offerings to exist in many states."

In October 2018, the Centers for Medicare and Medicaid Services (CMS) released a new report that found that 2019 premiums in Obamacare Silver plans would drop by 1.5 percent, the first recorded decrease in health insurance premiums since the ACA's enactment. This premium drop arises as CMS revealed in December 2018 that 300,000 fewer Americans had signed up for Obamacare compared to 2017.[9]

While this serves as a significant victory for President Donald Trump, individual health insurance premiums remain at record highs. Although President Trump repealed Obamacare's individual mandate, most of the ACA remains intact. This might explain why a majority of Americans still blame Obama, not Trump, for the current state of health care.

An October 2018 Morning Consult poll found that 53 percent of Democrats primarily blame, or credit, Obama for the state of health care, compared to 53 percent of independents and 59 percent of Republicans.[10]

Now that Democrats control the House of Representatives, and Obamacare repeal remains a campaign slogan for many Republicans, many Americans continue to look to ACA alternatives for their health-care needs.

Amid Republicans' failure to repeal Obamacare, President Trump signed an executive order in October 2017 to expand short-term health insurance plans and Association Health Plans (AHPs), which offer Americans more affordable options compared to Obamacare.

Short-term health plans often cost less than Obamacare because they do not have to comply with all of Obamacare's insurance regulations. Cato Institute health scholar Michael Cannon contended in May 2018 that Trump's expansion of short-term health plans could cost 90 percent less than Obamacare plans. AHPs allow small businesses to band together and benefit from the regulatory advantages that many large companies experience under current health insurance rules. AHPs can serve employees in a city, county, state, or particular industry across the nation.

Land O'Lakes created America's first AHP, which offers health insurance plans roughly 50 percent less expensive than Obamacare, while still protecting Americans with pre-existing conditions.

Avalere Health released a study in 2018 that found that AHPs could be approximately $2,900 lower yearly compared to the small-group market and $9,700 less compared to the individual market. President Trump's expansion of short-term health insurance plans and AHPs, both of which offer health insurance for far less than Obamacare plans, could allow Trump to fulfill the promise that Obama made by offering Americans lower health-insurance premiums.

6

SINCE 1950, 97.8 PERCENT OF MASS SHOOTINGS HAVE OCCURRED IN "GUN-FREE ZONES"

Compiling copious amounts of data, the non-profit Crime Prevention Research Center (CPRC) concluded that more than nine in ten mass shootings occurred in "gun-free zones" from 1950 through May 2018.[1]

The organization, headed by economist and author John Lott Jr., includes in its definition of *gun-free zones* any areas in which law-abiding citizens or concealed-carry permit holders are forbidden from carrying their firearms. Mass shootings—as defined by the FBI—are carried out by one or more shooters with the express intent to kill and in which four or more fatalities occur (not including the shooter). The CPRC excluded gang firefights and shootings that take place during the commission of other crimes, like robberies.

The CPRC also compiles an exhaustive list detailing the various types of gun-free areas and the headline-grabbing shootings that occurred in those respective locales. These include "places where only police or military police are classified as gun-free zones" and "places where it is illegal to carry a permitted concealed handgun." For example, the 2012 Aurora Movie Theater shooting, in which twelve people were killed and seventy others were injured, and the 2018 Waffle House shooting, in which four were killed, were committed in buildings exhibiting signage outside prohibiting concealed handguns. Mass shootings also occurred in "places where, by law, permit holders were banned." For example, Fort Hood (2009 and 2014), the Pulse Nightclub (2016), and the Borderline Bar & Grill (2018) fall under the category. The mass shooting at Marjory Stoneman Douglas High School in Parkland, Florida, where a gunman killed seventeen students and staff members and injured seventeen others, is categorized by the CPRC as occurring in "schools where permitted concealed handguns are banned."

In Parkland, an armed school resource officer was at the school during the shooting; however, trained, armed, and uniformed individuals are not always a deterrent to gun-toting killers intent on causing mass death. "Even if they're not in uniform but their job is to guard—and everybody knows their job is to guard—they are a target," Lott contends.[2] "If you're going to have an attack, they're going to be the first guys taken out."

The CPRC study has received pushback from the typical outfits, most notably Everytown for Gun Safety, an organization that supports gun control. The biggest points of contention are: 1) how to define mass shootings and gun-free zones, and 2) whether mass shooters target areas in which law-abiding gun carriers are barred from entering buildings or areas with their firearms.

"Most gunmen are smart enough to know that they can kill

more people if they attack places where victims can't defend themselves," Lott said. "That's one reason why 98 percent of mass public shootings since 1950 have occurred in places where citizens are banned from having guns."[3]

It is almost always safe to assume that if a mass shooting occurred, it happened in a place that prohibited so-called *good guys* from carrying their guns inside. Sadly, more times than not, the theory holds true. So, there's a reason why one might imagine that allowing concealed-carry permit holders would mitigate the number of mass shootings in America.

The Obama administration ordered the Centers for Disease Control and Prevention (CDC) to assess existing research on gun violence. The report, compiled by the Institute of Medicine and the National Research Council, found that firearms are used defensively hundreds of thousands of times every year. Among other things, the federal government's analysis revealed that there were "consistently lower injury rates among gun-using crime victims compared with victims who used other self-protective strategies."[4]

Openly advertising the words "gun-free zone" in front of a school is a "magnet for bad guys," says Erich Pratt, executive director of Gun Owners of America. "We would be much safer if all gun-free zones were dismantled as well."

7

DRUG OVERDOSES KILL MORE AMERICANS THAN GUN VIOLENCE

Drug overdoses killed more than 72,000 people in the United States in 2017—a new record driven by the deadly opioid epidemic, according to data from the Centers for Disease Control and Prevention (CDC).

The highest death rates occurred in West Virginia, Pennsylvania, and Ohio. The number of opioid-addicted patients is also on the rise elsewhere in the country, particularly in disaster-hit areas like Puerto Rico, where job prospects have collapsed, many have suffered injuries, and deadly opioids like heroin and fentanyl can often be easier and cheaper to acquire than FDA-approved alternatives.[1]

The rising overdose numbers make America's drug epidemic deadlier than gun violence, car crashes, global terrorism, or AIDS.

The shocking figures represent nearly 200 people dying from overdoses every day. The CDC estimates that 72,287 people died from overdoses, a 10 percent increase from 2016, with most of the deaths—nearly 49,000—caused by opioids.

For comparison, 39,773 people died as a result of gun wounds in 2017, more than 30,000 fewer than the number killed by opioids.

AGE-ADJUSTED DRUG OVERDOSE DEATH RATES: UNITED STATES, 1999-2016

	Total		Male		Female	
Year	Number	Deaths per 100,000	Number	Deaths per 100,000	Number	Deaths per 100,000
1999	16,849	6.1	11,258	8.2	5,591	3.9
2000	17,415	6.2	11,563	8.3	5,852	4.1
2001	19,394	6.8	12,658	9.0	6,736	4.6
2002	23,518	8.2	15,028	10.6	8,490	5.8
2003	25,785	8.9	16,399	11.5	9,386	6.4
2004	27,424	9.4	17,120	11.8	10,304	6.9
2005	29,813	10.1	18,724	12.8	11,089	7.3
2006	34,425	11.5	21,893	14.8	12,532	8.2
2007	36,010	11.9	22,298	14.9	13,712	8.8
2008	36,450	11.9	22,468	14.9	13,982	8.9
2009	37,004	11.9	22,593	14.8	14,411	9.1
2010	38,329	12.3	23,006	15.0	15,323	9.6
2011	41,340	13.2	24,988	16.1	16,352	10.2
2012	41,502	13.1	25,112	16.1	16,390	10.2
2013	43,982	13.8	26,799	17.0	17,183	10.6
2014	47,055	14.7	28,812	18.3	18,243	11.1
2015	52,404	16.3	32,957	20.8	19,447	11.8
2016	63,632	19.8	41,558	26.2	22,074	13.4

NOTES: Deaths are classified using the *International Classification of Diseases, Tenth Revision* (ICD–10). Drug-poisoning (overdose) deaths are identified using ICD–10 underlying cause-of-death codes X40–X44, X60–X64, X85, and Y10–Y14.

NCHS, National Vital Statistics System, Mortality

Nearly three times the number of people died in America of opioid overdoses than died in a terrorist attack in every country on the planet.[2] The latest year that the CDC published the death toll of HIV-positive Americans was 2016; that year, 15,807 people in that community died.[3]

The national opioid crisis may be the defining health challenge of the 2010s, but it began decades ago, in the 1990s, when pharmaceutical companies began encouraging doctors to use opioid prescription medications for conditions beyond cancer and chronic pain. Companies like Purdue Pharma, which manufactures Oxy-Contin (oxycodone), began expanding their marketing bases using aggressive promotion. Companies began hiring armies of promoters to woo doctors into prescribing opioids by offering free swag, lavish dinners, and even vacations, author Beth Macy describes in her book *Dopesick.* The more a doctor prescribed a drug, the more money its promoters made.

Macy notes the disconnect between the communities receiving the prescriptions and the price of the drugs. "Appalachia was among the first places where the malaise of opioid pills hit the nation in the mid-1990s, ensnaring coal miners, loggers, furniture makers, and their kids," she writes.[4] Yet OxyContin, for example, cost as much as $80 a pill in 1997, not exactly affordable for the average out-of-work coal miner.

As awareness of the addictive nature of these drugs grew, doctors began cutting off prescriptions at the turn of the 2010s, though it took years for the numbers to go down significantly. In 2012, for example, doctors prescribed 793 million doses of opioids in Ohio, the state with the highest number of overdose deaths. Cutting off their prescriptions did not diminish demand from hopelessly addicted Americans, most of whom came from underprivileged backgrounds and had struggled to pay for their pills.

Heroin—and later, fentanyl—filled that void.

Most of the world's opium, used to manufacture heroin, comes from Afghanistan, where it constitutes one of the biggest sources of revenue for the Taliban. The rise in opioid use in the United States has occurred simultaneously with record yields in opium cultivation in Afghanistan, beginning in the mid-2010s.[5] By 2017, Afghanistan was producing 9,000 tons of opium a year, most of it going into the heroin manufacturing process.

The government watchdog U.S. Special Inspector General for Afghanistan Reconstruction (SIGAR) has urged the White House to order a study on how much Afghan heroin enters the United States. In 2018, the Trump administration began an airstrike campaign specifically targeting Taliban heroin labs, although this strategy proved relatively ineffective because the Taliban can completely rebuild a destroyed lab in about four days.[6]

Every year, the CDC insists that only negligible amounts of heroin make it from Afghanistan into the United States despite the prodigious cultivation and several arrests of Americans attempting to smuggle the drug into the country. In contrast, most of the heroin smuggled into Canada is thought to come from Afghanistan.

There is one major reason to believe this is true: Mexico.

Mexico is the third-largest opium producing country in the world (after Afghanistan and Myanmar, which does not export at the rates that Mexico does) and is considered America's top supplier of heroin.[7] In 2016, the Drug Enforcement Agency (DEA) found that 93 percent of America's heroin supply came from Mexico. Heroin production by cartels in Mexico appears to have increased as demand for the drug skyrocketed north of the border, following the prescription drop.[8]

Experts studying the opioid epidemic in the mid- to-late 2010s found that demand had increased, but more importantly, customers increasingly sought out purer heroin, which presented a technological problem for the Mexican cartels. Prior to the opioid epidemic, Mexican heroin had about a 15 percent purity rating (compared to the Taliban product, which averages 50 to 70 percent pure). By late 2017, the Mexican cartels had begun producing 50 percent pure heroin, driving the American overdose death rate through the roof.[9] Users accustomed to 15 percent pure heroin are used to taking much larger amounts of the drug; doing so with the newly refined product could easily kill them.

Heroin tells only half the story. In 2017, the biggest driver of overdose deaths was the highly addictive synthetic opioid fentanyl, which killed more than 29,000 people that year. Far from the southern border—in opioid hotspots like Ohio and New Hampshire—fentanyl played a much larger role than heroin in killing Americans. In St. Louis, Missouri, fentanyl was responsible for 95 percent of opioid deaths in 2017.[10]

Fentanyl is typically up to 50 times stronger than heroin and it is legal to use to relieve extreme cancer pain. The American Pregnancy Association also lists it as among the drugs sometimes mixed with epidural anesthetics offered to women in labor—a far more common medical condition than cancer. Despite its legal status, unlike OxyContin, U.S. pharmaceuticals are mostly off the hook for legal fentanyl use.

Mexican traffickers have gotten keen on fentanyl. In a February 2019 bust near the California border, for example, police caught smugglers trying to traffic 13 pounds of pure fentanyl and another 14,000 fentanyl tablets into America. That bust also contained 17 pounds of heroin and a ton of methamphetamine. Yet the cartels have largely failed to compete with the world's largest manufacturer of the drug: China. China, Afghanistan's neighbor, is where most of America's fentanyl comes from.

The Chinese Communist Party claims to punish drug crimes more harshly than any other government in the world, openly encouraging other nations to embrace the use of capital punishment for drug suspects and supporting extrajudicial killings of drug suspects in neighboring Philippines with weapons donations.[11] Yet Chinese syndicates like the Zheng drug-trafficking group have sold illegal drugs online for years and maintain close ties to the same Mexican drug cartels that once competed for market share of heroin.[12] The cartels can profit by smuggling in the fentanyl at a markup, while the Chinese companies cash in on their cheaply made product. Meanwhile, Americans are believed to have purchased over $700 million worth of fentanyl online.

American officials have repeatedly demanded that China endeavor to stop manufacturing the drug. Chinese officials have typically responded with scorn, blaming America's "lax cultural attitude," and not Chinese companies' targeted advertising to opioid addicts, for the problem.

After intensified pressure from the Trump administration, China finally branded fentanyl a controlled substance, but not without praising its dictator, Xi Jinping, for the "wonderful humanitarian gesture." It expanded on that gesture in April 2019 by adding all fentanyl-related drugs to its controlled list, which prevents drug manufacturers from slightly tweaking the drug's chemical composition so that it is no longer technically fentanyl but offers the same high.[13]

With international criminals elbowing American pharmaceutical companies out of the opioid market, some have found a new niche: opioid overdose antidote drugs. Pharmaceutical products containing naloxone (Narcan), a reversal treatment that can save an addict if administered early enough during an overdose, have become a cash cow for companies looking to capitalize on the epidemic without running afoul of the U.S. government, which has begun allowing lawsuits against the companies selling opioids.

Opiant Pharmaceuticals, a partner company of nasal spray manufacturer Narcan, announced in 2018 that it had made a record $11.7 million in royalty payments in the latter half of 2017. The company's CEO, Roger Crystal, boasted at the time that "Opiant has a robust addiction-related pipeline with significant market potential," which the company was eager to execute on in light of Narcan's commercial success.

That market potential skyrocketed in September 2018 with the kind of promotion money can't buy: an unintended celebrity endorsement. Former *Barney & Friends* child-star–turned–pop-artist Demi Lovato, who has long been candid about her substance-abuse issues, overdosed on opioids and survived, thanks to Narcan. Adapt Pharma, Opiant's partner corporation, used the opportunity to launch "a media campaign to urge more people to keep the potential life-saving product on hand," according to Fox News.[14]

"We have to get enough naloxone out there to stop people from dying and, secondly, we have to get people into treatment," Mike Kelly, president of Adapt's U.S. operations, said at the time.[15]

The drug indeed saves lives but it also creates lifelong consumers of drugs such as methadone, used to wean addicts off heroin or other opioids, and of services such as counseling and therapy.

American officials in the most affected states have launched lawsuits against opioid producers, and the Trump administration has warned Chinese and Mexican drug cartels of planned legal action to curb illegal opioid imports. Meanwhile, national security experts have sounded the alarm on the use of drugs such as fentanyl, which produce a slow-motion terrorist attack. But the industries that have been built around the addiction—from the initial prescription of painkillers to the administration of overdose remedies—are vast and lucrative, uniting interests as diverse as the Taliban and the Sinaloa cartel. Little hope stands of ending the epidemic without dismantling the profit incentives for keeping it alive.

8

FALLING AND THE FLU ARE FAR DEADLIER THAN MASS SHOOTINGS

Americans who receive all their information from the mainstream media and anti-gun leftist politicians might live in dread of a mass-shooting every time they go out in public or put their kids on a school bus. In fact, Americans are far more likely to die from a fall or catching the flu than from a mass shooting.

Contemplating our demise, or that of our loved ones, is not the most pleasant thing in the world, but sometimes we have to examine dark topics, because manipulation of base fears is one of the government's favorite tools to control us.

In no way does this diminish the tragedy and horror of mass shootings. School shootings affect children and teens in the worst ways imaginable. The response to such incidents brings all Americans together in solidarity, and rescue and recovery efforts cross political lines. For example, following the Pulse Nightclub attack, in which an Islamic extremist shot up a gay nightclub, Chick-fil-A, a fast-food chain often demonized by LGBTQ activist groups, served free food at blood-donation stations.

As bad as mass shooting incidents are, the threat of these

nightmarish attacks is constantly overblown by the media and our government officials. For example, consider a *New York Times* report from June 2018. It breathlessly reported "at least 700 mass shootings" over the past two years. If true, this figure should cause all of us to reexamine the issue. After all, a horrific mass shooting practically every day for two years would bring a culture to its knees.[1]

Unfortunately for the *New York Times* (or maybe it's more accurate to say "unfortunately for anyone who believes the *New York Times*") its shocking number of mass shootings is a fantasy. To reach a number sure to scare readers, the *New York Times* conflated tragedies like the Parkland school shooting with incidents in which no one was killed. It also added in gang street crime from cities like Chicago, America's very own gang battleground. The FBI and other responsible organizations measuring crime do not include these crimes in mass shooting statistics. In the same breath, the *New York Times* says that "96 Americans die by firearms" daily, allowing at least some readers to conclude that gun murder accounts for this number. In fact, two-thirds of the 96 deaths are suicides.

Claiming 350 or more mass shootings per year is nothing new for the left. Rose McGowan and other leftists immediately tweeted that the San Bernardino terror attack was the 355th mass shooting of 2015. *Mother Jones* editor Mark Follman corrected them, explaining they were slightly off in their count. The San Bernardino incident was the 4th mass shooting of 2015, not the 355th.[2] That's not exactly a rounding error, but math has never been the left's strong suit. On a side note, imagine being a Hollywood leftist and getting fact-checked by the ultra-lefties at *Mother Jones* . . . embarrassing!

The truth is, you are extremely unlikely to die in a mass shooting. According to *Mother Jones*, who built and maintains a database to track these incidents, using FBI definitions instead of leftist fantasy, there were 816 deaths in 98 mass shooting incidents from 1982 to early 2018. That is 23 deaths per year, folks.

Compare the yearly death toll from mass shootings with that of the flu. Flu deaths fluctuate yearly based on the severity of the flu strains passed around in public, but they typically average between 12,000 and 56,000 U.S. deaths per year. In 2017, this figure spiked to 80,000 deaths in the United States.[3] Imagine if the media reported on this with the intensity and hysteria it applies to mass shootings. CNN viewers would be running around as scared of germs as Howard Hughes was.

Likewise, in 2015, 33,381 Americans died from falling. Another 29,668 fell to their death in 2016.[4] You won't see the media reporting on these deaths in between attacks on the Second Amendment. You never see #BanStairs trending on social media.

These stats don't diminish the very real problem of mass-shooting incidents, but they prove that the mainstream media and our politicians are more interested in ginning up mass hysteria than they are in fixing the issue. If they were serious about addressing the problem, they'd examine why mass-shooting incidents happen where they do and address those weaknesses.

According to an FBI report on mass shooting incidents from 2000 to 2017, 42 percent happen in the workplace and commercial buildings, while 21 percent happen in schools or other educational facilities.[5] These are so-called soft targets, because they are mostly "gun-free zones," with no armed people ready to fight back. President

Donald Trump recognizes this and has quoted research by the Crime Prevention Research Center (CPRC), which shows that 98 percent of mass shooting incidents happen in gun-free zones. The *Washington Post* claimed in a fact check that this figure is a partial untruth because by modifying the methodology used to reach the figure, they were able to lower it to 86 percent, which is still an overwhelming majority.

Unfortunately for the media and outspoken anti-gun politicians, even the federal government recognizes that good guys with guns are the best defense against mass shooting incidents, especially those targeting schools and other vulnerable populations. The CDC released a report in 2013 titled "Priorities for Research to Reduce the Threat of Firearm-Related Violence," which makes this point. The report stated, "Studies that directly assessed the effect of actual defensive uses of guns (i.e., incidents in which a gun was 'used' by the crime victim in the sense of attacking or threatening an offender) have found consistently lower injury rates among gun-using crime victims compared with victims who used other self-protective strategies."[6]

If good guys with guns stop bad guys with guns from wounding and killing children and the other targets of mass shooting incidents, why isn't the media advocating for more responsible armed citizens in our schools? You'll have to ask the *New York Times, Washington Post,* or CNN. I don't have the answer on this one.

Some schools are seeing the light on how to prevent mass shooting incidents. While experts and academics debate arming teachers or hiring guards, the Manatee School for the Arts in Palmetto, Florida, has hired two combat vets to act as armed security during school hours.[7] One of the vets will even carry a rifle to deter potential school shooters from thinking they will have a firepower advantage over the guards.

This program will protect students by acting as both a deterrent and expert defense should the worst happen. At the same time, it will provide jobs for combat veterans who badly need an income and a mission in life. The question you should be asking right now is: "Why isn't every school in America doing this immediately?"

9

THE U.S. RESETTLED MORE REFUGEES IN 2018 THAN ANY OTHER NATION

Despite the near-constant castigation from pundits and politicians on the left as being an anti-immigrant nation, the United States has taken in the lion's share of the world's refugees since the adoption of the 1980 U.S. Refugee Act. This country has done the heavy lifting, resettling three-quarters of the more than 4 million refugees resettled worldwide over the last three and half decades. While the rest of the nations of the world accept and resettle fewer and fewer refugees, the United States led all nations in 2018, resettling roughly 22,491 refugees in fiscal year 2018.[1] We led all other nations in 2017, too.

The United States resettled 33,000 refugees in 2017, significantly more than any other country in the world, a Pew Research Center analysis revealed. The same was true in 2016.

The United States also led all other nations in 2016, when it resettled around 97,000 refugees, many of them escaping war throughout the Middle East and poverty, primarily in northern Africa.

The Pew analysis also stated that "the global refugee population increased by 2.75 million, and reached a record 19.9 million in 2017, according to UNHCR. This exceeds the high in 1990, following the fall of the Berlin Wall."[2]

On the campaign trail, candidate Donald Trump promised to reduce the total number of displaced people allowed to resettle in the United States. The Republican White House hopeful's main concerns were over the ever-increasing financial burdens and the real security risks of accepting more Syrian refugees, whose backgrounds

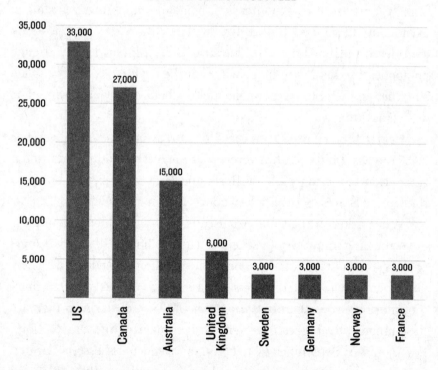

2017 REFUGEES RESETTLED

Source: https://www.pewresearch.org/fact-tank/2018/07/05/for-the-first-time-u-s-resettles-fewer-refugees-than-the-rest-of-the-world/

proved nearly impossible to fully verify—unlike the tens of thousands of Afghan or Iraqi people seeking asylum in the United States after war made their lands unlivable. Indeed, the United States spent more than $1 billion to settle 70,000 refugees from 2014 to 2015. That was before President Obama proposed adding another 15,000 refugees in the annual limit. Many liberal experts and media members lambasted even that move by Obama as inadequate. "The problem with the plan, no matter how quickly adopted, is how long it will take to have any effect," CNN analyst and *Washington Post* columnist Josh Rogin wrote in Bloomberg.[3] "Migrants applying for refugee asylum in the United States now will not have their applications considered until at least 2017 because of a long backlog. And once an application begins to be considered, the asylum seekers can face a further eighteen to twenty-four months before they are granted or denied asylum."

Nearly fifty House Democrats joined Republicans in November 2015 to pass a bill—with a veto-proof majority—adding additional restrictions on refugees from Syria and Iraq applying for entry to the United States. So, the safety concerns were palpable.

When asked at the time, Americans were ambivalent about their government's initial response to the rush of hundreds of thousands of migrants pouring into Europe, many of whom hoped to find a new home here in the United States. "By a narrow 51 to 45 percent margin, more approve than disapprove of the U.S. decision to increase the number of refugees it accepts to help deal with this situation," Pew noted in September 2015.[4] "When asked to assess the United States' response to the refugee situation more generally, 44 percent say the U.S. should be doing more, while 19 percent say it should be doing less; 31 percent say the U.S. is doing about what it should."

Thankfully, the European Commission declared in March 2019 that the migration crisis was over, after years of decline in the number of displaced people risking death to cross the Mediterranean into Italy in search of asylum.[5] Frans Timmermans, the European Commission's first vice president, said, "Europe is no longer experiencing the migration crisis we lived in 2015, but structural problems remain."

In 2018, 116,647 people were counted by the UN refugee agency, UNHCR, as crossing the Mediterranean, an 89 percent reduction compared with those who made the journey in 2015, at the height of the crisis. Some 171,635 migrants arrived in the EU by boat in 2017, down from 363,504 a year before, according to the International Organization for Migration.

"Overall, the world resettled 103,000 refugees in 2017, down from 189,000 in 2016," Pew noted. "The broad-based decline included decreases in other leading countries in refugee resettlement, such as Canada and Australia, though the drops in these countries were more modest than those in the U.S."

10

EIGHTY PERCENT OF CENTRAL AMERICAN WOMEN AND GIRLS ARE RAPED WHILE CROSSING INTO THE U.S. ILLEGALLY

For all the left's shrieks about a so-called *war on women* and a systemic *rape culture* pervasive throughout American society, the reality of sexual violence women and girls face during their dangerous trek from Mexico and South America to the U.S. southern border is met mostly with silence. Wanton brutality is another terrible cost many illegal immigrants pay in their attempt to gain access to our country.

In the case of women and girls making the dangerous journey to America from Mexico and Central America, that price, in part, is rape and sexual assault. An investigation into sexual assault of migrants by Splinter News, which is owned by Univision—an anti-Trump and anti-Wall outfit—revealed the stunning truth that 80 percent of Central American women and girls are raped during their journey, primarily while traveling through Mexico or when they cross the U.S. border.[1]

One woman profiled by the *New York Times* described being raped in Mexican brothels as well as in McAllen, Texas. She said, "They just told us, 'You guys don't have money, so you have to pay with your body.'"[2]

This sinister statement seems to be the rule, not an exception. According to the Splinter exposé, "The arrangement is so common there's a slang term for it—*cuerpomátic,* or *cuerpomático* (an apparent wordplay on Credomatic, a Central American credit-card processing firm), which means to use one's body—or *cuerpo*—as a source of currency."

Princeton Policy Advisors estimates that, in 2019, 103,000 women will be raped trying to reach the United States from Central America.[3]

This number could be much higher, as rape and other crimes against migrants skyrocket in Mexico and after they cross the border. And there are major questions about whether the rape of illegal immigrants stops once they are here. Increasingly, women are being moved by human traffickers directly into the sex trade. The National Human Trafficking Hotline reported 3,279 cases in 2012, which more than doubled to 7,572 cases by 2016.[4]

As in most violent crimes, children bear the worst of it. Then–DHS Secretary Kirstjen Nielsen testified to Congress in March 2019 that, "Of great concern to me is that the children are being used as pawns to get into our country. We have encountered recycling rings, where innocent young people are used multiple times to help aliens gain illegal entry. As a nation, we simply cannot stand for this."

Children are not only being used as props to help illegal aliens make it into the country as a fake family, they are also being raped and sexually abused along the way. Anecdotal evidence from numerous sources indicates that it is common practice for Central American families to give women and girls contraceptives before their journey to prevent unwanted pregnancies due to rape. Secretary Nielsen's opening statement included another sobering fact: every woman and girl that ICE comes in contact with at the border is given a pregnancy test because they run the very real risk of having been raped during their 1,000-mile trek from Central America to the U.S. border. "As you know, very unfortunately because of the increase of violence, at ICE, when we have families with children, we have to give every girl a pregnancy test over 10 [*sic*]. This is not a safe journey," Nielsen told the House Homeland Security Committee.

Timothy Ballard spent more than a decade fighting sex trafficking across the southern border as a DHS special agent. In an opinion piece for Fox News, he explained the importance of a border wall, saying that it would force human traffickers to attempt to bring children into the country through designated ports of entry, as opposed to being able to cross where they pleased. "For those children who are still kidnapped, the wall would provide hope. Had there been a wall, Liliana's traffickers would have likely been compelled to try their luck at any given port of entry, which are [*sic*] armed with advanced technology and well-trained officers," Ballard said. "In fact, at about the same time that Liliana was trafficked, I was participating in the rescue of a five-year-old boy, whose trafficker had kidnapped him in Mexicali, Mexico, where there actually was a wall."[5]

A wall isn't just for protecting Americans. It could protect the most vulnerable immigrants.

Alert officers, using their sharp skills and high-tech monitoring equipment, snagged the American trafficker at the Calexico Port of Entry, rescued the boy, and then identified an entire trafficking network, allowing officials to rescue countless more children.

This is how it's supposed to work. Roughly 10,000 children are being smuggled into the United States every year to be sold as sex slaves.[6] Do we not owe it to them to finish this wall and protect them from the monsters?

While elected leftists and the mainstream media insist that a border wall would be racist, xenophobic, and immoral, the brave men and women who protect the United States have a very different view. Perhaps stopping the rape of women and girls and the sex trafficking of children doesn't factor into leftists' definition of morality.

11

OBAMA DEPORTED MORE PEOPLE THAN ANY OTHER PRESIDENT

Between 2009 and 2015, the Obama administration had removed more than 2.5 million people through immigration orders. According to Department of Homeland Security data, the Obama administration had deported more people from the U.S. than any other in history.[1] By August 2016, Obama had deported more people than the total under all the presidents of the twentieth century. The record rates of deportation angered left-wing activists and earned Obama the nickname Deporter-in-Chief.

"Our message absolutely is: Don't send your children unaccompanied on trains or through a bunch of smugglers. That is our direct message to the families in Central America. Do not send your children to the borders. If they do make it, they'll get sent back," Obama said in June 2014.[2] But by the time he had issued that stern warning, the waves of migrants were already pouring into the United States. Obama's record deportation rates were in large part the result of the tens of thousands of adults and unaccompanied children who flooded the southern U.S. border illegally. The administration estimated a wave of 60,000 people illegally crossed the border in 2014 alone.

The number of destitute and desperate people making the long and dangerous trek from Central American countries to the United States had been on the rise for decades before Obama took office.

Bill Clinton brought his tough-on-immigration proposals before the American people, urging during his State of the Union address that "All Americans, not only in the States most heavily affected, but in every place in this country, are rightly disturbed by the large numbers of illegal aliens entering our country. The jobs they hold might otherwise be held by citizens or legal immigrants. The public services they use impose burdens on our taxpayers."

A month later in a memo, Clinton declared that his "administration shall stand firm against illegal immigration and the continued abuse of our immigration laws. By closing the back door to illegal immigration, we will continue to open the front door to legal immigrants."

Indeed, deportations skyrocketed from 69,680 in 1996 to 189,000 by the end of Clinton's second term in 2001.[3] The daily detention-center population more than tripled, from roughly 6,700 in 1994 to nearly 20,000 when Clinton left office.

Before he was lambasting President Trump's immigration policies from the pages of the *Washington Post*, Jeh Johnson was spearheading President Obama's much-maligned cross-country deportation campaign.

"As I have said repeatedly, our borders are not open to illegal migration; if you come here illegally, we will send you back consistent with our laws and values," Johnson said in a January 2016 statement about the crisis on the southwestern border.

"Since the summer of 2014 we have removed and repatriated

migrants to Central America at an increased rate, averaging about fourteen flights a week. Most of those returned have been single adults," the memo from Johnson, who served as secretary of Homeland Security from 2013 to 2017, continued. "This past weekend, Immigration and Customs Enforcement (ICE) engaged in concerted, nationwide enforcement operations to take into custody and return at a greater rate adults who entered this country illegally with children. This should come as no surprise. I have said publicly for months that individuals who constitute enforcement priorities, including families and unaccompanied children, will be removed."[4]

Protest against Obama's mass deportation agenda ramped up around the country in 2014. As late as June 2016, immigration advocates were being arrested while protesting Obama's push to remove more illegal immigrants. "We are defending the security and stability of our families, sending a direct message to the Obama administration," said Carlos Medina, a member of the Georgia Latino Alliance for Human Rights and one of the protesters who chained themselves to ladders in the middle of an Atlanta intersection in the summer of 2016. "We know that he has the ability to stop deportations at any given time. Our fight will not stop. The only thing that we will stop is the sinister machine that is the deportation machine created by this administration."[5]

In May of that year, House Democrats were railing against the Obama administration's proposal for a new wave of deportations targeting asylum seekers who were denied refugee status. "These are not illegal immigrants. These are children, these are people fleeing violence," Representative Luis Gutiérrez (D-IL) said. "They are asylum seekers."

"This is ill-advised, ill-timed and counterproductive on anything we're talking about in terms of galvanizing our community for the up-coming elections," said Representative Raúl Grijalva (D-AZ). "When we're trying to distinguish ourselves as being more humane . . . and trying to distinguish ourselves from . . . the rhetoric and what Trump is saying about this issue . . . here we are carrying out and proposing to carry out these raids, which I think are a huge mistake."

"These children and their families are fleeing extreme violence in Central America and they should have a chance to seek relief," declared Senate Minority Leader Harry Reid (D-NV).

Both Hillary Clinton and Bernie Sanders, who were battling each other for the Democratic Party's presidential nomination, slammed the Obama administration's mass-deportation plans. "I oppose the painful and inhumane business of locking up and deporting families who have fled horrendous violence in Central America and other countries," Sanders said in a statement.

Clinton concurred, saying that "large scale raids are not produc-tive and do not reflect who we are as a country."

Obama's deportation machine had removed nearly three million people from the United States by the time he left the White House.[6]

12

THE IRS DOCUMENTED 1.2 MILLION IDENTITY THEFTS COMMITTED BY ILLEGAL ALIENS IN 2017

The Internal Revenue Service said it uncovered roughly 1.2 million cases of "refund fraud" or "employment-related fraud" committed by illegal aliens in fiscal year 2017.[1] Refund fraud occurs whenever an individual tax return is filed using a Social Security Number that either doesn't match the filer's actual Social Security Number or is simply fabricated. "We identified 1,227,579 electronically filed tax returns, processed in FY 2017 through April 18, 2017, in which the Individual Taxpayer Identification Number (ITIN) on the return does not match the Social Security Number on the Form W-2," said the Treasury Inspector General for Tax Administration (TIGTA). "Note that a Social Security Number may have been used on Form W-2 for more than one of these returns."

Employment or tax-related fraud is among the most common kinds of identity theft in the United States, according to Lifelock, an identity-theft prevention company. "Nearly 60 million Americans have been affected by identity theft, according to a 2018 online survey by the Harris Poll. That same survey indicates nearly 15 million consumers experienced identity theft in 2017. . . . Nearly 1 in 14 cases of identity theft in 2017 were illegal alien–related."[2]

While most of the debate around illegal immigration is rightfully focused on the sheer number of foreign-born migrants and illegal immigrants entering the United States every year, often overlooked are the millions of cases in which an American's identity is stolen and used to gain employment or siphon social welfare benefits. Additionally, identity theft also poses a major national security risk, ruins the credit of citizens and children, and enables the baleful scourge of human trafficking. "Document and benefit fraud are elements of many immigration-related crimes, such as human smuggling and human trafficking, critical infrastructure protection, worksite enforcement, visa compliance enforcement, and national security investigations," says Immigration and Customs Enforcement (ICE), the agency charged with investigating and dismantling myriad document and benefit fraud schemes.[3]

Employment-related identity theft is anything but new. TIGTA, the agency that oversees the IRS, warned about the potential for fraud within the ITIN program (which began in 1996) as early as 1999, one year after the IRS Restructuring and Reform Act established TIGTA. "The Internal Revenue Service (IRS) made a policy decision to issue IRS Individual Taxpayer Identification Numbers (ITINs) to illegal aliens so tax filing obligations could be met. This IRS policy, to 'legalize' illegal aliens, seems counter-productive to the Immigration and Naturalization Service (INS) mission to identify illegal aliens and prevent unlawful alien entry," a 1999 TIGTA report said.[4] "The ITIN Program adversely affects effective and efficient tax administration. Providing illegal aliens with valid TINs allows for certain tax advantages and increases the potential for fraud. Fraudulent or invalid dependent claims on tax returns provide additional tax deductions and access to certain tax credits."

It took only a few years before the fraud forewarned to by to TIGTA took form. Between 2011 and 2016, the IRS documented roughly 1.3 million identity thefts committed by illegal aliens.[5] The cases stemmed from aliens given ITINs, numbers issued to individuals who are ineligible to receive a Social Security Number to work in the United States. Stealing or knowingly entering fraudulent Social Security information on tax forms, such as a W-2, is a felony. But the Obama administration never pursued or prosecuted the individuals who broke federal law. The IRS has remained mum about the specifics as regards the identity theft cases it referred to the Justice Department for criminal prosecution. "The IRS's Criminal Investigation division publishes an annual report stating how many 'prosecution recommendations' it makes each fiscal year and the crimes for which it makes them," notes Terence P. Jeffrey, CNSnews editor in chief. "In the six fiscal years from 2011 through 2016, according to these reports, IRS CI made 20,986 prosecution recommendations and 4,329 of them were for identity theft cases." In many of the instances in which an American's identity was stolen, the IRS did not notify them, although in recent years the agency has initiated programs and procedures to inform illegal alien identity theft victims.

Indeed, identity theft committed by illegal aliens is far more widespread than most Americans realize. Roughly 39 million Americans may have had their identities compromised by illegal aliens, according to government documents the Immigration Reform Law Institute (IRLI) sued the federal government to obtain.[6] The IRLI lawsuit revealed that between 2012 and 2016 there were nearly 40 million instances where names and Social Security numbers provided on W-2 forms failed to match corresponding data on file with the federal government.

The IRLI lawsuit was in response to the Obama administration's decision in 2012 to stop sending "no-match" letters to employers after the president unilaterally conferred amnesty on the 800,000 recipients of Deferred Action for Childhood Arrivals (DACA) status in 2012. DACA, which granted legal protections to nearly one million illegal immigrants brought to the United States as children, was revoked by President Donald Trump in September 2017. But for more than four years, no-match letters—which the federal government had relied upon since 1979 to prevent identity theft—were halted and cases of employer-related identity theft exploded. Indeed, many of the nearly one million DACA recipients had undoubtedly gained employment by using falsified information, often stolen or fabricated personal information.[7]

By 2019, the Trump administration had resurrected the practice of sending no-match letters to employers.

13

THERE ARE NO JOBS AMERICANS WON'T DO

The left loves to throw around the idea that immigrants—and especially illegal immigrants—are willing to do the dirty jobs that Americans aren't willing to take on. Like all the left's favorite lies, it does two things at once. First, it portrays illegal immigrants as noble people who want to work and improve the country and, second, it also slights American citizens of all races as pampered softies unwilling to get their hands dirty.

It's all a fantasy. Americans are willing to do any job, no matter how filthy, dangerous, or boring it might be to the average person.

This is backed up by hard federal data dissected by the Center for Immigration Studies, a non-partisan research organization whose motto is: "Pro-Immigrant, Low-Immigration."

In 2018, the think tank set out to determine once and for all if there are jobs that Americans won't do, analyzing the Census Bureau's American Community Survey data from 2012 to 2016. The data is devastatingly clear: There isn't a single occupation in the American economy that is more than 63 percent immigrant, and that combines both legal and illegal immigrants. In fact, there are only six occupations held by immigrants in more than half of the cases.[1]

The five occupations that are held by immigrants on a majority basis are:

- **Agricultural product sorters and graders (62 percent)**
- **Miscellaneous personal appearance workers (62 percent)**
- **Plasterers and stucco masons (58 percent)**
- **Sewing machine operators (52 percent)**
- **Miscellaneous agricultural workers, including animal breeders (51 percent)**
- **Tailors, dressmakers, and sewers (51 percent)**

Leftist politicians, the mainstream media, and the GOP establishment would have you believe that immigrants are the lifeblood of the economy. But the six majority-immigrant occupations account for about 1 percent of the U.S. workforce, and even within these six occupations, native-born Americans account for 46 percent of the workers.

Don't let them make the argument that young Americans are not willing to do these jobs either. CIS data shows that 34 percent of the native-born Americans in these occupations are under 30, as opposed to 29 percent on average in other jobs.

Think about some of the jobs that are part of the constant media drumbeat about the need for more immigrants and rights for illegals. They aren't as immigrant-heavy as you'd expect. Consider the CIS data for the jobs commonly associated with immigrants:

"maids and housekeepers" (51 percent native-born); "taxi drivers and chauffeurs" (54 percent native-born); "grounds maintenance workers" (66 percent native-born); "construction laborers" (65 percent native-born); "porters, bellhops, and concierges" (73 percent native-born); and "janitors" (73 percent native-born).

We've just exploded most of the myths about the immigrant workforce in a few short paragraphs. Feel free to put this book down for a few minutes if you need a breather.

The CIS report makes an important point about the actual dynamic between immigrants and native-born Americans in the economy: "The American economy is dynamic, and it would be a mistake to think that every job taken by an immigrant is a job lost by a native. Many factors impact employment and wages. But it would also be a mistake to assume that dramatically increasing the number of workers in these occupations as a result of immigration policy has no impact on the employment prospects or wages of natives. To talk about the labor market as if there were jobs done entirely or almost entirely by immigrants is not helpful to understanding the potential impact of immigration on American workers. It gives the false impression that the job market is segmented between immigrant and native jobs. This is clearly not the case."

Although it isn't as simple as saying every immigrant is taking a job from an American, there is clear evidence in the data that there is a relationship between immigrant labor and native-born unemployment. In high-immigrant occupations, the unemployment for native-born Americans averaged 14 percent, while other occupations at the time of the study averaged 8 percent. For example, the occupation with the highest percentage of immigrant workers, "graders and sorters, agricultural products," was 62 percent immigrant share, with an estimated illegal immigrant share of 30 percent. The native-born unemployment rate in that occupation was 24 percent; remember that 8 percent was average at the time. The agriculture example isn't a fluke either. "Plasterers and stucco masons," at 58 percent immigrant and 31 percent illegal immigrant, had a native-born unemployment of 17 percent.

These numbers show clearly that illegal immigration hurts native-born workers. "Miscellaneous personal appearance workers" are 62 percent immigrant but only 16 percent illegal immigrant, and the native-born unemployment is at just over 5 percent, exactly the average for all occupations. The native-born Americans hurt by illegal immigrants having jobs are not white-collar professionals, academics, and government workers. They are the black Americans, Hispanic Americans, and white Americans without college degrees who show up to work ready, every day, for difficult and often menial labor.

By this point, you're probably tired of statistical data, so how about a stark example of Americans taking dirty jobs that they supposedly won't do?

Jobs in meatpacking plants are dirty and dangerous, exactly the types of jobs that leftists believe only immigrants will do. And in the case of meatpacker Swift & Co., a considerable percentage of its employees in 2006 were in fact illegal aliens. The government conducted coordinated immigration raids on six Swift & Co. plants that year, arresting 1,300 illegal aliens, or roughly 9 percent of the company's entire workforce.[2]

Even before the raids, Swift & Co. fired 400 illegal immigrants— and this is where it gets interesting. Even before the raids, the company had to raise hourly wages nearly $2 an hour to attract legal workers. Following the raids, lines of applicants for jobs at Swift & Co. plants reportedly stretched "out the door." And the people lined up for these dirty jobs were native-born Americans.

Americans are ready and willing to do dirty, tough jobs. When leftists who think being a Starbucks barista is backbreaking labor and sermonize to you about "immigrants doing the jobs Americans won't do," feel free to correct them—native-born Americans are willing to do any job on the planet . . . for fair pay.

14

FOR EVERY $1 A NETFLIX EMPLOYEE DONATES TO A REPUBLICAN, $141 GETS DONATED TO DEMOCRATS

Netflix has morphed from a U.S. DVD mail-order service into one of the premier progressive big-tech institutions in the world. Hollywood is one of the largest collections of crazy leftists in the country. But what you may not know is that the only way you could make Hollywood even more progressive is through the marriage of Hollywood and the other big asylum of left-wing progressives in California, Silicon Valley. That is exactly what has occurred at Netflix, the dominant power player in entertainment production.

Some people remember the old Netflix, which offered films that were on the silver screen or went direct to video on a variety of platforms. But the new Netflix focuses on producing original content exclusive to the platform; *Stranger Things* is one popular example.

Original content for Netflix is now big business in Hollywood. According to *Forbes*, of the $13 billion the company spent on content in 2018, more than $11 billion was to create original movies and series.

There's just one problem with what would otherwise be an interesting story about the convergence of tech and entertainment. Netflix is left wing to its core . . . and the content it creates is, too.

Netflix employees are astonishingly left wing, even by Silicon Valley's standards. During the 2018 election cycle, Netflix employees donated $190,592 to Democrats, while donating just $1,350 to Republicans. The second largest donation ratio among the Silicon Valley giants was at Apple, at 27 to 1.[1] Billionaire and progressive propagandist George Soros purchased 148,500 shares of Netflix stock in early 2018, making the far-left financier a leading shareholder. Soros sold the stock later that year, profiting by millions just before tech stock values plummeted by nearly a trillion dollars.

Of course, employees introduce their political positions into their work, but what about the senior executive? Surely, he's donating to both sides? Netflix CEO Reed Hastings donated $500,000 in 2018 to the left-wing Senate Majority PAC. That's just the money he put into one PAC in one election year! Besides running Netflix, Hastings is on Facebook's board of directors along with Peter Thiel, Donald Trump's biggest supporter from the tech world. Hastings reportedly emailed Thiel during the 2016 election cycle to advise him that supporting Trump showed "catastrophically bad judgment."[2]

Speaking of corporate boards, Netflix added former U.N. Ambassador and longtime Obama crony Susan Rice to its board of directors in 2018.[3] It seems like a strange hire, as Rice doesn't have much of a resume in the world of fictional stories, unless you count the Benghazi incident. But look how CEO Reed Hastings fawningly described her: "We are delighted to welcome Ambassador Rice to the Netflix board. For decades, she has tackled difficult, complex global issues with intelligence, integrity, and insight and we look forward to benefiting from her experience and wisdom."

You are probably asking one big question right now, "So Netflix employees are left-wing from top to bottom, but does it show up in the content?" The answer is a resounding yes.

The most obvious example is the company's multiyear production deal with Barack and Michelle Obama. Barack Obama's description of the deal seems innocuous—the former president described it as an opportunity to tell stories "we think are important, and lift up and identify talent, that can amplify the connections between all of us. I continue to believe that if we are hearing each other's stories and recognizing ourselves in each other, then our democracy works." In practice, one of the first projects mentioned publicly to come from Obama was an adaption of the anti-Trump book *The Fifth Risk.*[4] Surprise, surprise!

Opinions about Obama's involvement in Netflix are mixed. Roseanne Barr, never one to mince words, called it an "unholy alliance." Netflix Chief Content Officer Ted Sarandos, the guy in charge of all content on the platform, had a different view. He said, "This is not the Obama Network. There's no political slant to the programming." But Sarandos, like other Netflix executives, is a six-figure donor to Democrats. He was also a key fundraiser for Obama during his presidential years, reportedly hosting a dinner in 2009 that raised $700,000 for the president. He is also married to Nicole Avant, who was Obama's ambassador to the Bahamas before she became a fundraiser for his campaign. In that light, Sarandos's denial of bias sounds like the plot of a bad Netflix original movie.

The bias in Netflix content isn't limited to Obama. The streaming platform announced in February that it was paying $10 million for the rights to *Knock Down the House*, a documentary about new socialist darling Alexandria Ocasio-Cortez (AOC). AOC and the Obama examples are explicitly political, but only scratch the surface of Netflix's bias.

The company has consistently propped up the career of unfunny comedian and professional Trump-hater Chelsea Handler. After finally axing Handler's boring talk show *Chelsea* after two seasons, the platform gave her carte blanche to develop a documentary on "white privilege," for which she attempted to crowdsource material by posting to Twitter: "Tonight I start shooting my documentary for #Netflix on white privilege. Starting with my own privilege and my own whiteness. To learn more about what it's like to be a person who isn't white in this country. Please message me your questions on the topic and I will incorporate."[5]

After pulling the plug on Chelsea Handler's talk show, the company took a different course with another anti-Trump comedian, this time choosing Hasan Minhaj. Minhaj hosted the 2017 White House Correspondents' Association Dinner, where he called President Trump the "liar-in-chief" and "the orange man behind the Muslim ban." But when Minhaj criticized Crown Prince of Saudi Arabia Mohammed bin Salman on his Netflix show, the company sang a very different tune. It pulled down the episode within the country at the behest of the government in a move Amnesty International called "further proof of a relentless crackdown on freedom of expression."[6]

Another short-lived leftist Netflix talk show experiment was *The Break with Michelle Wolf*, which was canceled after ten excruciatingly unfunny episodes. Some of *The Break*'s worst moments saw Wolf comparing Immigration and Customs Enforcement (ICE) to the murderous jihadists of ISIS, referring to First Lady Melania Trump as part victim of spousal abuse, part gold digger, comparing Ivanka Trump to bloody "vaginal mesh," and drum-majoring a marching band in a "Salute to Abortions."

These are just a few of the obvious examples. Progressive politics and social-justice-warrior values are creeping into every area of Netflix's original content and become obvious as soon as you start scrolling through the platform's original programming. Watch sci-fi mystery series *Altered Carbon* and see what sticks out at you.

All of this bias matters because Netflix continues to grow as a major force in entertainment. Besides elbowing its way into Hollywood's most sacred territory, including the Academy Awards, the company continues to pick up subscribers as more and more Americans "cut the cord" on traditional TV offerings. And Netflix is doing quite well for itself financially; it reported a 2018 profit of $845 million, which it didn't pay a single penny of taxes on.

15

HALF OF FEDERAL ARRESTS ARE RELATED TO IMMIGRATION

Illegal immigration is so rampant that 50 percent of the more than 165,000 federal arrests made in 2014 were for immigration offenses, according to the Pew Research Center's analysis of Bureau of Justice Statistics' most recent available data.[1] Because illegal immigration is out of control, federal law enforcement officials are spending less time making arrests for drugs, guns, and interstate property crimes.

- **Percentage of federal arrests in FY 2016 involving immigration offense as the most serious arrest offense: 45 percent**
- **Percentage of all federal arrests in FY 2016 that took place in the five federal judicial districts along the U.S.–Mexico border: 58 percent**
- **Percentage in FY 2006: 45 percent**

Americans, especially the older generation, like to think about federal law enforcement officers as the brave G-men fighting organized crime and busting up drug rings. These are the agents who formed the Untouchables to take down Al "Scarface" Capone. But the facts show that federal law enforcement agencies are so consumed with immigration crimes, including human trafficking and smuggling operations, that they don't have the time or the manpower to make busts for drugs or embezzlement.

Immigration arrests grew to 50 percent of all federal arrests from just 28 percent a decade earlier. The Department of Homeland Security (DHS) accounted for 59 percent of all 2014 federal arrests, up from 37 percent in 2004. The arrests made by Customs and Border Protection, just one agency of the DHS, totaled more than all of the DOJ agencies combined. Those agencies include: the FBI, DEA, ATF, and the U.S. Marshals Service.[2]

Although this may be obvious, it's important to point out that they aren't arresting Americans for these crimes. Whether it is an illegal border crossing, smuggling, or horrific crime like human trafficking, 61 percent of these arrests involve non-citizens. The share of U.S. citizens arrested fell to 39 percent from 57 percent a decade earlier.

Reflecting on our dated vision of federal law enforcement as the guys in suits looking to bust gangsters and racketeers, we let our imaginations run wild with scenes from classic movies: U.S. Marshals tracking a murder suspect through a forest; feds in Los Angeles finding clues to rescue a starlet kidnapped by a crazy fan; G-men in Chicago staking out an Italian restaurant where crime lords do their dirty work. Of course, these things happen—federal law enforcement agencies are present in all 50 states—but the large and increasing emphasis on immigration crime has focused much of their efforts along the southern border.

Sixty-one percent of all federal arrests occurred in just over 5 percent of the federal judicial districts. The five hot spots for federal immigration arrests include one each in California, Arizona, and New Mexico, and two in Texas. And they say there is no border crisis!

"From fiscal years 2011 through 2016, the criminal alien proportion of the total estimated federal inmate population generally decreased, from about 25 percent to 21 percent,"[3] said a United States Government Accountability Office Release in July 2018. "During this period, the estimated number of criminal aliens incarcerated in federal prisons decreased from about 50,400 to about 39,500, or 22 percent. Ninety-one percent of these criminal aliens were citizens of one of six countries, including Mexico, Honduras, El Salvador, Dominican Republic, Colombia, and Guatemala." It doesn't take a genius to figure out that these five border districts would be the best place to build a big beautiful wall.

Perhaps if human traffickers and others intent on breaking our federal laws are stopped in their tracks by a secure barrier or wall, our federal law enforcement agencies can devote their resources to stopping the drug epidemic sweeping the country.

16

AMAZON PAID $0 IN TAXES ON $11.2 BILLION IN PROFITS IN 2018

While it's well known that tech giants such as Amazon, Apple, Google, and Tesla generate massive amounts of revenue, what many people don't know is just how many tax breaks these companies enjoy.

An analysis by watchdog group Good Jobs First found that tech giants received approximately $9.3 billion in state and local subsidies over a five-year period. One of the most recent subsidies was given to Taiwanese manufacturer Foxconn, which received at least $4.1 billion to construct a production plant in Wisconsin.[1]

Much of this money comes from the budgets of cities and states attempting to promote growth within their communities. The number of subsidies handed out is only expected to increase as cities endeavor to further attract high-tech firms.

So why are these states and cities so desperate to have tech companies set up shop in their neighborhoods? Many have argued that these tax breaks are necessary to attract high-paying tech jobs to these areas, but it appears that these massive handouts have often not resulted in much significant job creation in recent years—at

least not enough to justify the billions in tax incentives these companies receive.

While facility construction can result in the creation of short-
term construction jobs, once the facility has been completed these
jobs disappear. This is beneficial to contractors in the short term but
it hardly justifies massive tax subsidies. For example, Apple received
a $214 million tax break to construct its data center in Iowa, which
resulted in the creation of 550 construction jobs to build the $1.3
billion facility.[2] Ultimately, the facility will only produce 50 full-time
jobs.[3] Nortel Networks received a $2 million tax subsidy from the
state of Massachusetts in 2008 with the aim of keeping 2,200 jobs
in the area and adding 800 more to the facility located in that state.
However, by 2010 there were only 145 jobs filled at the facility while
the tax incentive for the company was scheduled to last another four
years.[4]

Greg LeRoy, the executive director of Good Jobs First, co-
wrote an op-ed in *The Guardian* with his colleague Maryann Feldman. In it, they stated, "The 'lots of eggs in one basket' strategy
is especially ill-suited. But many public leaders haven't switched
gears yet, often putting taxpayers at great risk, especially because
some tech companies have become very aggressive about demand-
ing big tax breaks. Companies with famous names are even more
irresistible to politicians who want to look active on jobs."[5]

One company that has used the allure of its "famous name" to
guarantee tax breaks and benefits is the e-commerce giant Amazon. Run by Jeff Bezos, whose $100 billion personal fortune makes
him the richest man in the world, Amazon has managed to not only
receive several tax benefits but has also avoided paying any federal
income tax for 2017.

In an annual report filed to the SEC in February 2018, Amazon estimated that not only would the company not be paying anything in federal income taxes for 2017 but it would, in fact, be receiving $137 million in a tax refund.[6] During that year, Amazon reported a $5.6 billion profit.

For 2018, Amazon once again paid no federal income tax whatsoever.[7] Despite doubling its profits from the year previous to $11.2 billion, due to a number of tax write-offs and stock payments, the company is set to receive around $129 million in tax rebates.

Amazon's gaming of the tax system has been happening for so long that Good Jobs First runs a regularly updated tracker of Amazon's latest tax subsidies and write-offs. But while Amazon is a world leader in taking tax subsidies, it certainly isn't alone.

Tesla CEO and SpaceX founder Elon Musk has successfully built many of his companies using taxpayer money and government subsidies. According to a 2015 article in the *Los Angeles Times*, these companies have benefited from approximately $4.9 billion in government funding.[8] Musk's space exploration company, SpaceX, has perhaps benefited the most from tax incentives and government funding; the company is now competing with Boeing to receive high-paying government contracts. Musk was a huge supporter of California bill AB-777, proposed in 2014, which would make space exploration and flight companies such as SpaceX exempt from paying property taxes. The *Wall Street Journal* noted in an article that "SpaceX could have sought an appeal of a property tax bill it received last year for engines built at its headquarters, but instead jumped the queue and petitioned the legislature for a tax reprieve."[9]

Shortly after Musk's attempts to have SpaceX exempt from property tax, the company was offered a $100 million incentive package by the state of Texas. Unsurprisingly, the company took this offer and moved to Brownsville, Texas, where it received $15 million for making the move and another $85 million to put toward infrastructure investments. Brownsville has previously been known as one of the poorest cities in America.

Many of SpaceX's projects and launches have been funded using money generated by government contracts. A report from May 2018 claimed that SpaceX has received approximately $5.5 billion in government contracts from both NASA and the U.S. Air Force. Since then, SpaceX has undertaken new contracts for the government, likely pushing this figure well over the $6 billion mark.

Citizens for the Republic, a PAC started by Ronald Reagan, is running an initiative called "Stop Elon from Failing Again." The organization has previously commented on Musk and his various ventures, stating, "Elon Musk is a phony and a fake. He is stealing billions from taxpayers because he gets good press from his fellow Millennials and because of his Washington lobbyists. Despite billions in profits, Musk is leaning so heavily on government subsidies and support that he can't even test an engine without the taxpayer holding their hand. This is a lose-lose situation. We can't continue to waste large amounts of taxpayer money on Elon Musk's failed schemes. There needs to be a congressional investigation of Elon's Musk's continued waste and continued failures."[10]

Elon Musk doesn't just rake in taxpayer dollars with SpaceX; he also received $750 million from the state of New York to build Tesla's Gigafactory 2. Hundreds of millions in tax dollars were given to Tesla as part of an initiative by Governor Andrew Cuomo. The money came with the provision that if Tesla didn't employ

1,460 workers in the factory, the company could face state penalties of almost $41.2 million. Currently, the plant employs around 800 workers split between Tesla and Panasonic, which also operates out of the facility.

However, some former employees have doubted whether New York's investment in the company is worth it. One former employee, Dennis Scott, commented on the issue, saying: "That $750 million could have been spread out a lot better to a lot of other companies to stay here in Buffalo than sinking it into one big company."[11]

Tesla provided a tour of the Gigafactory 2 to members of the media under extremely controlled conditions, which allegedly included walls built to block idle areas of the factory. Former employees have claimed the whole tour was a PR operation. Former Gigafactory 2 employee Dale Witherell commented on the tour, saying, "It was all fabricated for show. There was no actual production that day so some of the teams in their specific area were instructed to make sure they looked busy and they actually were working on the same module over and over again." Dennis Scott has also questioned the official current employee figure at the factory. "If you took all of our shifts, there are about 50 people, maybe 60 people at best per shift, there are four shifts," Scott said. "You do the math. Are you going to tell me there are 200 people up in the front office?"[12]

Good Jobs First calculates that Google's parent company, Alphabet Inc., has received $860,574,286 since the year 2000. Social media giant Facebook has received $332,585,266 from the federal government in a similar timeframe. In 2018, Facebook's revenue amounted to $55.8 billion, while Alphabet's revenue was around $136.8 billion.[13]

So, the question remains, what is there to be gained from the government handing over billions of dollars to companies already generating billions in revenue? The general idea seems to be that these companies will at some point bring more jobs into cities and states, but so far, all evidence appears to show that this is rarely the case.

Why are American taxpayers being forced to finance the latest SpaceX rocket or Amazon's new headquarters? And how much longer will politicians throw money at these firms before they realize that there is little to no long-term benefit? It appears that it's up to the American taxpayers themselves to draw attention to this issue and bring an end to this particular brand of crony capitalism.

17

AMERICA HAS SPENT $22 TRILLION FIGHTING THE WAR ON POVERTY

Fifty-five years ago, President Lyndon B. Johnson delivered his 1964 State of the Union Address and announced that his "administration today, here and now declares unconditional war on poverty in America." In the years since, American taxpayers have spent over $22 trillion to eradicate poverty.[1] It's been an utter waste of wealth. Adjusting for inflation, America's fifteen-figure anti-poverty spending spree, which does not include Social Security or Medicare, amounts to over three times the cost of all our wars since the American revolution.

Means-tested federal welfare spending exploded by more than 40 percent between 1980 and 1987, while the number of Americans living in poverty rose by millions.

President Johnson's Great Society created a slew of new poverty programs and agencies: Medicare, the government health-care program for elderly Americans; Medicaid, the government health-care

program for low-income Americans; the Economic Opportunity Act; the Office of Economic Opportunity Community Action Agencies, the Elementary and Secondary Education Act; the Higher Education Act; the Model Cities Program; the Housing and Urban Development Act, which created the Department of Housing and Urban Development; the Urban Mass Transit Act; the Supplemental Nutrition Assistance Program (SNAP), otherwise known as food stamps; the National Endowment for the Arts (NEA); the National Endowment for the Humanities; and the Wilderness, Endangered Species and Federal Water Pollution Control Acts.

Despite the litany of new programs, poverty, as measured by the U.S. Census Bureau, has hardly diminished since LBJ declared his infamous war. Contrary to his administration's lofty legislative schemes, a sizable portion of the population still struggles to make ends meet, and remains dependent on the same programs Johnson helped create to solve the problem of poverty. Incredibly, the poverty rate in America had been on a steady decline for nearly twenty years before Johnson declared his "unconditional war on poverty in America." For most of the post–World War II period, the poverty rate was falling drastically despite the absence of Great Society programs. In 1950, the American poverty rate was 32.2 percent. By 1965, that number had fallen by nearly half, to 17.3

percent, without any sweeping government intervention and new anti-poverty programs.

The most recent U.S. Census Bureau data placed the official poverty rate at 12.3 percent. Put another way, in 2017, there were about 39.7 million people living in poverty. This means that since Johnson's war, the poverty rate fell by roughly five points in fifty-five years. Robert Rector, a senior scholar at the Heritage Foundation, found that as of 2013, the federal government ran over 80 means-tested welfare and entitlement programs that provided cash, food, housing, medical care, and other social services to low-income Americans.

This figure does not include state-provided welfare and entitlement services. Furthermore, roughly 100 million Americans, which amounts to approximately one in three citizens, received government benefits from at least one of these programs. Federal spending is roughly sixteen times higher today, adjusting for inflation, than when the War on Poverty began nearly sixty years ago. As Rector notes, "But as welfare spending soared, the decline in poverty came to a grinding halt." Then, he asked rhetorically, "How can this paradox be explained? How can the government spend $9,000 per recipient and have no apparent impact on poverty? The answer is that it can't."

The disastrous results of the Great Society programs belie Johnson's intended goal. He promised the nation that his plan to erase poverty would strike "at the causes, not the just the consequences of poverty." "Our aim is not only to relieve the symptom of poverty, but to cure it and, above all, to prevent it," the president said.[2] But Johnson might have aided low-income Americans better by simply handing out bags of money to alleviate their economic ills. Instead, Great Society programs stagnated the post-World War II progress of eliminating poverty that was already occurring. But Johnson planned to reduce, not increase, dependence on American welfare. "We want to give the forgotten fifth of our people opportunity, not doles," he said, while also suggesting that the War on Poverty would help America make "important reductions" in future entitlement spending. He also said his initiative would be "making taxpayers out of tax eaters" and added that it would serve as an "investment" that would "return its cost manifold to the entire economy."

As welfare spending steadily increased, the various poverty programs began to serve as a substitute for a stable, two-parent household. Even worse, many welfare programs penalized low-income couples who married by eliminating or substantially reducing government benefits. Rector contended that this phenomenon created a perverse incentive for single-family households. He wrote, "The War on Poverty created a destructive feedback loop: Welfare promoted the decline of marriage, which generated the need for more welfare." What's more, there has been no significant increase in the number of married-couple families with children since 1965. Rector also contends that unwed childbearing and single-parent households are the most important factors for increasing childhood poverty. He notes, "If poor women who give birth outside of marriage were married to the fathers of their children, two-thirds would immediately be lifted out of official poverty and into self-sufficiency.

"Welfare wages war on social capital, breaking down the habits and norms that lead to self-reliance, especially those of marriage and work," Rector wrote. "It thereby generates a pattern of increasing intergenerational dependence. The welfare state is self-perpetuating: By undermining productive social norms, welfare creates a need for even greater assistance in the future."

Perhaps more tragic than the trillions wasted to end poverty is the moral cost of Johnson's massive expansion of the welfare state. Not only did American poverty stagnate in the decades after Johnson's Great Society took form, but the state of America's nuclear families also began to disintegrate. High school graduation rates, which had increased rapidly throughout the twentieth century, started to plateau after 1970. At the dawn of Johnson's War on Poverty, roughly 7 percent of American children were born outside marriage. Today that number has ballooned to 40 percent. Marriage stagnated, and single-parent households exploded as the welfare state expanded.

The result? A deadly darkening of the nation's inner cities. America was slowly littered with neighborhoods where shattered families and unwed (usually teenage) mothers produced unruly youths. With father figures and role models rare, these children were more likely to be born into poverty and were too often housed by HUD, doctored by Medicaid, taught in tattered schools, and fed using food stamps. The values and morals that make one an upstanding citizen fell by the wayside. What replaced them was a corrupt culture that shunned shame and perpetuated a panoply of repulsive self-defeating behavior: lawlessness, dropping out, and drug abuse. "Urban crime rates rose rapidly from the 1960s through the early 1990s, at which point the public got angry, rebelled against soft-on-crime progressives, and cracked down hard on criminals," author and investor Louis Woodhill wrote in *Forbes*.[3] "The result was an exploding prison population, with the majority of those incarcerated being young, fatherless males." Indeed, the legacy of the War on Poverty is nothing short of generational misery for the millions of Americans who had been reduced to the playthings of social engineers and progressive elites who'd spent decades dimensioning the poor down to the most shrunken scope of existence, one that endorsed poverty both moral and spiritual. Despite the Johnson administration's many promises, millions remain mired and dependent almost entirely on the state for their very survival. Instead of helping to cure "inequality," expanding government benefits compounded the problems.

Leading academic and civil rights establishment figures have spent decades arguing that America's legacy, Jim Crow laws and a persistent and systemic racism are the root causes of so much of the economic maladies many poor blacks still suffer. But the facts simply belie that logic.

"According to the 1938 *Encyclopedia of the Social Sciences*, that year 11 percent of black children were born to unwed mothers. Today about 75 percent of black children are born to unwed mothers," economist Walter Williams notes.[*] "Is that supposed to be a delayed response to the legacy of slavery? The bottom line is that the black family was stronger the first 100 years after slavery than during what will be the second 100 years." Newly liberated slaves sought out the long-separated loved ones and rushed to marry and start families, data shows. Williams writes that "from 1890 to 1940, a slightly higher percentage of black adults had married than white adults. Today about twice as many blacks have never married as whites."

No sociopolitical factor other than Johnson's Great Society—not even the real scourge of racial terrorism that persisted throughout twentieth-century America—can so neatly explain how black people who had maintained strong families, worked, saved, and secured varying degrees of education suddenly began to fall out of the mainstream of America's middle class just as those brutal racial barriers to success began to fall away. Economist Thomas Sowell summarized in stark terms the devastation that Johnson's welfare expansion exacted on black Americans. "The black family survived centuries and generations of Jim Crow, but it has disintegrated in the wake of the liberals' expansion of the welfare state."[5]

How could a people who had overcome so much misery, centuries of barbarity, be so easily seduced by social programs that sapped their self-worth and plunged its progeny into unspeakable despair? There are now two generations of black Americans trapped in a never-ending cycle of suffering. Despite all this, we still know that two parents mean twice the chance that a black child won't fall victim to the string of social pathologies that plague so many American inner cities. Indeed, author Charles Murray has spent years documenting how Johnson's welfare expansion encouraged the same pathological behaviors that have ravaged poor whites.

Rector proposes one solution to reducing American poverty: mandating that "able-bodied, non-elderly adult recipients in all federal welfare programs be required to work, prepare for work, or at least look for a job as a condition of receiving benefits." Republicans and conservatives have called for implementing work requirements for Medicaid as well as food stamps so that Americans can receive help while at the same time find the ladder that may help them climb out of poverty.

Robert Doar, a poverty scholar at the American Enterprise

Institute, advocates for work requirements for food stamps, which he says will help "fight poverty at its roots." An April 2018 poll from the Foundation for Government Accountability (FGA) found that Americans highly approve of work requirements as a condition for Americans to continue receiving food stamps. FGA found that more than 82 percent of Americans, including 94 percent of Republicans and 71 percent of Democrats, support work requirements for food stamp recipients. Perhaps it's an idea whose time has come.

18

AMERICA'S TRADE DEFICIT GREW 600 PERCENT AFTER NAFTA

During the 1992 presidential campaign, candidate Bill Clinton and then-president George H. W. Bush were aligned on one issue: that the proposed North American Free Trade Agreement, or NAFTA, would produce untold jobs and wealth for American workers, secure free trade with Mexico and Canada, and create amazing new opportunities and markets for American products. Only one candidate disagreed—Ross Perot. Perot might be best remembered for mocking impersonations on *Saturday Night Live*, but he was firm in his opposition to NAFTA.

Perot famously said during a debate that NAFTA would create a "giant sucking sound" of jobs pulled from America to the cheap labor of Mexico. Although most people laughed at him at the time, Perot was 100 percent correct about NAFTA. If anything, a "giant sucking sound" downplays the level of devastation experienced by both white and black American workers in the decades following NAFTA.

But even Ross Perot would never have predicted that shortly after entering NAFTA, China would be allowed to join the World

Trade Organization (WTO) and sap the American economy of even more jobs.

Economist Eric D. Gould of the Institute of Labor Economics presented the sobering facts of free trade in research he released in 2018. According to Gould, there were fewer American men working in manufacturing in 2010 than there were in 1960.[1] Gould described the situation like this: "The loss of these jobs represented a significant worsening of economic opportunities." That may seem a bit dry to you, but for an economist, this is like running around screaming with your hair on fire.

Factory jobs should never be discounted, no matter what coastal elites say. Gould explains that in 1970, factory work was the third highest-paying job for both white and black men. By destroying the American manufacturing sector, the free trade crowd vaporized the middle class for both blacks and whites. Indeed, as NAFTA gutted the middle class and annihilated millions of jobs, it also ushered in a nearly 600 percent increase in U.S. trade deficits, according to the U.S. Census Bureau.[2]

At least a million manufacturing jobs were lost to Mexico due to NAFTA. The losses accelerated after China entered the WTO in 2000, roughly another five million jobs from 2000 to 2014. Michael Stumo, CEO of the Coalition for a Prosperous America—a trade policy think tank—explained the China trade problem succinctly. "When you have China, for example, subsidizing energy, free land, subsidized employment, low-cost or free credit loans that become grants, and can undercut you by half, that's really big. It's an unearned advantage because of subsidies."

To really understand NAFTA, which President Donald Trump

called "the single greatest jobs theft in the history of the world" during the 2016 campaign, we must zoom in on some case studies of how free trade agreements devastated middle-class America.

One such example is Weirton, West Virginia. You may have never heard of it, but Weirton was once called one of America's steel capitals. It hosted one of the largest private employers in the state, and its largest taxpayer. It even served as the backdrop for the film *The Deer Hunter.*

But then NAFTA happened and Weirton, West Virginia, lost 94 percent of its steel jobs. Ninety-four percent of the best paying jobs in the state of West Virginia were shipped off to Mexico. The town shrank from a high of 33,000 residents to fewer than 20,000.[3]

The town was affected not only by the loss of steelworkers. The plant, like all large manufacturing companies, had employed doctors, nurses, lawyers, and all sorts of other support positions. The company had also plowed the town's streets and put up its Christmas lights every year.

A city government worker told the *Independent* that "nothing had replaced the steel jobs." And nothing would, as long as free trade deals like NAFTA made it economically foolish to produce steel in America.

Journalist Chadwick Moore documented a similar case in a story titled "Left for Dead in Danville: How Globalism Is Killing Working Class America," which explains the effects of free trade on Danville, Virginia.[4] Danville was once home to Dan River Mills, a thriving textile manufacturer that supplied 33 percent of bedding products sold in Walmart. But free trade demolished the business. The company's factories closed in 2006, and the Danville plant became one of 650 textiles-manufacturing plants that closed in the South between 1997 and 2009.

The town has suffered terribly from its free-trade nightmare. Murder has tripled, drug use and suicide rates have soared, and gang problems plague many neighborhoods. Violent crimes are 211 percent higher than average in Virginia, and crime in general is 66 percent higher than the national average.

One reason is clear—after the jobs left, incomes plummeted. Danville's median income is about half that of the state of Virginia as a whole. And the town is roughly evenly split between white and black Americans—free trade is color-blind and robs Americans of all races of their well-paying jobs.

There are untold numbers of towns and cities just like Danville and Weirton. The jobs left, and plentiful opioids took their place.

This downward spiral of manufacturing jobs would have continued under Hillary Clinton, a committed globalist and just as supportive of free trade as her husband. During the 2016 election, President Obama agreed with Clinton that the jobs were gone for good. Describing then-candidate Donald Trump, Obama said, "He just says, 'Well, I'm going to negotiate a better deal.' Well, what, how exactly are you going to negotiate that? What magic wand do you have? And usually the answer is, he doesn't have an answer."[5]

Despite Obama's skepticism, President Trump has found his magic wand, which took the form of scrapping NAFTA and slapping tariffs on China. And the jobs have started to come back, as it suddenly makes sense to make everything from steel to TVs in the United States again.

If you're a manufacturing worker who just got back to the business of building America's economic engine, or if your business suddenly has new customers with wallets fat from well-paying jobs, I'd humbly suggest sending a prayer to heaven for giving us a leader who recognized the damage that free trade did to America. And while you're at it, throw in a prayer for Ross Perot, who recognized the danger and tried to warn our nation back in 1992.

19

TAXPAYERS DOLED OUT $2.6 BILLION IN FOOD STAMPS TO DEAD PEOPLE

In the waning years of the Great Recession, billions of American taxpayer dollars not only went to millions of people struggling to feed their family, but were also paid out to dead people who had spent years lingering on the public dole.

A January 2017 U.S. Department of Agriculture (USDA) inspector general audit noted that taxpayers had spent $2.6 billion on food stamps for the deceased in a span of twenty months.[1] The USDA's inspector general sifted through billions of transactions from the Supplemental Nutrition Assistance Program, or SNAP, the federal government program known more commonly as food stamps.

It turns out, the inspector general's review of more than $23 billion in SNAP transactions between October 2013 and June 2015 revealed that 3,394 retailers authorized to accept food stamps were using the Social Security numbers of dead people when reporting their food stamp transactions to the federal government. The retailers then used the Social Security numbers of the deceased to cash in on food stamp benefits, redeeming $2.6 billion worth of welfare aid. These dubious transactions amounted to three times the yearly amount of fraud USDA officials reported between October 2013 and June 2015, according to the audit.

But the fraud within these stores during that time period did not stop there.

An additional 193 retailers authorized to accept SNAP benefits used birthdates of people under the age of eighteen when reporting certain SNAP transactions to the federal government, the audit showed. According to the inspector general's audit, $41 million in taxpayer money was claimed in the name of people who are not legally allowed to receive welfare benefits. According to the most recent government guidelines for food stamp eligibility from the USDA's Food and Nutrition Service, minors under the age of eighteen cannot receive food stamps in their name, leaving it to their parents or legal guardians to apply for on their behalf.[2]

It didn't take long for some shrewd state investigators to take a deeper look at their food stamp rolls before they found massive mismanagement and similar abuse. In 2018, the state of Missouri conducted an audit of its food stamp program and found that consumers conducted "3,668 food purchases" using information of SNAP recipients who had been dead for more than a month.[3] The audit also found 2,358 instances where another person made purchases using the food stamp benefits of incarcerated individuals, who cannot legally use food stamps while in prison.

It would seem that the economic downturn in America, caused by the housing market crash, triggered a massive rush of retailers seeking authorization to accept food stamp benefits from consumers carrying government-issued EBT (or food stamp) cards.

Indeed, a majority of the retailers busted for committing food stamp fraud with taxpayer dollars were approved to operate as licensed SNAP retailers during the first four years of the Obama administration, when enrollment in SNAP skyrocketed to record highs.

An October 2018 report from the Government Accountability Institute (GAI) found that between 2008 and 2012, the Obama-run USDA gave the green light for 71,000 SNAP retailers to operate, increasing the number of food stamp–eligible retailers by a whopping 41 percent.[4] But the increase in government-approved SNAP retailers did not go through the most stringent screening process. The USDA did not make it a requirement for these retailers to undergo background checks during the application process, leading to a bevy of bad apples slipping through the cracks. Between 2012 and 2014, nearly 36,000 retailers, or 11.8 percent of Obama USDA-approved SNAP retailers, took part in food stamp fraud each year, according to the GAI report.

- There were 216,738 firms authorized to accept SNAP benefits in 2010 and 40.3 million American on food stamps that year.
- There were 261,150 authorized firms accepting SNAP benefits in 2014 and 46.6 million Americans on food stamps that year.
- There were just more than 250,000 authorized SNAP retailers in fiscal year 2017 and 42 million Americans on food stamps that year.

By September 2018, 38.6 million Americans were on food stamps. A decline of more than 3.8 million fewer people on the program since President Donald Trump took office.

Around this same timeframe food stamp fraud exploded, jumping to $592.7 million in 2016. That represented an astounding 61 percent increase from $367.1 million in 2012, according to Department of Agriculture data. The number of fraud investigations in 2016 totaled 963,965, up more than 30 percent from 2012. Amazingly, fraud in the program increased just as the total cost of the SNAP benefits disbursed decreased. In 2016, $66.5 billion in benefits were doled out, down from $74.6 billion in 2012.

Still, the poverty program's integrity has long been a major issue. And sadly, most states' fraud investigation units, the offices that police benefit recipients, are severely understaffed. The same is true for fraud units in the Agriculture Department, which are tasked with monitoring retailers. "According to the USDA's website, the federal food stamp program has 'over 100' inspectors to police the nearly 200,000 retailers nationwide that accept EBT cards," wrote GAI President and Breitbart News editor-at-large Peter Schweizer.[5]

During the recession, food-stamp enrollment reached its highest level—47.6 million SNAP recipients—since the federal government first started recording data for the food stamp program in the late 1960s. But back then, food stamps were stamps. For decades, poor Americans handed a retailer an actual stamp in exchange for food. But thanks to the 1996 welfare reform, states were required to issue SNAP benefits on debit cards. The mandate made accessing cash benefits like Temporary Assistance for Needy Families (TANF) as easy as swiping a credit card. It also created a huge incentive for financial institutions to create and regulate the millions of welfare benefits being issued to these EBT cards.

Today, just a handful of companies manage most of the EBT transactions in America, according to the Agriculture Department. Among them are J. P. Morgan Electronic Financial Services, Inc., which has contracts with twenty-four states and two U.S. territories. Affiliated Computer Services (ACS), a subsidiary of Xerox, holds another fifteen state contracts. And eFunds Corporation, a subsidiary of Fidelity National Information Services (which is in no way connected to Fidelity Investments), administers EBT cards in ten states and one U.S. territory. To be sure, it had been several years since the Great Recession hit, but food stamp usage continued to rise long after the recession ended. The number of people enrolled in the food stamp program increased by 70 percent between 2008 and 2013, even though the Great Recession ended in June 2009, according to the National Bureau of Economic Research.[6] During the latter part of those years, the Obama administration also allowed people with incomes above the poverty level to take part in the program.

"This business is a very important business to J. P. Morgan," Christopher Paton, the financial firm's managing director of treasury services, told *Bloomberg News* in 2011. "It's an important business in terms of its size and scale. We also regard it as very important in the sense that we are delivering a very useful social function. We are a key part of this benefit delivery mechanism. Right now, volumes have gone through the roof in the past couple of years or so. . . . The good news from J. P. Morgan's perspective is the infrastructure that we built has been able to cope with that increase in volume."

An "important business" indeed. And it's one that amounted to hundreds of millions of dollars in revenue for the country's largest financial firms. "Just how lucrative J. P. Morgan's EBT state contracts are is hard to say, because total national data on EBT contracts are not reported," Schweizer observed. "But thanks to a combination of public records requests and contracts that are available online, here's what we do know: eighteen of the twenty-four states J. P. Morgan handles have been contracted to pay the bank up to $560,492,596.02 since 2004. Since 2007, Florida has been contracted to pay J. P. Morgan $90,351,202.22. Pennsylvania's seven-year contract totaled $112,541,823.27. New York's seven-year contract totaled $126,394,917."

The Wall Street banks that induced the housing market crash that wiped out the life savings of millions of Americans became the very same financial institutions now tasked with feeding a record number of newly poor people.

As is the case with most government initiatives, cronyism and self-enrichment appear to have permeated the political process by which those few wealthy companies positioned themselves to serve the new need of administering transactions for an ever-expanding poverty program. "Prior to the 2002 EBT implementation mandate, J. P. Morgan's political donations to members of the House and Senate agriculture committees were modest. But since 2002, they've been on a steady climb upward, rising from $82,302 to $332,930 in just the span of eight years," Schweizer wrote, pulling from government disclosures. "Adding to the unseemliness is the fact that three senators and six representatives who are agriculture committee members had, as of 2010, investments in J. P. Morgan; one senator, meanwhile, had money invested in Xerox. And in March 2012, the

White House disclosed that President Obama has money in a J. P. Morgan Chase private client asset management checking account."

But things did begin to change in 2014, when recipients slowly began dropping out of the program. The Obama administration's decision to accept some slight cuts to SNAP in the 2014 Farm Bill coincided with a precipitous decline in food stamp participation. Soon, state legislatures began proposing policies aiming to curb dependence on the program.

Obama signed the bill into law, allowing $8.7 billion worth of food stamp cuts, a move seen at the time as an appeasement to the bolstered House Republican majority that had lobbied hard to force more cuts to the entitlement program a year before.[7] States also tried to implement or reinstate work requirements for people receiving food stamp benefits, although many states put off these reforms due to the Great Recession. Maine led the way in these cost-cutting reform efforts when the state's Department of Health and Human Services began implementing work requirements in July 2014. Maine officials said the state's government would require able-bodied food stamp recipients between the ages of 18 and 49 to work, volunteer, or participate in public service activities to receive benefits, according to a 2014 *Bangor Daily News* report.[8]

A snowball effect began to take form. Other states moved to enact similar reforms, and some of the changes began producing desired results. The state of Georgia, for instance, reported a whopping 62 percent drop in food stamp usage after it gradually implemented its work requirement reforms in January 2016, the *Atlanta Journal-Constitution* reported in 2016. Soon, SNAP enrollment started to drop nationwide.[9]

A November 2018 study from Children's HealthWatch noted that food stamp usage among immigrants who came to the U.S. over the past five years declined by 10 percent.[10] The study added that the enrollment drop among recent legal immigrants took place because of a proposed Trump administration policy aiming to limit recent immigrants' ability to apply for permanent U.S. residency if they participated in SNAP or other federal welfare programs.

Although enrollment in the nation's food stamp program reached record lows during Trump's time in office, the number of government-approved SNAP retailers remains higher than ever before—and so does the number of food stamp fraud cases.

GAI obtained a 2017 fiscal year USDA summary, which found that even though SNAP enrollment dipped to historic lows, the federal government allowed more SNAP retailers to operate than in years when enrollment in food stamps reached its peak. It's as if no one learned the lesson from a few years prior. But why should Americans have faith in bureaucrats to competently monitor a multi-billion-dollar poverty program like food stamps? After all, millions of food stamp fraud dollars have funded deadly acts of terrorism, from the 1993 World Trade Center bombings to the 2013 Boston Marathon Bombing that left three dead and wounded more than 260 others.

20

WORLD LEADERS FLEW TO DAVOS IN A FLEET OF 1,700 PRIVATE JETS TO DISCUSS THE IMPACT OF GLOBAL WARMING

A fleet of some 1,700 private jets flew into Davos, Switzerland, in January 2015 to devise a plan to "limit our environmental impact" and mitigate the existential threat of global warming at the annual World Economic Forum.[1] That figure eclipses the number of aircraft that flew in seven of the ten largest air-to-air combat battles in modern warfare since the early 1900s.[2] In fact, the flock of private jets was so vast that the Swiss Armed Forces was forced to open up a military air base for the first time ever to absorb the sheer assemblage of super-rich, climate-conscious global elites converging on the remote Alpine region of Switzerland. Add to the massive carbon footprint produced by those flying from afar on commercial airliners into the elite global gathering, the countless helicopter commutes between the surrounding airports and Davos, or the increased auto activity for everyone from socialites to VIPs attending the event. The *Huffington Post*, a publication certainly sympathetic to the notion that we earthlings are diving headfirst toward manmade self-destruction, acknowledged in 2015 that "it's a bit ironic to discuss climate change at Davos, a remote location in Switzerland that requires a tremendous carbon footprint to even get to."[3]

Jeff Greene, the American real estate mogul who made billions by betting against subprime mortgages, "flew his wife, children and two nannies on a private jet plane to Davos for the week" in 2015, according to *Bloomberg News*.[4] Greene, a failed Democratic U.S. Senate candidate, established himself that year as the face of the annual event's dizzying hypocrisy by audaciously declaring that "America's lifestyle expectations are far too high and need to be adjusted so we have less things and a smaller, better existence. We need to reinvent our whole system of life."

In January 2018, another 1,300 carbon-pumping private planes landed at a handful of regional airports near Davos for the forty-eighth World Economic Forum. A year later, another 1,500 private jets descended on Davos carrying the assembled to tackle the planet's impending global climate catastrophe.[5]

The massive amount of greenhouse-gas–spewing private aircrafts it takes to convene this critical annual confab is bad for PR, admits Oliver Cann, head of strategic communications at the World Economic Forum. "How many private jets are going to Davos in 2019? It's a question that always gets asked. And so it should," Cann wrote. "From an environmental perspective, taking a private jet is the worst way to travel to Davos."

By now you might be wondering why the world's wealthiest influencers, heads of state, entertainers, CEOs, and politicians—poised to plot and debate policies with the express purpose of eradicating poverty and saving our planet from the "major threat" of a carbon-induced death—wouldn't just use Skype? The hypocrisy on display here is baffling, stunning even. A true profile in how the *haves* conceive the scripture from which they preach down to the rest of us about the consequences we all will face for failing to dramatically reduce our carbon footprint all while their weeklong soiree emits what amounts to thousands of carbon nuclear bombs. It's precisely the kind of insincerity that goes a long way to explain why so few American adults are overly concerned with climate change.

Less than half of independent voters, people not beholden to one political party or another, said in December 2018 that more action should be taken to address climate change. That's up from 22 percent in 1999.[6]

Three months after the 1,700 jets flew into Davos, President Barack Obama and Bill Nye flew from DC to the Florida Everglades for an empty talk about climate change's negative effect on the U.S. economy.[7] "Heading down to DC to catch an #EarthDay flight on Air Force One tomorrow with the president. We're going to #ActOnClimate," Nye wrote on Twitter.[8] Two years later, Obama boarded a private jet and was accompanied by a fourteen-car convoy to attend a climate change conference in Milan.[9]

Of course climate-alarmists like Obama and Al Gore warn that we can't "continue to put 90 million tons of global warming pollution into the atmosphere every day, as if it's an open sewer."[10] But America's leading elected officials who lecture voters about their need to cut their carbon footprint are some of the world's worst carbon-pumping perpetrators. Gore, for example, claims to live a "carbon-free lifestyle" but has had to repeatedly defend the power suck his sprawling 10,000-plus-square-foot Nashville, Tennessee, mansion musters. It's "more electricity in one year than the average American family uses in twenty-one years," according to one study.[11]

Speaker of the House Nancy Pelosi, who warned the world in January 2019 to "face the existential threat of our time: the climate crisis," had spent years burning through millions in taxpayer dollars flying thousands of miles around the world.[12] "Milan, Rome and Naples, Italy, and Kiev, Ukraine, for herself, her husband, several members of Congress, and their spouses," Judicial Watch president Tom Fitton noted.[13] "The Italy trip included Milan, Rome, and Naples with visits to the Vatican Museum, Sistine Chapel, Duomo, and viewing Da Vinci's *Last Supper*."

Senator Bernie Sanders, who has declared climate change "the single greatest threat facing our planet," traveled thousands of miles via private jet to campaign for candidates from South Carolina to California in the waning day of the 2018 midterm election.[14]

New York Democrat Alexandria Ocasio-Cortez, the author of the Green New Deal, which has the express goal to "replace every combustion-engine vehicle," spent $29,365.70 on ride-hailing apps such as Uber and Lyft between May 2017 and December 2018, federal filings showed.[15]

Why should Americans concern ourselves with the warnings from wealthy elites and our elected betters about the jeopardy our carbon production is putting the planet in when those same elites prove time and time again to be the planet's primary polluters?

21

NINETY PERCENT OF PLASTIC WASTE COMES FROM ASIA AND AFRICA

Today, there are some five trillion pounds of plastic pollution floating around in various oceans around the world. Every year, more than eight million tons, or sixteen billion pounds, are dumped into the planet's waterways.[1] "Indonesia's Citarum River, blackened by debris beyond recognition, has been dubbed the most polluted river in the world. The situation has gotten so bad that the army was recently called in to remove the plastic waste—and prevent further dumping in the waterways," *Forbes* staff writer Hannah Leung noted. "It's just one sliver of the massive pollution problem in Asia. China, Indonesia, [the] Philippines, Thailand, and Vietnam are dumping more plastic into oceans than the rest of the world combined, according to a 2017 report by Ocean Conservancy."[2] About 90 percent of the planet's plastic pollution comes from a few rivers in Asia and Africa.[3]

A groundbreaking study conducted by a team of researchers at Germany's Helmholtz Centre for Environmental Research pored over data on debris from 79 sampling sites along 57 rivers and found that just a handful of rivers in a couple of countries account for an overwhelming majority of the pollutants piling up in our oceans.

"The 10 top-ranked rivers transport 88–95 percent of the global load into the sea," Christian Schmidt, a hydrogeologist who headed the study, told the *Daily Mail* after the research was published in 2017.[4] "The rivers with the highest estimated plastic loads are characterized by high population—for instance the Yangtze with over half a billion people."

The study, published in the journal *Environmental Science & Technology*, said that by cutting plastic pollution in China's Yangtze River—the third-longest river in the world—and the Ganges River, located in India, ocean pollution could be reduced by half.

What's more? Of the top ten rivers that carry the most pollution, eight of them are in Asia and two, the Nile River and the Niger River, are in Africa.

"The 192 [coastal countries] with a coast bordering the Atlantic, Pacific, Indian Oceans, Mediterranean and Black Seas, produced a total of 2.5 billion metric tons of solid waste," concluded a groundbreaking study titled "Production, Use, and Fate of All Plastics Ever Made," published in *Science Advances* and conducted by Jenna Jambeck, who is an environmental engineer at the University of Georgia, and a team of experts.[5] "Of that, 275 million tons was plastic, and an estimated 8 million metric tons of mismanaged plastic waste entered the ocean in 2010."

"We all knew there was a rapid and extreme increase in plastic production from 1950 until now, but actually quantifying the cumulative number for all plastic ever made was quite shocking," Jambeck told *National Geographic*.[6]

The growing problem of plastic pollution is a "planetary crisis," declared Lisa Svensson, Director for Ocean at United Nations Environment. "In a few short decades since we discovered the convenience of plastics, we are ruining the ecosystem of the ocean."

In June 2018, the United Nations Environment Program released its first-ever "state of plastics" report, which outlined actions the world's governments had taken to reduce plastic waste. "The assessment shows that action can be painless and profitable—with huge gains for people and the planet that help avert the costly downstream costs of pollution," head of UN Environment Erik Solheim said in the report. "Plastic isn't the problem. It's what we do with it."

But the report showed that United Nations–backed bans on plastic and other measure meant to lower plastic use have produced poor results.

Half of the sixty countries that implemented bans or financial disincentives couldn't produce data to show the environmental impact. Of the remaining thirty participating countries, about nine saw significantly reduced plastic use in the first year while another six countries experienced little impact. The report chalked up the meager results to a lack of enforcement.

Environmental activists, meanwhile, have little faith in the proposal and plans of action put forward by the United Nations. "We welcome that they are looking at a stronger statement, but with billions of tons of plastic waste entering the oceans we need much more urgent action," Tisha Brown of Greenpeace told BBC News. "We need manufacturers to take responsibility for their products— and we need to look at our consumption patterns that are driving all this."[7]

Plans to pare plastic consumption took off at the turn of the century. Multinational corporations and whole countries jumped on the bandwagon to ban everything from plastic bags to plastic straws. American Airlines banned plastic straws and stirrers on its flights and also banned plastic flatware in its lounges in the United States and around the world. The Walt Disney Company began to ban plastic straws and stirrers at nearly all its theme parks and resorts around the world in 2018. From Chile to Peru to California and Seattle, Washington, to Washington, DC, to the European Union, measures to ban plastic and Styrofoam have popped up in nearly all four corners of the planet.[8]

But cutting consumer consumption and levying fines, fees, taxes, and bans on plastic will do little to curtail the stream of waste piling up in our oceans, says Rob Kaplan, CEO of Circulate Capital, a New York City–based investment firm that has committed tens of millions to plastic waste collection. "There's no silver bullet to stop plastic pollution," says Kaplan. "We're not going to be able to recycle our way out of the problem, and we're not going to be able to reduce our way out of the problem."

22

NEARLY 70 PERCENT OF MUSLIMS (1.2 BILLION) SUPPORT SHARIA LAW

The mainstream media and politicians have spent decades trying to convince us that the majority of Muslims around the world are "moderate Muslims" who embrace mainstream Western values. But quite the opposite is true—in fact, the majority of Muslims around the world support oppressive Sharia law enforced by the government. You don't need to take my word for it; Muslims are perfectly comfortable answering poll questions about their true beliefs.

The Pew Research Center published a comprehensive study of global Muslims' opinions in 2017. One of the topics covered by Pew was Muslims' desire for Islamic Sharia law as the official law for the country they live in. Pew reported results by country, with answers ranging from 99 percent support in Afghanistan to 8 percent in Azerbaijan.[1] But when we combine the Pew data with census data about the global Muslim population, the true opinion of the global Muslim population is revealed. Some 70 percent of the world's Muslims, or approximately 1.2 billion people, support Sharia law.

The evils of Sharia law are worth their own book but can be

summarized as being completely out of alignment with Western values. Sharia law is based on strict observance of the Quran and other Islamic teachings. It includes tenets that forbid alcohol and gambling, and well-known laws against insulting or drawing the prophet Muhammad. Several crimes under Sharia law are punished by death, especially blasphemy.

So much of the brutality behind Sharia law is found in its treatment of women. Under Sharia law, women lose most of their civil rights, including the rights to an education, voting, driving, and inheritance. In countries that currently observe Sharia as the law of the land, women and girls suffer from honor killings, female genital mutilation, child marriage, and sex trafficking. Shariah also authorizes murder against non-believers, called *infidels*, who refuse to convert to Islam. It mandates the execution of gays and lesbians, and sanctions killing Jews and anyone who dares draw the prophet Muhammad.

Rabia Kazan, the founder of the Middle East Women's Coalition and a resident of Turkey, has witnessed the horrors of Sharia law firsthand. She talked about the threat of Islamic law at an event in Washington, DC. "Unfortunately, the whole world ignores our pain. They torture our girls; they stone women; kill our women in the name of Sharia law under the Islamic regime," Kazan said. She explained the reason that women must speak out against Sharia succinctly: "Silence is killing us."[2]

Numbers are one thing but they don't begin to illustrate the horrifying and deadly reality of Sharia law.

Take Saudi Arabia, where an Egyptian hotel worker was arrested in September 2018. His crime? Eating breakfast with a female coworker. The absurdity didn't stop there. The hotel owner was brought in for questioning for "failing to adhere to spatial controls for employing women." Egypt is no better. Popular actress Rania Youssef was arrested for wearing a dress that exposed her legs at the Cairo International Film Festival.[3] One of the worst things a woman can do under Sharia law is show her femininity, uncovered body parts in public, which partly explains the ubiquity of burkas and hijabs in Muslim culture.

Sharia apologists push the opinion that these examples of the law's asininity are germane only in the Middle East, where Sharia is both ingrained throughout society and strictly enforced. But the headlines from other Muslim countries are just as grotesque. Indonesia has the largest Muslim population in the world, but Sharia law is not official countrywide. It is observed as law in a province called Aceh, which has been a steady source of stories detailing the violence meted out against both men and women since Sharia law became commonplace in 2001. In 2014, a woman accused of "improper sexual relations" with a married man was gang-raped by eight "vigilantes," emboldened to act by Sharia law. The man she was dating was beaten; then the eight men dumped sewage on them. Following this horrific attack, the gang of criminals dragged her to the police station, where she was charged for breaking Sharia laws against extramarital sex. The police caned the rape victim.[4]

Canings and whippings are a common part of life in Aceh under Sharia law. In January 2019, a teenage couple suffered a whipping for being caught cuddling in public. It was reported that hundreds of spectators watched the two eighteen-year-olds whipped seventeen times for transgressing Islamic law. These whippings are not slaps on the wrist. After six unmarried couples were whipped after being arrested in a hotel raid in March 2019, two of the women were injured so severely they couldn't walk away afterward.

Many Muslims believe that Sharia law should also be applied to non-Muslims. This varies widely from country to country but is about a fifty-fifty split in the Middle East. In the case of Indonesia, Christians in Aceh have been punished under Sharia law since 2016. In the first case that saw a non-Muslim punished under Sharia law that year, a sixty-year-old Christian woman was whipped thirty times with a rattan cane for violating Islamic law. Her crime was selling alcohol.[5]

Sharia law is steadily creeping into the west, in some cases in an official legal capacity, and in others, by the actions of individuals whom Western governments appear unwilling to shut down. For a perfect illustration of Sharia law's unfair treatment of women, we need look no further than Sweden. Shocking? Sure, Sweden has a reputation for being a progressive country that embraces feminism and equality. But Sweden also has a "lay judge" system, in which members of the community can work alongside professional judges and replace juries in certain situations. These lay judges have introduced Sharia law in Muslim communities in the country. In a March 2018 case, lay judges found a man not guilty of beating his wife. Their reasoning was that he came from a "good family" and his wife did not.[6]

The former president of the Swedish Bar Association, Bengt Ivarsson, wrote on Twitter, "This is one of the most prejudiced and strange judgments I have read. Not completely unexpectedly dictated by two lay judges. Still, no one in charge wants to do something about the lay judge system."

European governments have routinely neglected or flat-out failed to thwart the spread of Sharia law. In March 2019, Mohammed Amin, a Muslim man living in London and working at a health center, harassed and threatened a female Muslim coworker who was not dressing as conservatively as he believed Sharia law dictates. When a doctor intervened, Amin threatened him for being a Christian and warned him against going to the police. Although Amin was arrested, he only faced community service and a fine of £85. Meanwhile, British police often raid the homes of people who make social media posts that criticize Islam.[7]

Western governments steadfastly devoted to the pernicious idea of "multiculturalism" have turned a blind eye to some of the most horrific outgrowths of Sharia. Bureaucrats and elected officials in Europe often actively cover up crimes against women and girls. One example is the United Kingdom's sweeping under the rug of widespread sex abuse and the "grooming" of girls by Muslim men, which has infamously occurred in Rotherham and other cities.[8] Some lawmakers in Western countries insist that Sharia "honor killings" do not occur on their land, despite a growing body count.

Too many Americans insist on wearing blinders, claiming none of this could come to our country. But that just isn't true. Twitter, an American tech company, has begun sending notices to users that they have violated Pakistan's Sharia law against blasphemy. Author and conservative commentator Michelle Malkin is one of many who have received the notice, which ominously adds, "This notice is not legal advice. You may wish to consult legal counsel about this matter."[9]

Will violating Sharia law become the latest excuse for Silicon Valley tech companies to ban conservative users from the platform? It doesn't seem like a stretch. Beyond the Internet, what we know is that the great majority of Muslims around the world support Sharia law, and if they migrate en masse to the West, they're more likely to cling to their religious beliefs and shun mainstream Western culture. Any claims to the opposite by the media and politicians are nothing more than dangerous politically correct platitudes.

23

JIHADISTS FROM IRAN, PALESTINE, AND SYRIA TOOK HOME BILLIONS IN U.S. MONEY AND WEAPONS DURING THE OBAMA ERA

Through the disastrous Iran nuclear deal—formally called the Joint Comprehensive Plan of Action (JCPoA)—Iran secured over one billion dollars in funding, paid in cash, from the White House. The Palestinian Authority (PA), an entity that openly pays the families of terrorists for their "martyrdom," received a last-minute windfall from the Obama administration just as the president was on his way out. In Syria, the Free Syrian Army (FSA), the "moderate" group President Obama touted as an example to overthrow Assad's tyranny, defected to al-Qaeda in 2015, bringing their U.S.-provided weapons and equipment with them.[1]

Both as a senator and president, Obama made clear his stance on the sovereignty of Palestine and the legitimacy of the Palestinian Authority, its government. In a 2009 speech in Cairo, Obama asserted, "the situation for the Palestinian people is intolerable. And America will not turn our backs on the legitimate Palestinian aspiration for dignity, opportunity, and a state of their own."[2]

In a subsequent speech in 2013, delivered before Palestinian Authority president Mahmoud Abbas in Ramallah, Obama declared, "the United States is deeply committed to the creation of an independent and sovereign state of Palestine."[3]

The Obama administration acted on this commitment largely through funding the Palestinian Authority. Much of the money came through an Economic Support Fund (ESF) that disbursed money to both the Palestinian Authority directly and to programs aiding the PA through the U.S. Agency for International Development (USAID). According to Congressional Research Service reports, the Obama administration gave $776 million to that ESF in 2009, $400 million in 2010, $395 million in 2011, and one million more in 2012.[4]

In 2013, President Obama ordered the release of frozen assets to the Palestinian Authority. These had been frozen following a PA attempt to secure a seat at the United Nations, despite not being a sovereign state. (Contested nations with much clearer sovereign claims, such as Taiwan, do not have a seat at the United Nations.) The released money totaled $500 million.[5]

In the waning hours of his presidency, Obama quietly allocated yet another $221 million to the Palestinian Authority, this time overriding complaints from GOP members of Congress who had blocked the move. Congress presides over funding appropriations as per the Constitution, but the president made the move anyway. Then–Secretary of State John Kerry told Congress about the money hours before the inauguration of President Donald Trump.[6] These funds never ended up in the hands of the PA. Trump froze the transfer shortly after taking office. But, experts have reason to believe much of the other millions offered to the PA as aid has fallen into the hands of terrorists.

The PA does not attempt to hide its payments. It runs a bureau-cratic entity called the Palestinian Authority Martyrs Fund, which pays the families of Palestinians killed, injured, or arrested in inter-actions with Israeli police. The program does not exclude the families of jihadists who die in suicide attacks. Among those imprisoned, the longer the sentence (i.e., the worse the crime), the more money they receive.[7]

The group has spent years funneling cash to terrorists jailed in Israel or their families if the terrorist died in his (and it's almost always his) attack. Not coincidentally, the PA seemed to have more money to spend on its "martyrs fund" every year as new American aid was made available. In 2017, payments rose to $158 million—compared to $135 million in 2016. Disbursements for family mem-bers of dead terrorists totaled $197 million in 2017, up from $183 million a year before.

These terrorists have killed not just Israelis, but Americans—meaning Americans are funding payments to the families of their compatriots' murderers. The most high-profile incident of such a case is the killing of Taylor Force, who was stabbed to death in Tel Aviv by a Palestinian "martyr." Republicans in Congress have at-tempted to cut U.S. funding for these payments through the Taylor Force Act, which would freeze aid to the PA until it dissolves the "martyrs fund."

The Obama administration was just as transparent about its preference in the ongoing Iran–Saudi Arabia proxy war as it was about its support for Palestine. Candidate Obama said he would negotiate with the Iranian regime "without preconditions."[8] The novelist Ben Rhodes—who inexplicably rose to become one of

Obama's top foreign policy advisers—said in the aftermath of the Iran nuclear deal that those who considered Iran to operate under the iron fist of Supreme Ruler Ayatollah Ali Khamenei were wrong. "The insistence that everyone in Iran's government is a hardliner, cut from the same cloth, willfully rejects any opportunity for Iran's own leaders to move in a different direction. It's self-defeating," Rhodes said.[9]

The game-changing provision of the Iran nuclear deal was the lifting of millions in sanctions on Iran. Initial estimates suggested that Iran stood to gain $7 billion in assets frozen in response to the development of its illegal nuclear program; Iran had an estimated $100 billion in foreign assets frozen abroad in 2015.[10] The United States handed over $400 million up front in euros, Swiss francs, and other foreign currency, flown in on pallets on the same day that Iran released four U.S. hostages—a move that made many question whether the payments were related to the nuclear deal at all or was just a ransom.

After much outrage fueled by unverified reports, the Obama administration finally admitted that the $400 million was just a taste of what Iran received directly in cash: a total of $1.7 billion, officially the settlement of a decades-old arbitration claim between the United States and Iran.

That nearly two billion was separate from the $150 billion Iran has "parked outside the country," as Obama put it, also ready to be released in the aftermath of the deal.[11]

Iran needed the money. Its sluggish economy, growing poverty levels, and the aftermath of the 2009 Green protests had left it a nation in anguish. Naturally, Khamenei invested in absolutely none of that. The money went to Syria, where Hezbollah forces ensured the prolonged tenure of Bashar al-Assad; to Yemen, where the Shiite Houthi movement overran the capital, Sana'a; to Lebanon, where Hezbollah now has a stranglehold on the government; to Iraq, where the Iran-backed Popular Mobilization Forces (PMF) now threaten to engulf the native Kurdish population; and to Hamas and the Palestinian Authority.

Whether it was smart for Iran to invest in colonizing its neighbors remains to be seen. It certainly did not sit well with average Iranians, who took to the streets in late 2017 and late 2018 chanting "death to Palestine" and "leave Syria alone."[12] But it may have been the deciding factor in cementing Assad's control over his country after brutal chemical weapons assaults in Daraa, Homs, Hama, and other areas failed to keep rebels from seizing one of the country's largest cities, Raqqa.

The irony of this is that Iran revived a dictatorship on life support after Obama funneled millions to the rebels trying to take it down. While the money to stop Iran's belligerence went into helping Assad, the money to stop Assad ended up in the hands of al-Qaeda.

Obama took an interest in the Syrian Civil War in 2012, following Assad's comments warning he would not hesitate to use chemical weapons. "We cannot have a situation where chemical or biological weapons are falling into the hands of the wrong people," Obama declared.[13] "We've been very clear to the Assad regime, but also to other players on the ground, that a red line for us is if we start seeing a whole bunch of chemical weapons moving around or being utilized."

Assad ultimately used the chemical weapons with no direct response from Obama, turning the red line into a punch line. The
attacks motivated Obama to seek congressional help to arm the rebels fighting against Assad in Syria, directly embroiling the United
States in that war. In 2014, Obama requested $500 million to fund
the "moderate" wing of the FSA, one of the many militias now par-
taking in the Syrian melee.[14] The White House promised to strictly
vet militia members for ties to al-Qaeda and its then-ascendant off-
shoot, the Islamic State of Iraq and Syria. The result? A year later, the
United States had found a total of 60 rebels who passed vetting,
meaning the fighters were receiving $4 million in U.S. aid each.[15]

U.S.-funded subgroups of the FSA like the New Syrian Forces
began defecting to the al-Qaeda associate the Nusra Front, finding it impossible to fight Assad's forces alone. Naturally, they took
their U.S.-funded weapons with them. Some FSA fighters, rather
than joining al-Qaeda, turned to Turkey, helping Turkish forces attack America's most reliable ally in the country, the Syrian Kurdish
People's Protection Units (YPG).[16]

We may never know how much Obama-era funding fell into the
hands of al-Qaeda. As recently as January 2019, reports began to
surface that al-Qaeda allies in Syria were in possession of antitank
guided missiles (ATGMs) the United States offered Syrian rebels
beginning in 2013.[17] Such missiles, if abandoned following lost battles, could also fall into the hands of the dwindling Islamic State, a
potential source of munitions for the terrorists.

24

THE TAXPAYER COST OF ILLEGAL IMMIGRATION WILL EXCEED $1 TRILLION BY 2028

We are familiar with many of the downsides of illegal immigration, from increases in crime and the spread of disease to depressing wages for low-skilled black, white, and Hispanic-American workers. But there is one other downside worth mentioning—illegal aliens will cost taxpayers more than $1 trillion over the next ten years.

A 2017 study by FAIR, a non-partisan public interest organization focused on illegal immigration, ran the numbers of our government's expenditures on illegal aliens.[1]

According to FAIR, the first challenge is figuring out how many illegal aliens there are in the country. It turns out, nobody knows, because nobody keeps an accurate count. The majority of data sources available rely on self-reported data. In other words, to go in the database, illegal immigrants have to admit they are illegal immigrants. Sounds more like an IQ test than an immigration check to me.

Despite the lack of accurate data, FAIR estimates that there are 12.5 million illegal immigrants in the country. We'll work with their number, but keep in mind if you ask ten prominent pundits or elected officials how many illegal immigrants are in the United States, you'll get at least ten different answers. But if you disagree with FAIR and think the population of illegals is significantly higher, it just makes the numbers more grim—the more illegals, the faster we'll waste a trillion dollars on them.

FAIR pins federal spending on illegals at just under $46 billion. This includes federal education programs, medical costs, the justice system, and welfare programs for illegal aliens.

As if that wasn't bad enough, FAIR then adds in just under $89 billion in state funding in the same categories.

That puts the total taxpayer expenditures at nearly $135 billion a year. In a decade, that adds up to $1.3 trillion taxpayer dollars spent on people who came to our country illegally. Of course, a lot of that spending is on the children of illegals born in this country as citizens, which FAIR estimates at 4.2 million kids.

Leftists make the argument that illegals are a boon for taxpayers, as they pay taxes just like the rest of us. FAIR buries this argument about a mile deep with the real facts. Tax contributions from illegal immigrants total $15.4 billion to the federal government; another $3.5 billion are paid in state and local taxes. That's $18.9 billion in taxes paid versus $135 billion in taxpayer funds received. Even a Democrat can do the math on who wins in this equation.

In business, "opportunity cost" refers to decisions or opportunities we cannot pursue due to what we've chosen to invest our time, energy, and funds into. For example, the opportunity cost for a restaurant chain that decides to open a new location in downtown Atlanta might be that it cannot open a location in the suburbs until the following year. Take a second and think about the opportunity cost of America spending more than a trillion dollars in a decade on illegal aliens.

What would you invest that trillion in, if the government didn't give it to illegal aliens?

Many globalists would be eager to spend another trillion on a decade of endless wars in the Middle East.

But the people who believe it is time to "Make America Great Again" know that we should be using the trillion bucks wasted on illegal aliens to rebuild our crumbling infrastructure: good functional airports, bridges that don't collapse, and of course, a big, beautiful border wall.

25

AMERICA PROTECTS AND FOOTS THE BILL FOR BORDER WALLS AROUND THE WORLD

CNN's Chris Cuomo made his feelings about walls clear: "The president went to the heart of what I call his 'brown menace theory,' saying these migrants, they're dirty people, they bring disease." He isn't alone either—CNN commentator Angela Rye shares an opinion that would be considered moderate on the left: "It is not about securing the borders. It is about xenophobic, racist, bigoted beliefs."

When Democrats aren't claiming a wall on the southern border would be racist or comparing it to Nazi Germany, they are repeating the mantra that "walls don't work."[1] But the funny thing is, leftists don't make any of these arguments about the border walls America funds all over the world for our allies.

America has been in the border-wall business for years, but for some reason, we're spending our money and expertise protecting the borders of other countries instead of ours. In fact, the 2019 budget put forth by Senate Republicans spends ten times more money on the defense of other countries than it proposed to spend on our southern border—$54 billion versus $5.7 billion.[2]

Reading about some of the border security projects around the world that American taxpayers are subsidizing is the geopolitical version of Oprah Winfrey's famous giveaways: "You get a border! You get a border! Everybody gets a border!" The 2018 omnibus budget included $500 million to build a border wall for Jordan. This wall stretches along its 287-mile border with Iraq and Syria, and its primary purpose is to stop jihadists from entering Jordan. Imagine a rancher in Rico, Arizona, whose family faces constant danger from Mexican drug cartel wars and destitute and desperate illegal immigrants. What's fair about him footing the bill to stop jihadists from infiltrating Jordan?

The contractor for the wall in Jordan, Raytheon, bragged that "In total, the systems we have installed protect 4,500 miles of borders." That's wonderful for Raytheon, but how many of those miles are along the borders of your home country?

Vice News had an in-depth report on the wall in Jordan, called the Jordan Border Security Program (JBSP). Here's how they describe the border security America paid for: "The first phase of the JBSP, the erection of the towers, was completed in September 2009. Phase 1B, the beginning of the fence, was completed in March 2014. Phases 2 and 3, the building of a fully integrated and networked fence running along a 275-mile (442 km) stretch of Jordan's borders with Syria and Iraq and costing some $300 million, are scheduled to be fully operational this year," Vice's William Arkin explained.[3] "Further phases will extend the fence along the entire border and improve surveillance and detection gear. Mobile surveillance stations and quick reaction forces will be stationed at vulnerable points or emerging hot spots."

And the 2018 omnibus didn't stop there. It allocated an additional $1.7 billion for security in Jordan and other countries, "that these funds may be used in such amounts as the Secretary of Defense may determine to enhance the border security of nations adjacent to conflict areas including Jordan, Lebanon, Egypt, and Tunisia resulting from actions of the Islamic State of Iraq and Syria."

When walls are being built far away from America's southern border, the money flows like water and no one is screaming racism.

America has also been instrumental in the building of border walls in Israel. Although we did not directly fund a wall there as we did in Jordan, America's massive foreign aid to Israel, including a new security act that would send the country $38 billion over ten years to fund its defense, means that the United States was a big financial driver of Israel's security efforts.

Israel has multiple walls. One is a 150-mile-long wall along Israel's border with Egypt, designed to keep illegal aliens coming from Africa out of the Jewish state. Must be nice, stopping illegal aliens, don't you think? The wall cost about $415 million and was completed in early 2013.[4]

The wall on Israel's border with Egypt reduced illegal immigration from 16,000 people in 2011 to 20 people in 2016. For those who are not math inclined, that is a 99 percent drop in illegal immigration. You can't get much better than that—if those twenty people are so intelligent and determined to live in your country that they can defeat your best security measures, you ought to welcome them in.

"President Trump is right. I built a wall along Israel's southern border. It stopped all illegal immigration. Great success. Great idea."

—Prime Minister Benjamin Netanyahu[5]

At this point, the standard leftist response is "But our borders are different!" Except, they aren't. The American border is much longer than Israel's, but also has the advantage of natural barriers along certain stretches. No one can argue with a straight face that an Israel-style wall wouldn't be a great improvement over the wide-open border we have today.

The more famous border wall in Israel is the West Bank Barrier, a 440-mile-long multilayered fence system designed to control the flow of people in and out of Israel from the Palestinian territories and to prevent terrorist bombers from entering.

Guess what? Like the border wall with Egypt, it has been stunningly effective. Terrorist attacks crossing the border into Israel cost 452 lives in 2002, before the fence was built.[6] Attacks since have dwindled to almost zero. According to the Israeli Ministry of Foreign Affairs, the West Bank Barrier caused "an absolute halt in terrorist activities."

And the bad guys seem to agree. In a 2008 interview with a Qatari newspaper, Palestinian Islamic Jihad leader Ramadan Shalah complained that the West Bank barrier "limits the ability of the resistance to arrive deep within [Israeli territory] to carry out suicide bombing attacks, but the resistance has not surrendered or become helpless."

President Trump recognizes that the Israeli model would work here. In early 2017, he commented, "Do walls work? Just ask Israel about walls. . . . Just ask Israel."

We know walls work from the examples of Israel and other countries we've built walls for around the world. We also know there is nothing racist about wanting to keep illegal immigrants out of our country, and not able to enter at will.

Leftists in the media and Democrats in Congress have to answer some hard questions: Why do walls work there, but not here? Why are walls racist here, but not there? Even House Democrats afraid to condemn the anti-Semitism of Representative Ilhan Omar (D-MN) wouldn't be willing to claim Israel should tear down its fences and walls.

Until the Democrats are forced to answer these questions, and until we realize that many Republicans in Congress love open borders as much as their colleagues across the aisle, we will be stuck in the frustrating position of watching America secure the borders of other countries while we hope President Trump can find enough funding under the White House sofa cushions to secure our border.

26

U.S. GREENHOUSE GAS EMISSIONS HAVE PLUMMETED FOR DECADES WITHOUT FEDERAL LAWS OR A MASSIVE CARBON TAX

As if it were ripped from the cutting-room of a *Saturday Night Live* studio, a major news organization proposed a jaw-droppingly ludicrous question to its millions of readers in November 2018: Is dimming the sun the answer to global warming? The article came from CNN, not *The Onion,* and was based on research by scientists at Harvard and Yale.[1] The idea: Pump large amounts of sulfate particles into the Earth's lower stratosphere via plane, balloons, or large guns. The hypothetical plan would cost around $3.5 billion. It was merely the latest in a long line of senseless ideas to save the planet from peril. Political solutions to global warming, however, have long-proved equally half-baked and just as far beyond parody.

Republican lawmaker Carlos Curbelo shunned prevailing political wisdom in July 2018 when he introduced a bill that would impose a heavy tax on industrial carbon dioxide emissions.[2] Curbelo had hoped that his "bill or legislation similar to it will become law" one day. Unfortunately for the Florida native, the odds of his measure making its way out of the United States House of Representatives were infinitely slimmer than the likelihood that he'd be there to see it happen. You see, Curbelo shared the same fate as Bob Inglis, a six-term Republican from a southern state, who was booted out of office mere months after introducing a carbon tax bill. But unlike Inglis, Curbelo had unveiled his plan to tax the planet into cooler temperatures almost a month after data showed that the amount of American carbon dioxide pumped into the atmosphere had continued to steadily decline for more than a decade.

Indeed, according to Environmental Protection Agency (EPA) data released in June 2018, greenhouse gas emissions—which scientists say are the main driver of man-made global warming—nosedived without the enactment of a massive federal law mandating such decreases.[3] Though global warming alarmism hit a fever pitch after Al Gore failed to become president—and remained remarkably irrelevant to voters when they were surveyed—the U.S. was the world's leader in reduction of greenhouse gas emissions in 2017. "Carbon emissions from energy use from the U.S. are the lowest since 1992," said a June 2018 BP Statistical Review of Global Energy report detailing the state of America's CO2 output in 2017.[4] Of all countries, "declines were led by the U.S. (−0.5%)," the report acknowledged, adding that "this is the ninth time in this century that the US has had the largest decline in emissions in the world. This also was the third consecutive year that emissions in the US declined, though the fall was the smallest over the last three years."

Often overlooked and seldom reported, the United States' carbon emissions output stands in sharp contrast with major polluters like Russia, Iran, the European Union, and China, whose increases in greenhouse gas emissions were more than three times the United States' decreases. Despite the gains America has made in reducing our carbon footprint, most of the planet is falling far short of the goals set by the United Nations in cutting greenhouse gas emissions. And it's not for lack of trying. From California to Kazakhstan, countries and provinces and cities around the world have implemented ambitious policies meant to pare the pollutants pumped into the atmosphere. But to no avail. And while failing to constrain carbon output, a bevy of these bureaucratic boondoggles have succeeded only in pissing off the people who pay for the costs of cutting emissions.

The Golden State, the world's fifth largest economy, approved a plan calling for 100 percent carbon-free electricity by 2045.[5] But Californians need only look to their northern neighbors for confirmation of the kind of calamity creating a carbon-free fairyland can bear. In 2008, British Columbia became the first North American region to implement a carbon tax. In the decade since, the legislation has forced the government to report how it repeatedly failed to meet its goal to reduce emissions.[6]

Food and Water Watch, a Washington, DC–based nonprofit environmental group, called the Canadian carbon tax on 70 percent of emissions a "failed experiment."[7] "The real-world record fails to demonstrate that British Columbia's carbon tax reduced carbon emissions, fossil fuel consumption or vehicle travel," the group said. Its data, which tracked greenhouse gas emissions in British Columbia from 1990 to 2014, actually showed that greenhouse gas pollutant levels were falling for several years before the government passed its regressive tax plan. "During the years that the tax was in place for the entire year, from 2009 to 2014, greenhouse gas emissions from taxed sources rose by a total of 4.3 percent," the group noted. "During this same time period, emissions from non-taxed sources fell by a total of 2.1 percent."

In just a few short years since Prime Minister Justin Trudeau of Canada put a new plan in place forcing provinces to tax CO2 generated by businesses, foreign companies began "to invest in other countries to avoid Canada's carbon taxes," noted Ethan Allen Institute policy analyst David Flemming.[8] Citing *Wall Street Journal* analysis, Flemming writes that "foreign direct investment in Canada fell 56 percent(!) from 2013 to 2017, which has caused Canada's prospects for economic growth to decrease. As a result, Trudeau has been forced to decrease his demands out of fear that his party would lose in the 2019 election." To date, the British Columbian carbon tax has been an utter disaster. And the province hasn't come close to meeting its goal to reduce emissions 33 percent by 2020.

Despite an ever-expanding amount of evidence that taxing CO2 does nothing to reduce a population center's greenhouse gas output, more countries are implementing policies that do just that. But some countries are beginning to shift course. "Australia rescinded its carbon tax after massive public outcry, which led to a change in government," noted Jonathan Lesser, president of Continental Economics.[9] "Britain's carbon tax is hated, and its subsidies for wind and solar power, like those in Germany and Spain, have led to soaring electricity prices, increased energy poverty, and reduced industrial competitiveness."

Meanwhile, China and India are the driving forces behind a

world where carbon emissions continue to rise. Ignoring the United Nation's dire demand that countries impose hefty taxes on CO_2, these populous mega-countries have no incentive to tax their pollution. It would increase their energy costs and make them far less competitive on a global scale. Poor and developing nations also have no incentive to reduce emissions. For example, in Ethiopia and Tanzania, cotton and coffee are critical economic drivers and generate a giant carbon footprint from farm to storefront. Uzbekistan, home to the world's seventh largest gold producer and fourth largest mining reserves, would also suffer from emissions penalties. The world's fastest-growing economies and historically destitute nations will never enact feel-good carbon taxes that don't cut CO_2 emissions and only raise the price of everything.

27

HILLARY CLINTON SUPPORTED A "STRONG, COMPETENT, PROSPEROUS, STABLE RUSSIA" BEFORE BLAMING IT FOR HER ELECTION LOSS

Hillary Clinton advocated for a "strong" Russian Federation in an extensive interview in 2010 with Russian-American journalist and former Soviet propagandist Vladimir Pozner.[1] Asked how the United States plans to challenge Russia for its myriad human rights abuses while also building a strategic partnership between the two nations, Clinton said, "One of the fears that I hear from Russians is that somehow the United States wants Russia to be weak. That could not be farther from the truth. Our goal is to help strengthen Russia. We see Russia with the strong culture, with the incredible intellectual capital that Russia has, as a leader in the twenty-first century. And we sometimes feel like we believe more in your future than sometimes Russians do.

"I mean, we want very much to have a strong Russia because

a strong, competent, prosperous, stable Russia is, we think, in the interests of the world," the former secretary of state added.

That was in March 2010. In the year leading up to Hillary Clinton's face-to-face with Pozner, scores of Russia's most prominent human rights advocates were kidnapped, murdered in cold blood, or openly threatened. More than a week before her sit-down with Pozner, Clinton's State Department released a blistering annual report, which cited international experts who "reported that the March 2008 election for president in Russia was neither fair nor free, and failed to meet many international standards for democratic elections."[2] In fact, the State Department's report on human rights practices in Russia should have made it impossible for Hillary Clinton to endorse the idea that the United States was eager "to help strengthen Russia."

Clinton's State Department cited "numerous reports of governmental and societal human rights problems and abuses during the year." These included:

- **Killing human rights activists**
- **Physical abuse by law enforcement**
- **Searches without court warrants**
- **Interference with political speech on major television networks**
- **Murders of eight journalists, with more beaten**
- **Political instructions to government-owned media outlets**

- Pressure on major independent outlets to abstain from critical coverage
- Limited freedom of assembly, with police using violence on peaceful protesters
- Discrimination, harassment, and violence against religious minorities
- Continuing anti-Semitism, while acknowledging that the number of anti-Semitic attacks decreased
- Corruption with impunity throughout the executive, legislative, and judicial branches
- Restricting the activities of some nongovernmental organizations (NGOs)
- Human trafficking
- Xenophobic, racial, and ethnic attacks and hate crimes, particularly by skinheads, nationalists, and right-wing extremists
- Forced labor

Given the grossly atrocious state of civil society on virtually every level of life for marginalized Russian people, minorities, human rights advocates, and journalists, among others, as noted by the State Department, there's no wonder Hillary Clinton's interview with Pozner went unnoticed by America's media and the world for years. It would seem that the Obama administration didn't want the world to read Hillary Clinton's remarks about making Russia great again, given that a U.S. Department of State website link showing a transcript of Clinton's interview with Pozner wasn't created until well after she left her State Department post in February 2013.

As it were, just a few years after declaring that the United States doesn't "see Russia as a threat," Clinton responded to the Kremlin's 2014 annexation of Crimea by comparing Vladimir Putin to Adolf Hitler.[3] And three years later, in her 2017 book, *What Happened*, Hillary Clinton placed part of the blame for her presidential election loss to Donald Trump at the feet of the Russian president. "What Putin wanted to do was [. . .] influence our election, and he's not exactly fond of strong women, so you add that together and that's pretty much what it means."[4]

28

HILLARY AND BILL CLINTON MADE MILLIONS AND RUSSIA GOT 20 PERCENT OF ALL U.S. URANIUM

In June 2010, former president Bill Clinton received a half-a-million-dollar speaking fee for an event in Moscow attended by high-ranking Russian officials. The six-figure check was furnished by a Russian government–connected investment bank, Renaissance Capital, which stood to gain financially from the sale of 20 percent of America's uranium supply. At the time, the uranium was owned by the Canadian company Uranium One and it was going to be sold to the Kremlin-controlled nuclear energy company Rosatom.[1] The sale of a controlling interest in Uranium One to the Russians was approved by the Nuclear Regulatory Commission, an independent U.S. agency. But the deal involved a fifth of America's uranium supply, American uranium mines, and exploration fields and, therefore, required the approval of the Committee on Foreign Investment in the United States (CFIUS). Hillary Clinton's State Department was one of the nine U.S. agencies and committees that made up CFIUS.

As first documented by Peter Schweizer in his best-selling book *Clinton Cash*, millions of dollars were funneled by beneficiaries of the Uranium One sale to the Clintons' family foundation around the time that Hillary Clinton's State Department was being asked to approve a transaction that had huge diplomatic and national security implications.[2]

Pulitzer Prize–winning *New York Times* reporter Jo Becker broke down the deal thus:

> As the Russians gradually assumed control of Uranium One in three separate transactions from 2009 to 2013, Canadian records show, a flow of cash made its way to the Clinton Foundation. Uranium One's chairman used his family foundation to make four donations totaling $2.35 million. . . . Other people with ties to the company made donations as well.

"Those contributions were not publicly disclosed by the Clintons, despite an agreement Mrs. Clinton had struck with the Obama White House to publicly identify all donors," the *New York Times* reported. The *New York Times* also confirmed that "shortly after the Russians announced their intention to acquire a majority stake in Uranium One, Mr. Clinton received $500,000 for a Moscow speech from a Russian investment bank with links to the Kremlin that was promoting Uranium One stock."

When asked to defend what looked like his trading on the currency that was his wife's position as Secretary of State, Bill Clinton said he doesn't take every speaking gig offered to him, noting, in 2015, that "if there's something wrong with it, I don't take it."

"Something wrong," in this case, might have been the timing. But perhaps more troubling is that nine foreign investors involved in the uranium deal donated a combined $145 million to Hillary and Bill Clinton's family foundation. No such charitable contributions were made to the family foundations belonging to the other eight agency chiefs who approved the uranium transfer. There's no shortage of serious questions raised by this shady transaction. The first is the most obvious: Why did Bill Clinton cash a six-figure check from a bank tied to the Kremlin while his wife was secretary of state? Why did the Clintons' family foundation accept $145 million from foreign funders looking to profit from the sale of a company with assets linked to twenty percent of America's uranium? Why did the Clintons fail to publicly disclose the millions donated to their foundation from the former chairman of the uranium-owning company, breaking a promise Hillary Clinton made to the Obama administration? That these questions exist smacks of despotic political corruption at worst and a credulity-contorting confluence of coincidences at best.

But perhaps the most troubling aspect of this story is that before the Obama administration approved the sale of Uranium One to the Kremlin, the Justice Department had uncovered a Russian scheme involving bribery, extortion, and money laundering launched by high-ranking Russian officials with the express goal of growing Vladimir Putin's nuclear-energy footprint inside the United States. According to court records, the racketeering scheme saw millions of dollars sent to the Clinton Foundation, the FBI said, at the same time Hillary Clinton's State Department was set to approve the Uranium One deal. "Rather than bring immediate charges in 2010, however, the Department of Justice (DOJ) continued investigating the matter for nearly four more years, essentially leaving the American public and Congress in the dark about Russian nuclear corruption on U.S. soil during a period when the Obama administration made two major decisions benefiting Putin's commercial nuclear ambitions," *The Hill* reported.[3]

> - **Donations to the Clinton Foundation in 2013, her final year as secretary of state: $143 million**
> - **Donations to the Clinton Foundation in 2017, after Hillary Clinton lost the 2016 presidential election: $27 million[4]**

Schweizer scored the Uranium One deal as a winner for the Russians and the Clintons: "Everyone got what they wanted in this deal: the uranium investors made a nice profit; the Russians acquired a strategic asset; and the Clinton Foundation bagged a lot of money."[5]

As to the aforementioned questions the U.S. media never posed to the Clintons, the American people are still waiting for answers.

29

PRESIDENT OBAMA AND HILLARY CLINTON ENCOURAGED U.S. INVESTORS TO FUND TECH RESEARCH USED BY RUSSIA'S MILITARY

One of the Obama administration's first major international initiatives, as part of the much-maligned "Russian reset," saw then–Secretary of State Hillary Clinton initiate and champion a massive program known as Skolkovo.

Barack Obama visited Moscow in July 2009 and announced the creation of the U.S.-Russia Bilateral Presidential Commission. Four months later, then–Russian president Dmitry Medvedev unveiled the idea behind Skolkovo, a nonprofit initiative funded by the Russian government and American investors with the goal of building a vast high-technology and research hub intended to be the Russian version of Silicon Valley. Medvedev formally launched the Skolkovo Foundation in 2010.

"We have 40,000 Russians living in Silicon Valley in California,"

Clinton said in a March 2010 interview with Russian-American journalist and former Soviet propagandist Vladimir Pozner.[1] "We would be thrilled if 40,000 Russians were working in whatever the Russian equivalent of Silicon Valley is, providing global economic competition, taking the Internet and technology to the next level."

By June of that year, Medvedev was touring California's Silicon Valley, wooing tech titans to invest in and support the restoration of the Kremlin's crippled technology industry. For Medvedev, technological innovation in Russia was "a personal passion," President Obama said at the time.[2] Under the direction of Hillary Clinton, the State Department helped spearhead a recruitment campaign that enlisted dozens of American tech giants—including Google, Intel, and Cisco, whose CEO John Chambers signed a 10-year "commitment to invest $1 billion USD to drive entrepreneurship and sustainable innovation in Russia"—and some major American universities into the partnership.

The Massachusetts Institute of Technology (MIT) entered into a $100 million agreement with the Skolkovo Foundation, on behalf of the Russian government, that established the Skolkovo Institute for Science and Technology, or Skoltech, which ultimately saw MIT professors and researchers working out of the Skolkovo campus, which is located just 30 minutes outside Moscow. In 2011, an office near Stanford University was established for the Skolkovo Foundation.

By 2012, more American tech behemoths like Boeing, General Motors, Microsoft, and IBM had signed on to the effort and had made major financial contributions to the project. Skolkovo Foundation vice president Conor Lenihan soon announced that Skolkovo had assembled 28 Russian, American, and European "Key Partners."[3]

Of those 28 corporations, 17 made large financial commitments to the Clinton Foundation, totaling tens of millions of dollars. Some even sponsored high-dollar speeches delivered by Bill Clinton.[4]

Fearing the Obama-Clinton-Kremlin pet project could put America's national security at risk, the U.S. Army Foreign Military Studies Program warned in 2013 that "Skolkovo is arguably an overt alternative to clandestine industrial espionage."[5] The research and analysis center warned U.S. tech firms involved that Skolkovo could be a "vehicle for world-wide technology transfer to Russia in the areas of information technology, biomedicine, energy, satellite, and space technology, and nuclear technology. . . . The Skolkovo Foundation has, in fact, been involved in defense-related activities since December 2011, when it approved the first weapons-related project— the development of a hypersonic cruise missile engine. . . . Not all of the center's efforts are civilian in nature," the report cautioned.

In 2014, Lucia Ziobro, a senior FBI agent in Boston, Massachusetts, warned that her agency "believes the true motives of the Russian partners, who are often funded by their government, is to gain access to classified, sensitive, and emerging technology from the companies."[6]

Indeed, several Skolkovo research projects included both civilian and military application technologies. The Skolkovo Foundation published, in a 2014 document, the development of the Atlant, an advanced multifunctional airship being developed in the Skolkovo Aeronautical Center.[7] "Particularly noteworthy is Atlant's ability to deliver military cargoes," the publication said of the hybrid aircraft. "The introduction of this unique vehicle is fully consistent with the concept of creating a mobile army and opens up new possibilities for mobile use of the means of radar surveillance, air and missile defense, and delivery of airborne troops."

Cybersecurity experts warned in 2010 that U.S. companies working at Skolkovo "may . . . inadvertently be harming global cybersecurity," Radio Free Europe noted at the time.[8] The security centers of the Russian Security Service (FSB), which administer information warfare for the Russian government, just happen to be located in Skolkovo.

"It is here that the Russian government runs information warfare operations against the Ukrainian government," Vitaliy Naida, head of the Internal Security (SBU) department for the Ukrainian government, told *Newsweek*.[9] "It starts with the FSB's security centers 16 and 18, operating out of Skolkovo, Russia. These centers are in charge of information warfare. They send out propaganda, false information via social media. Recaptioned images from Syria, war crimes from Serbia, they're used to radicalize and then recruit Ukrainians."

In the end, as GAI president Peter Schweizer noted in the *Wall Street Journal*, "What is known is that the State Department recruited and facilitated the commitment of billions of American dollars in the creation of a Russian 'Silicon Valley' whose technological innovations include Russian hypersonic cruise-missile engines, radar surveillance equipment, and vehicles capable of delivering airborne Russian troops."

30

TOP DEMOCRATS BLAMED OBAMA FOR DOING LITTLE TO STOP RUSSIA'S 2016 ELECTION MEDDLING

"There is no serious person out there who would suggest somehow that you could even—you could even rig America's elections, in part, because they are so decentralized and the numbers of votes involved," a defiant President Obama declared during a press conference at the White House in October 2016. Chastising Donald Trump, Obama told the Republican presidential nominee to "stop whining" about the possibility that the election could be "rigged."[1]

"There is no evidence that that has happened in the past or that there are instances in which that will happen this time. And so I'd invite Mr. Trump to stop whining and go try to make his case to get votes."

Nearly a year later, however, high-ranking Democrats and even former Obama administration officials were publicly calling out their former boss, blaming him for being too hesitant and too timid toward Russia in the face of its covert campaign to interfere in the 2016 elections.

Representative Adam Schiff (CA), the top Democrat on the House Intelligence Committee, said the Obama administration failed to establish a "more forceful deterrent" against Russia's cyberattacks against the U.S. election in 2016.[2] "We should have called them out much earlier," Schiff said in February 2018. "While I respect the motive in terms of the Obama administration, they didn't want to be seen as meddling, the American people had a right to know what was going on and could be trusted to do the right thing with it. And they should have defended being more public and aggressive at the time, at least in my view."

A senior Obama administration official quoted in the *Washington Post*, in June 2017, said this of the Obama White House's failure to stop Putin's election meddling: "It is the hardest thing about my entire time in government to defend. I feel like we sort of choked."[3] High-ranking Democratic lawmakers agreed, scolding the Obama administration for failing to stop Russia.

Democratic senator Ron Wyden (OR) told CNN in June 2017 that he was "troubled . . . that the Obama administration didn't do more."[4] Michael Morell, the acting director of the CIA during the Obama administration, said it appears President Obama "did nothing" after learning that Russia has continued to interfere with the election after being warned by the president to "cut it out."

Indeed, Russia had been engaged in a full-throated hacking campaign against the United States for years before Barack Obama ever publicly acknowledged the national security threat that his administration had full knowledge of all along.

In 2014, Russian hackers penetrated sensitive parts of the Obama White House computer system. Hackers gained access to real-time information, including details about President Obama's non-public schedule. The breach was considered by the FBI and the Secret Service to be among "the most sophisticated attacks ever launched against U.S. government systems."[5] Russia's cyber war on America only intensified in the ensuing months, as President Obama downplayed the threat.

In February 2015, Russian hackers breached the Pentagon's network.[6] By July, the United States' highest-ranking military officials had crowned the Kremlin our greatest enemy. General Joseph Votel, head of the U.S. Special Operations Command, told the Aspen Security Forum in July 2015 that Russia "could pose an existential threat to the United States."[7] Within weeks, chairman of the joint chiefs of staff, General Joseph Dunford, told the U.S. Senate, during his confirmation hearing, that "Russia presents the greatest threat to our national security."[8] That month, Russian hackers compromised the email network of the joint chiefs of staff.[9]

In the summer of 2015, Russia hacking group Cozy Bear broke into the Democratic National Committee (DNC) servers and spent months monitoring email communications. In April 2016, Kremlin-linked hackers known as Fancy Bear compromised the DNC's servers, and later weaponized the stolen information after similar attempts to hack the Clinton and Trump campaigns had failed.[10] These breaches were met for months with little to no action by Obama and his intelligence chiefs, CIA Director John Brennan, National Intelligence Chief James Clapper, and FBI Director James Comey.

It wasn't until December 29 that the FBI and Department of Homeland Security released a thirteen-page report, titled "Grizzly Steppe: Russian Malicious Cyber Activity," that detailed the

Kremlin's election meddling scheme.[11] While the document was widely reported as being presented to President Obama, he was apparently well aware of its findings for months. And nearly every detail of the FBI–Homeland Security report had been published by private security firms months before Obama reportedly received it. U.S. intelligence agencies were "confident that the Russian government directed the recent compromises of emails from U.S. persons and institutions, including from U.S. political organizations," an October report stated.[12]

"These thefts and disclosures are intended to interfere with the U.S. election process. Such activity is not new to Moscow—the Russians have used similar tactics and techniques across Europe and Eurasia, for example, to influence public opinion there," the October statement continued. "We believe, based on the scope and sensitivity of these efforts, that only Russia's senior-most officials could have authorized these activities."

"Meanwhile, the Obama-era targeting of the Trump team involved the Clinton campaign and the DNC hiring an opposition research firm, Fusion GPS, which contracted with a former British spy, Christopher Steele, who used Kremlin-linked sources, among others, to produce a dubious dossier that may have served as the basis for the Foreign Intelligence Surveillance Act (FISA) warrants on the Trump team and, perhaps, for the entire special counsel investigation," wrote author and London Center for Policy Research senior fellow Monica Crowley.[13] "Seemingly, the Clinton and DNC teams were willing to collude with some sources in Moscow to hit Trump.

"As Russia ramped up its cyber espionage, the Obama team refused to say or do anything to address it until its first public statement in October 2016. Until that moment, they assiduously avoided rocking the boat with Russia in order to achieve their ultimate goal—the Iran nuclear deal," Crowley continued. "That also meant appeasing Moscow in areas beyond cyber: canceling planned missile defense systems in eastern Europe, negotiating away U.S. advantages in arms control, disclosing specifics of our nuclear arsenal, looking the other way when Russia annexed Crimea, invaded eastern Ukraine and re-entered the Middle East."

31

DONALD TRUMP WON THE 2016 ELECTION BY WINNING MICHIGAN, A STATE RUSSIA DIDN'T ATTEMPT TO HACK

The media-induced rancor around Russian election meddling had all but consumed the political landscape in 2016. But there's very little evidence to suggest that Vladimir Putin's propaganda machine had a substantial effect on the outcome of the 2016 election. There is no "evidence that vote tallies were manipulated or that voter registration information was deleted or modified," read the U.S. Senate Intelligence Committee's Russia report.[1] While there were several attempts to hack elections systems in nearly two dozen states by "Russian government cyber actors," Donald Trump beat Hillary Clinton in Michigan (by more than 10,000 votes), a state that wasn't targeted by Russian hackers and had eluded Republicans in presidential elections for decades. Hillary Clinton's lead over Donald Trump increased in July 2016 after a Russia-linked hacker released internal Democratic Party emails that embarrassed their presidential candidate, according to real-time polling data published by Real Clear Politics.[2] Sure, Russia raised an army of fake Facebook and

Twitter accounts that often spewed false and fiery headlines and advertisements. But two Ivy League professors, armed with reams of empirical data, reveal that "homegrown 'fake news' is a bigger problem than Russian propaganda.

"State-sponsored propaganda like the recently unmasked @TEN_GOP Twitter account is of very real concern for our democracy," wrote Brendan Nyhan and Yusaku Horiuchi, both professors of government at Dartmouth College. "But we should not allow the debate over Russian interference to crowd out concerns about homegrown misinformation, which was vastly more prevalent during and after the 2016 election." [3]

Another batch of embarrassing emails, this time from Clinton campaign chairman John Podesta (who had unwittingly clicked on a phishing email), coincided with Clinton's polling numbers increasing, yet again. What did hurt Hillary Clinton's election chances was FBI Director James Comey's October 28 announcement (in a letter to Congress) that he was reopening the federal investigation into her use of a private email server while serving as secretary of state.

The failed candidate has not shied away from firing shots at Comey. "I was on the way to winning until the combination of Jim Comey's letter on October 28 and Russian WikiLeaks raised doubts in the minds of people who were inclined to vote for me but got scared off. And the evidence for that intervening event is, I think, compelling [and] persuasive," Clinton said in May 2017, referencing the Russia-led DNC server hack. [4] She took a wider swing at Comey in her 500-plus-page election postmortem, *What Happened*, writing on her election loss that "the determining factor [in her losing the election] was the intervention by Comey on October 28 . . . but for that intervention, I would have won."

To be clear, Clinton's chances to win the White House had already begun to decrease in the days before Comey's announcement. But her election odds cratered a week after the FBI director's decision to reopen the email probe hit the news. What's more? When on October 7 the *Washington Post* published the infamous *Access Hollywood* tape, in which Trump made lewd remarks about women, his election odds hit a near-campaign low (though his odds, similar to Clinton's, had begun to decline before the tape was made public).

Media hyperventilating aside, so-called Russian interference into elections or ballot initiatives didn't begin during the 2016 election cycle. Researchers at the University of Toronto looked back and found that the Kremlin had launched no fewer than 16 attempts to influence the results of a major election since 2015. "Of these, two—Brexit in 2016 and the Czech Republic in 2017—turned out the way the Kremlin apparently hoped, and seven had results that partly reflected Russian interests," wrote Lucan Ahmad Way, a professor of political science, and Adam Casey, a PhD candidate in political science.[5] "One example from the second group is the 2017 French presidential election. The National Front won an unprecedented amount of support—but the pro-European Union Emmanuel Macron won. Similarly, in the United States, Hillary Clinton was defeated, but U.S. sanctions against Russia remain in place. The others were the 2016 elections in Austria, Bulgaria, a referendum in the Netherlands, and the 2017 elections in Germany and the Netherlands."

In many cases, the researchers acknowledged, Russia's interference campaign failed. And it was unclear what effect, if any, the

Kremlin had on the outcome of the election. "It's true that Russia has been increasingly trying to meddle in Western elections. But it hasn't gotten much for its efforts—and these efforts have often back-fired," Way and Casey wrote. "For instance, the U.S. uproar about Russian interference has almost certainly made it less likely that the United States will lift its sanctions. Thus, on balance, Putin's expansion of Russian interference may not be in Russia's interests."

It's also worth noting that while America is exceptional, it's not special when it comes to Internet-based foreign influence into its political elections.

Extensive research from Washington, DC–based independent watchdog Freedom House found that elections in 18 nations were influenced by online disinformation campaigns.[6] While China and Russia led all nations in employing armies of social media bots and paid opinion makers, other politically questionable to crooked na-tions, including Syria and Ethiopia, Turkey, and the Philippines, have all adopted similarly subversive tactics.

32

GOOGLE COULD SWING AN ELECTION BY SECRETLY ADJUSTING ITS SEARCH ALGORITHM, AND WE WOULD HAVE NO WAY OF KNOWING

In the modern digital age, a few major tech giants have risen to a special level of prominence, not only becoming household names, but also wielding enormous power over the Internet as a whole. The most powerful of these Masters of the Universe is Google. Initially created as a search engine that aimed to index the vast number of websites on the Internet to make them findable by the average person, Google has become a tech juggernaut, and its worldwide influence has continued to grow to frightening levels over the past decade.

Google has become much more than a simple search engine; it now produces a wide variety of products from online file storage to digital assistants and in-home smart speakers. Google also controls advertising on the Internet, in what prominent figures in the industry consider a duopoly, with Facebook as the other leader. Despite this, the company is still primarily known for its search feature, and it is in the search engine that its power to move elections can be found.

It has been estimated by Robert Epstein of the American Institute for Behavioral Research and Technology that tech firms such as Google could have shifted upward of 12 million votes in the 2016 U.S. presidential election if they wished to do so.

"As it happens, 90 percent of search around the world is conducted on just one search engine," noted Epstein during a radio interview on SiriusXM's *Breitbart News Daily* radio show. "There's never been a precedent for anything like this, ever. You've got one company that's controlling search around the world."[1]

Epstein continued, "That's a power to shift opinions that's in the hands of a handful of people in one particular town in Northern California, affecting people around the world, with no way to counteract what they're doing, with no competitors out there."

A study conducted by Epstein during the 2016 election cycle revealed that Google favored positive search "autocomplete" suggestions—Google's recommended guesses for what you want to search for based on the words you've already typed—relating to Democratic presidential candidate Hillary Clinton.[2] Often, positive results for Clinton were suggested to users even if negative search terms were more popular at the time. For example, when a user typed "Hillary Clinton is," Google would suggest searches such as "Hillary Clinton is great," as opposed to "Hillary Clinton is corrupt," despite research showing negative searches about Hillary Clinton were more popular at the time.

Epstein and his colleagues first noticed this phenomenon after a video published by Matt Lieberman of SourceFed caught their attention. Lieberman's video claimed that Google's search engine was actively suppressing negative information about Clinton while competing search engines such as Microsoft's Bing and Yahoo were regularly returning negative results for terms relating to Clinton. Epstein's report states, "It is somewhat difficult to get the Google search bar to suggest negative searches related to Mrs. Clinton or to make any Clinton-related suggestions when one types a negative search term. Bing and Yahoo, on the other hand, often show negative suggestions in response to the same search terms. Bing and Yahoo seem to be showing us what people are searching for; Google is showing us something else—but what, and for what purpose?"

Google attempted to explain Epstein's findings, stating that Google's search bar is programmed to filter out negative results for most high-profile individuals; however, Epstein and his research team claim that Google suppresses negative suggestions selectively. For instance, it was quite easy to have Google's search bar return negative suggestions for President Trump and a host of other conservative personalities.

It would appear, based on Epstein's research, that Google was biased toward showing positive results for Hillary Clinton. It may seem odd to some onlookers that a huge Silicon Valley company would be more interested in politics than in making money, but with Google, you have to understand the relationship between the tech giant's executives and the Clintons. Eric Schmidt, the now former executive chairman of Google's parent company, Alphabet Inc., and the former CEO of Google, stated during the 2016 campaign that he would like to work for Hillary Clinton, specifically requesting to fill the role of "head outside advisor" to the campaign. This was discovered in emails leaked by whistleblowing group WikiLeaks, which showed correspondence between Clinton's campaign chairman John Podesta and campaign manager Robby Mook.

In the emails, Podesta writes, "I met with Eric Schmidt tonight, as David reported, he's ready to fund, advise, recruit talent, etc. He was more deferential on structure than I expected. Wasn't pushing to run through one of his existing firms. Clearly wants to be head outside advisor but didn't seem like he wanted to push others out."[3]

Podesta described to Mook his conversations with Schmidt, saying, "The thing [Schmidt] really pressed me hard on was geography. Very committed to the idea that this be done in a city where young coders would want to be, preferably outer borough NYC. Thought No Cal was priced out of the market and too into itself. Thought DC lacked talent in this arena."

Schmidt outlined his plan for the Clinton campaign in previous correspondence with campaign officials; a key issue that was discussed was the location of the Clinton campaign's headquarters. Schmidt wrote to Clinton's lawyer Cheryl Mills, "The campaign headquarters will have about a thousand people, mostly young and hardworking and enthusiastic. It's important to have a very large hiring pool (such as Chicago or NYC) from which to choose enthusiastic, smart and low paid permanent employees."

Ultimately, the Clinton campaign placed the campaign headquarters in Brooklyn, New York. This could be an example of Schmidt's influence on Clinton.

Following the election of President Trump, Google executives were dismayed to the point of being choked up, as revealed by leaked internal footage of a Google meeting published by Breitbart News.[4] The footage showed Google staff at an all-hands meeting acting visibly upset at the election of President Trump, with many discussing ways to prevent such an outcome in the future.

The tape features Google co-founders Larry Page and Sergey

Brin, VPs Kent Walker and Eileen Naughton, CFO Ruth Porat, and CEO Sundar Pichai. At one point, Porat appears to begin to cry when discussing the election result, and Brin stated that the all-hands meeting is "probably not the most joyous we've had" and added that "most people here are pretty upset and pretty sad." Overall, the video adds further credence to claims of Google's bias against conservatives. It's hard to imagine what the meeting would have been like if Clinton had won the presidential election, but it's reasonable to expect there would have been a lot less Kleenex.

In August 2018, Epstein warned that Facebook could have easily influenced the November midterm elections. Epstein said companies like Facebook and Google could shift upward of 12 million votes if they chose to do so. More alarming is that Epstein believes the companies could do this while leaving little to no paper trail. "I calculate that these companies will be able to shift upwards of 12 million votes in November with no one knowing that they're doing so . . . and without leaving a paper trail for authorities to trace."[5]

"If on election day of 2016, if Mark Zuckerberg had chosen to send out what we call a 'targeted message,' a message saying, 'Go out and vote,' that went only to supporters of Hillary Clinton, no one would have known that was being done. No one would have known that the message was going only to supporters of Hillary Clinton, and it would have given her an additional 450,000 votes," Epstein explained.

Epstein concluded the interview by asking a very simple question, "Who on earth gave the executives at these companies the power to decide what 2.5 billion people around the world get to see or [not] see?"

So how do we prevent this mass manipulation by Silicon Valley liberals at Google? What should we look out for and guard against in the 2020 presidential election? Epstein, for one, is taking action. "With people on three continents, we're working on a system that will preserve these ephemeral events, so we will eventually have very, very good ways to track this kind of thing.

"But at the moment . . . what I'm very much afraid of is the midterm elections, we might not be fully operational by then, and that would be a shame, because there are no records left of these kinds of shenanigans, these manipulations," he continued. "If we don't get our systems up and running at least a month before the elections, Google will be able to do all kinds of things to shift votes, with no record and no one aware that they're doing this."

Epstein's team continued their work on the issue of big tech control and Google's influence extensively in hopes to be better able to measure just how powerful Google's influence could be in the next few elections. Epstein performed further analysis of Google search results related to three congressional races in Southern California. Democrats won all three races and, according to Epstein's research, Google's search results may have helped them win those races.

Similar to the evidence shown in the 2016 election cycle, which proved that Google pushed positive stories relating to Hillary Clinton, Epstein's research showed that users searching for topics relating to the three congressional races in 2018 were significantly more likely to see positive search results related to Democrat-related stories at the top of their results.

Epstein's analysis showed that at least 35,455 undecided voters in the three different districts could have been influenced to vote for a Democratic candidate over a Republican one due to Google's search results.[6] As a result, 70,910 votes could have been lost by Republicans across the three districts. In district CA 45, the margin of victory for Democrats was only 12,000 votes. The Democrats' total victory margin across all three districts was 71,337, which means that Google's altered search results could account for most of the Democratic votes. If this data is applied to the midterm races across the U.S. at the time, this could have accounted for 4.6 million undecided voters influenced to support Democrats during the elections.

Epstein's findings are also quite conservative in their estimates, assuming for instance that voters only perform one election-related Google search per week; it's actually more likely that a voter conducts 4–5 searches per day, meaning that the effect of Google's search bias could be even more influential that Epstein estimated.

Donald Trump's 2020 campaign manager Brad Parscale is well aware of these issues and has begun crafting a campaign strategy to work around the big-tech Masters of the Universe. Google, Facebook, and their compatriots in Silicon Valley can operate with impunity and have continued to shape users' opinions without most people noticing.

33

GOOGLE WORKS WITH THE OPPRESSIVE CHINESE GOVERNMENT TO BUILD A CENSORIAL SEARCH ENGINE BUT REFUSES TO WORK WITH THE U.S. GOVERNMENT

It was revealed in 2018 that search giant Google had been working on a side project in China for some time as the company attempted to further break into the massive Chinese market. This project, codenamed Dragonfly, was revealed to be a Chinese search engine with direct government oversight, leading many to worry not only about its censorship of searches related to democracy, religion, and criticism of communism, but also its use as a surveillance tool over the Chinese public.

One of the most troublesome and dystopian aspects of Google's Chinese censored search engine was the fact that it would block search results relating to certain human rights violations, democracy-related information, and protests that took place in the country. This was first reported by The Intercept, which revealed that Project

Dragonfly "will comply with the country's strict censorship laws, restricting access to content that Xi Jinping's Communist Party regime deems unfavorable."[1] It's enough to leave the typical Google user in the West wondering, "Why is the largest company on the Internet working to censor the Chinese people and willing to help that oppressive government 'disappear' dissidents?"

Senior staff at Google seemed aware that the project might not be well received by the public and, according to multiple reports, employees involved in the project were ordered to "keep quiet" and "deflect questions" about Project Dragonfly. One employee stated, "We were told to avoid referencing it around our team members, and if they ask, to deflect questions." Other employees were reportedly ordered to "delete a memo revealing confidential details" about the project, showing that Google was aware of the optics of the situation.

In an open letter, over a dozen human-rights organizations, including Human Rights Watch, Amnesty International, and Reporters Without Borders, condemned Project Dragonfly, stating that it was "an alarming capitulation by Google on human rights." The open letter further stated, "The Chinese government extensively violates the rights to freedom of expression and privacy; by accommodating the Chinese authorities' repression of dissent, Google would be actively participating in those violations for millions of internet users in China."[2]

In August 2018, Google employees wrote an open letter to management requesting further information on Project Dragonfly and its operations in China. "Currently we do not have the information required to make ethically-informed decisions about our work, our projects, and our employment. That the decision to build Dragonfly was made in secret and progressed with the [artificial intelligence] Principles in place, makes clear that the Principles alone are not enough," the letter stated. "We urgently need more transparency, a seat at the table, and a commitment to clear and open processes: Google employees need to know what we're building."[3]

Senior Google research scientist Jack Poulson, in what seems a legitimate act of sticking to ethical principles (a Silicon Valley rarity), resigned from the company in protest of its involvement in the Chinese censored search engine. In his resignation letter Poulson said, "Due to my conviction that dissent is fundamental to functioning democracies, I am forced to resign in order to avoid contributing to, or profiting from, the erosion of protection for dissidents. I view our intent to capitulate to censorship and surveillance demands in exchange for access to the Chinese market as a forfeiture of our values and governmental negotiating position across the globe. . . . There is an all-too-real possibility that other nations will attempt to leverage our actions in China in order to demand our compliance with their security demands."

Many public figures were vocal about their opposition to Project Dragonfly, including Vice President Mike Pence, who urged the company to end the project during a speech before the Hudson Institute in October 2018. Pence stated that other U.S. companies should be hesitant to enter the Chinese market "if it means turning over their intellectual property or abetting Beijing's oppression."

Pence openly called for Google to end the project, stating, "For example, Google should immediately end development of the Dragonfly app that will strengthen Communist Party censorship and compromise the privacy of Chinese customers."[4] In Pence's view, potential profits do not outweigh what companies like Google are forced to give up for the price of entering the Chinese market, namely their soul.

Chinese policy expert Michael Pillsbury told Fox News host Tucker Carlson that the Internet giant was "highly embarrassed" over the leaked information relating to the project. Reports at the time claimed that the project had been in development since spring 2017, but development was pushed ahead of schedule in December 2017 after Google CEO Sundar Pichai met with top Chinese government officials.

Google had already developed custom apps called "Maotai" and "Longfei," which were demonstrated to Chinese officials and could reportedly be launched within a year. In the interview, Pillsbury noted that Google had previously taken a strong stance against China, refusing to do business with the Chinese government, an act that one employee previously called one of the "greatest things" the company had ever done. "Fast forward eight years and Google has reversed itself, but done so secretly," said Pillsbury.

During a September 2018 hearing before Congress, alongside representatives from other major tech firms, Google's Keith Enright told the Senate Commerce, Science, and Transportation Committee that there "is a Project Dragonfly," but added that "we are not close to launching a product in China."[5] Similarly, Ben Gomes, Google's search engine chief, said in an interview with the BBC at Google's twentieth-anniversary celebration event, "Right now, all we've done is some exploration, but since we don't have any plans to launch something, there's nothing much I can say about it."

But according to sources who spoke to The Intercept, that simply wasn't true. One source said that Gomes's comments to the BBC were simply "bullshit" and that Gomes had in fact informed employees in July that Google had active plans to release a version of Dragonfly as soon as possible.[6] Gomes instructed employees to prepare the search engine to be "brought off the shelf and quickly deployed" once they received approval from officials in Beijing.

Gomes reportedly told employees that the Chinese censored search engine was "extremely important" to Google and that the Chinese market was a huge growth area for the company. "We are talking about the next billion users" for Google, said Gomes. He further referred to China as "the most interesting market in the world today," and told staff that "by virtue of working on this, you will act as a window onto this world of innovation that we are otherwise blind to."

In the same year, Google workers walked out in protest of the company's decision to work on a contract for the U.S. government, specifically the Pentagon. Over 3,000 Google employees signed an open letter requesting that the company refuse to work on "Project Maven," which was a customized surveillance engine, based on artificial intelligence (AI), with the capability to utilize data captured by military drones to track vehicles and other objects.[7] Such information is extremely valuable to the Department of Defense in identifying threats and civilians in war zones.

The letter from Google employees asked company bosses to cancel all involvements with Project Maven and to "draft, publicize, and enforce a clear policy stating that neither Google nor its contractors will ever build warfare technology."[8] The employees warned that if Google did not do this, their plan would irreparably damage Google's brand and its ability to compete for talent.

In short, Google employees protested working with the U.S. government on technology that could save the lives of American troops and innocent civilians, but the vast majority of them were happy to help the Chinese government stop teenagers from searching for information on the Tiananmen Square protest and to locate dissidents who could be "unpersoned" in the traditional communist way.

A separate letter published by the Tech Workers Coalition reads, "We believe that tech companies should not be in the business of war, and that we as tech workers must adopt binding ethical standards for the use of AI that will let us build the world we believe in." As a result of Google's involvement with Project Maven, approximately a dozen employees reportedly quit the company.

Following the mass protest over Google's involvement in the Pentagon contract and the company's subsequent refusal to work on Project Maven, Bob Work, former deputy defense secretary, criticized Google for its continued operations in China while refusing to work with the U.S. government. Discussing Project Maven, Work said, "I fully agree that it might end up with us taking a shot, but it could easily save lives. It might save 500 Americans or 500 allies or 500 innocent civilians from being attacked."[9] Work added that asking Google to teach an AI system to "look for things on video" was "what we [the U.S. military] considered to be the absolutely least objectionable thing" for the company to do. Work further noted that Google was operating a new AI center in Beijing with several hundred Chinese engineers. Work said that due to China's "civil-military fusion," in which all private companies have an obligation to share their information with the Chinese government, "anything that's going on in that center is going to be used by the military."

Following the massive outcry from both the right and the left over Project Dragonfly, Google claimed to have shuttered the censorship effort, with no plans to launch in China. The tech giant announced in June 2018 that it would no longer be taking part in Project Maven and would not be renewing the Pentagon contract in 2019. The company, however, has continued to work on Project Dragonfly. In fact, some employees' latest performance reviews were based on their work on the Chinese censored search engine.

In March 2019, The Intercept reported that Google was "carrying out a secret internal assessment" of Project Dragonfly.[10] The Intercept stated, "A small group of top managers at the internet giant are conducting a 'performance review'" on progress on the project so far. These performance reviews are completed annually to evaluate employees' level of output and development on a project. The reviews often include a peer-review component but The Intercept notes that in the case of Dragonfly, this aspect has been removed.

A source told the outlet, "Management has decided to commit to keeping this stuff secret," and are "holding any Dragonfly-specific documents out of [employees'] review tools, so that promotion is decided only by a committee that is read in on Dragonfly." If Google has no plans to launch the project in China, why is development still reportedly under way and being watched so closely by upper management?

Google executives are well aware that the repercussions for their refusing to work with the U.S. government are minimal, a slight loss in revenue, perhaps, but nothing that will have a massive effect on the firm long-term. But the repercussions for pulling out of a deal with the Chinese government shortly after establishing new research centers in the country and promising them a whole new method of spying on their citizens? Well, those costs could be far greater.

34

FACEBOOK CHANGED ITS ALGORITHM, LEADING TO A 45 PERCENT DROP IN USERS INTERACTING WITH PRESIDENT TRUMP

In early 2018, Facebook announced a change to the algorithm governing the site's newsfeed. Algorithms are complex software functions that, in Facebook's case, dictate for the social media giant what posts are seen by what users at what time. CEO Mark Zuckerberg announced that the algorithm would emphasize posts from "friends and family" and local news over those from business, brands, and the media.[1]

Facebook did, however, promise to promote "broadly trusted" news sources on their platform—unsurprisingly these sources consisted of left-leaning mainstream outlets.[2]

One of the most notable effects of this algorithm change was the sudden drop in engagement for President Donald Trump. Social media analytics firm NewsWhip reported that the president's engagement rate, or whatever percentage of his followers saw and interacted with his posts, dropped by a massive 45 percent following the new algorithm update.[3]

Democratic politicians such as Bernie Sanders and Elizabeth Warren appeared to face nowhere near the decline in engagement that the president did. They also have a much smaller reach than the president, meaning they have less engagement to lose.

Facebook appeared to be aware that this was taking place, saying in a post relating to the algorithm change, "Pages may see their reach, video watch time and referral traffic decrease. The impact will vary from page to page, driven by factors including the type of content they produce and how people interact with it."[4] But the president wasn't the only one negatively affected by this sudden change in Facebook's newsfeed; conservative media outlets suddenly found their reach on the platform declined significantly as well.

NewsWhip noted in April 2018 that mainstream media outlets such as CNN, NBC, Fox News, the *New York Times*, and the *Huffington Post* were dominating Facebook in terms of publishing for March.[5] In particular, CNN had seen their engagement increase by 30.1 percent, a jump that did not follow the usual pattern for a mainstream news site. In general, NewsWhip noted that a small number of viral articles could help boost a publisher's rankings for a short period—but CNN saw a sustained boost across all of their articles. NewsWhip noted that CNN's average engagement per article had been around 4,982 in February; this figure jumped to 7,010 a month later. NewsWhip also found that many other mainstream media sources saw a boost across the board.

Fox News and NBC saw a boost of a few million interactions while the *New York Times* saw a huge jump, from 9.3 million interactions on average to 27.3 million. Suspiciously, many alternative outlets saw a significant drop in their interactions at the same time. Breitbart News dropped from the ninth largest publisher on Facebook in December to the twenty-first largest just a few months later. NewsWhip stated quite clearly that this was likely due to the algorithm change, observing, "It seems highly likely that these changes are predicated on the ongoing news feed algorithm changes, which took effect around the end of January. It's not clear whether these increases have resulted in more traffic for the sites concerned, and it's not to say that all sites will have benefitted."

This was in line with Facebook CEO Mark Zuckerberg's commentary about promoting "trusted sources" on the platform. In a post from his own Facebook page, the CEO stated that he "asked our product teams to make sure we prioritize news that is trustworthy, informative, and local. And we're starting next week with trusted sources."[6]

To define these "trusted sources," Facebook stated that they "surveyed a diverse and representative sample of people using Facebook across the US to gauge their familiarity with, and trust in, various different sources of news."

In an interview with Vox, Zuckerberg discussed how Facebook was going to begin prioritizing publishers on the platform differently, saying, "Take the *Wall Street Journal* or *New York Times*. Even if not everyone reads them, the people who don't read them typically still think they're good, trustworthy journalism. Whereas if you get down to blogs that may be on more of the fringe, they'll have their strong supporters, but people who don't necessarily read them often don't trust them as much."[7]

In that quote alone, Zuckerberg makes it clear: the *Wall Street*

Journal and the *New York Times* will be among the lucky anointed to receive preferential treatment on Facebook.

In an interview with Breitbart News, *Western Journal* executive editor George Upper discussed the effect of Facebook suddenly intervening directly in publishers' engagement rates, saying, "Facebook's Campbell Brown has said that Facebook now has a 'point of view' when it comes to news. . . . They are, in other words, making editorial decisions rather than allowing users to choose what posts get the most traction through likes, shares, and other interactions," Upper continued.[8] "Facebook is saying to users that they don't care what sites or people or news outlets a user has liked on Facebook— they will determine what news users get to see. Those seem like the words and deeds of a publisher to me—and not only that, but a publisher with an agenda."

Unfortunately for Facebook, the sudden change to the site's newsfeed did not have a positive effect on its users.

While the company promised to promote "trusted sources" for news, they also promised to show users more posts from their friends and families in an attempt to "bring people together."

According to a survey taken by Ypulse in May 2018, the change in the site's algorithm made users unhappier. Ypulse surveyed 2,100 U.S. citizens aged between 13 and 35 years old, asking them how they felt when using different social media services such as Facebook, Twitter, YouTube, Reddit, Instagram, Spotify, and Snapchat. The survey revealed that fewer than one in three users felt better and more positive after using Facebook while most users felt better after using apps such as Spotify and Netflix. Although it may be hard to believe, 36 percent of users felt better after using Twitter while 44 percent enjoyed their time on Instagram. Facebook's figures were not so generous. Only 29 percent of Facebook users felt more positive after using the platform while only 23 percent felt their time on the social media site was "well-spent."

The vice president of research at Ypulse, Jillian Kramer, said at the time, "Entertainment platforms are giving [users] something to be happier, instantly lifting the mood and changing the conversation, whereas ones that are focused on self-identity and personal branding are not winning in that arena."[9]

In an attempt to benefit establishment media outlets and left-wing politicians, Facebook damaged their platform for the average user.

Explaining his site's new rule changes, Zuckerberg said the modifications would reward posts from "friends, family, and groups" and less so from "businesses, brands, and media." Facebook had promised to promote what the tech giant called "broadly trusted" news sources. It turns out that "broadly trusted" translated to *not conservative*. Indeed, Facebook's January 2018 algorithm change hit conservative news outlets hardest. A report from the Outline finds that conservative sites including Breitbart News and Fox have also seen dramatic dips in engagement, while mainstream left-wing news sites like CNN and the *New York Times* were virtually unaffected by the change. Frequency of posts did not affect engagement declines for conservative brands. The dramatic drop in engagement caused by Facebook's algorithm adjustment went far beyond President Trump and leading conservative news sites. The rate of interactions on the Facebook pages of Republican congressmen declined by an average of 37 percent, 10 percent more than their Democratic counterparts, according to data from *Western Journal*. Facebook has since admitted that it reduces the reach of material it considers "fake news" by up to 80 percent. Those who raise questions about Facebook's political impartiality don't do so in bad faith. Indeed, it was Facebook's COO Sheryl Sandberg who, in May 2015, told Clinton campaign manager John Podesta that she wanted to "help" Clinton "win badly."

As if Facebook didn't face enough bad news in 2018, Breitbart News has clawed back up to almost the top ten in engagement rankings on the platform, despite algorithm changes and all manner of dirty tricks meant to suppress Breitbart and sites like it.[10]

35

GOOGLE AND FACEBOOK ENLISTED BIASED "FAKE NEWS" FACT-CHECKERS WHO WERE OFTEN WRONG

Shortly after President Trump's election as president of the United States, the mainstream media turned its ire toward social media and "fake news." As a result, social media websites and tech companies from Google to Facebook decided to employ "objective fact-checkers" to police the content on their platforms.

There was only one issue: Nearly every fact-checker appointed as a social media arbiter of truth was overwhelmingly biased and often made massive mistakes. The fact-checking groups that Facebook partnered with included Snopes, ABC, PolitiFact, and FactCheck.org, all of which displayed left-wing partisanship throughout the 2016 election cycle.

For example, Hillary Clinton famously endorsed the concept of open borders in a paid speech in which she stated, "My dream is a hemispheric common market, with open trade and open borders."[1] One would think that Clinton's endorsement of open borders could not be more clear cut, yet PolitiFact claimed that it was "mostly false" when President Trump claimed during one of the presidential debates that Clinton had called for open borders.[2] When President Trump accurately claimed that Russia had 1,800 nuclear warheads and had expanded their nuclear stockpile while the United States had not, PolitiFact rated this statement "half true," adding that Trump was "missing the big picture."[3]

Elsewhere, fact-checking website Snopes claimed that the "general idea" of a widely debunked meme that claimed that thirty-three Republican lawmakers who voted to repeal Obamacare lost their seats to Democrats was "correct." It was pointed out by many that some of the individuals whose faces had been marked with a red X in the meme had never served in Congress, making it impossible for them to lose a seat to a Democrat, yet Snopes still rates the meme as true.[4]

ABC News, another trusted fact-checker, has a long history of bending the truth to fit its agenda. The most blatant example was when the news agency set up a fake police crime scene in an attempt to fool their viewers into believing that ABC was at the site of a kidnapping in Woodruff, South Carolina.[5] ABC reporter Lindsey Davis appeared on a segment for *Good Morning America* standing before a yellow strip of crime scene tape reading SHERIFF'S LINE DO NOT CROSS. The crime scene tape had been strung between two tripods on either side of the reporter by ABC News. Is this the sort of organization that should be deciding what is "fake news"?

Popular Internet fact-checking website Snopes.com was also revealed to be one of the trusted fact-checkers for Facebook, but Snopes has a well-known history of left-wing partisanship. Snopes employs a staff of nearly entirely left-wing fact-checkers, some of whom wrote for the online publication *Raw Story*, which was described as a "progressive news site that focuses on stories often ignored in the mainstream media."[6]

Many of Snopes' other employees have openly espoused their left-wing views. This includes its managing editor, Brooke Binkowski, who said in a tweet that supporters of Brexit were "pandering to racist mouth-breather 'Britain First' types." Snopes' bias against conservatives became extremely obvious when it began to fact-check satirical articles by the conservative parody-news website the Babylon Bee. The parody-news site published an article titled, "CNN Purchases Industrial-Sized Washing Machine to Spin News Before Publication." Sane individuals saw this article for what it was—an obvious joke at the expense of CNN. But Snopes felt it was their duty to ensure that the public knew that CNN had not, in fact, purchased a washing machine to rinse their news cycle. Snopes declared in a fact check that the article was "false."[7] But the result of Snopes marking stories by the Babylon Bee as "false" is that the site's Facebook page ran the risk of being penalized. The admin of the Babylon Bee Facebook page received a message shortly after the CNN story was rated false, which read, "A page you admin (the Babylon Bee) recently posted the link (CNN Purchases Industrial-Sized Washing Machine to Spin News Before Publication) that contains info disputed by (Snopes.com), an independent fact checker."[8] Then the important part of this warning is revealed: "Repeat offenders will see their distribution reduced and their ability to monetize and advertise removed."

So as a result of Snopes' dedication to marking any articles remotely critical of liberal news outlets like CNN as false (even when they're admittedly satirical) the Babylon Bee risked having their page reach be severely diminished, and even risked losing the ability to run ads on its Facebook articles. "Demonetizing," or removing the ability to make advertising revenue, is one of Silicon Valley's favorite weapons against conservatives and others they want to silence.

But all was not well between Facebook and its fact-checkers. Issues between Snopes and their Silicon Valley allies began to arise. In December 2018, some fact-checkers began to express their displeasure at how they had been treated during their time at Facebook. Some even went to the press. Binkowski told *The Guardian*, "They've essentially used us for crisis PR. They're not taking anything seriously. They are more interested in making themselves look good and passing the buck. . . . They clearly don't care."[9]

It became clear that the fact-checkers felt as if Facebook didn't actually have the best interests of their users at mind when they began the fact-checking program. Instead, the company was under immense pressure to do something about the issue of "fake news" to pacify the mainstream media and was being blamed by the cannibalistic left for the electoral success of President Trump. "Why should we trust Facebook when it's pushing the same rumors that its own fact checkers are calling fake news?" an unnamed Facebook fact-checker asked *The Guardian*. "It's worth asking how do they treat stories about George Soros on the platform knowing they specifically pay people to try to link political enemies to him? [. . .] Working with Facebook makes us look bad."

Unsurprisingly, in February 2019, Snopes announced that they would be ending their partnership with Facebook entirely. "It doesn't seem like we're striving to make third-party fact-checking more practical for publishers—it seems like we're striving to make it easier for Facebook. At some point, we need to put our foot down and say, 'No. You need to build an API,'" Snopes' vice president of operations, Vinny Green, told Poynter.org. "The work that fact-checkers are doing doesn't need to be just for Facebook—we can build things for fact-checkers that benefit the whole web, and that can also help Facebook."[10]

Now a new so-called fact-checking service has entered the online fray, this time with the partnership of old-school tech giant Microsoft. NewsGuard takes fact-checking to a new level. Rather than appearing alongside a single article or video link, NewsGuard rates news outlets on overall "trustworthiness." The fact-checking service provides sweeping judgment of entire news outlets rather than focusing on single incorrect or inaccurate articles.

The organization, which claims to be dedicated to fighting fake news, is backed by such swamp monsters as Tom Ridge, the first secretary of Homeland Security in the George W. Bush administration; Richard Stengel, the former editor of *Time* magazine and undersecretary of State for Public Diplomacy in the Obama administration; and Don Baer, the chairman of Burson, Cohn & Wolfe and former White House communications director in the Clinton administration.

NewsGuard's site "trustworthiness" ratings don't always make sense. For example, *BuzzFeed* has received a green shield of trustworthiness from NewsGuard despite incorrectly claiming that President Trump ordered his lawyer Michael Cohen to commit perjury, a claim later disputed by special counsel Robert Mueller.[11]

However, popular conservative websites such as Breitbart News and the Drudge Report are branded with a red warning indicating that the sites are "untrustworthy" and spread "fake news." NewsGuard comes automatically installed with Microsoft's Mobile Edge browser, only requiring activation, and can be installed on most other web browsers. The shaping of political narratives under the guise of fact-checking doesn't just stop at social media.

Which of these fact-checkers can be trusted? Who should the average Internet user look to when defining what is true? The answer is simple: Look in a mirror.

Blindly trusting any of these so-called fact-checkers is a fool's game that will result in an increasingly limited and easily influenced worldview. The only person who can decide what information is accurate is you. Do your research, and come to your own conclusions—not the ones that the Silicon Valley gods, political elite, and the mainstream media want to force on you.

Below is a brutally honest instant message exchange between a nineteen-year-old Zuckerberg and a friend shortly after Facebook launched:

Zuck: Yeah so if you ever need info about anyone at Harvard
Zuck: Just ask
Zuck: I have over 4,000 emails, pictures, addresses, SSN
[Redacted Friend's Name]: What? How'd you manage that one?
Zuck: People just submitted it.
Zuck: I don't know why.
Zuck: They "trust me"
Zuck: Dumb fucks.

36

FACEBOOK RECEIVES YOUR MOST SENSITIVE PERSONAL INFO FROM YOUR PHONE'S OTHER APPS

Based on Facebook's treatment of user data, you can safely assume Mark Zuckerberg's company doesn't believe in any traditional concept of privacy. Every shred of data you've put onto your profile, every profile you've liked, and every conversation you've had on Facebook Messenger is collated and used to sell to advertisers.

Most Facebook users believe if they keep sensitive information off the platform, then it remains private. Unfortunately, this couldn't be farther from the truth. A *Wall Street Journal* investigation found a wide variety of popular smartphone apps send the most personal information inputted by Americans directly to Mark Zuckerberg's multimillion-dollar advertising machine.[1] Even your menstrual cycle, ladies, isn't safe from Facebook's all-seeing eye. Indeed, Flo Period & Ovulation Tracker sends its users' menstrual-cycle data into Facebook's vast information systems, despite having a privacy policy that says it will not share "information regarding your marked cycles, pregnancy, symptoms, notes and other information that is entered by you and that you do not elect to share."

Women aren't the only Facebook users being put at risk here. Some health and fitness apps send your personal health goals, caloric intake, and exercise habits to Facebook, which then uses that information to cater ads to your interests and behaviors, even if they are extremely personal. In the *Journal*'s test, fitness app Lose It! couldn't wait to gossip with Zuckerberg's platform. "When a user entered having completed 45 minutes of 'sexual activity' during one test, the app sent that information to Facebook along with an estimate of how many calories the activity burned."

Imagine what advertisers would pay to know that you regularly have 45 minutes of sexual activity on Monday afternoons at 3:00 p.m.. Especially if they could cross-reference that with your significant other's profile that shows them working until 5:00 p.m. Do you think Mark Zuckerberg doesn't know who your secretary is?

This hypothetical example may be terrifying, but it isn't far off from the current state of mass social-media surveillance. Applications caught sending data to Facebook include fitness apps, the aforementioned menstrual cycle tracker, real estate apps including Trulia and Realtor.com, a sleep cycle tracker, and even Glucose Buddy, an app for diabetic people.

According to the *Wall Street Journal*, apps found sending sensitive data to Facebook include:

- Flo Period & Ovulation Tracker
- Weight Loss Fitness by Verv
- BetterMe: Weight Loss Workouts

- **Lose It!**
- **GetFit: Home Fitness & Workout**
- **Instant Heart Rate: HR Monitor**
- **BetterMen: Fitness Trainer**
- **Realtor.com Real Estate Search**
- **Trulia Real Estate: Find Homes**
- **Breethe: Sleep & Meditation**
- **Glucose Buddy**

All these apps, except Glucose Buddy, have had millions of downloads in just the past year.

Interestingly, the finance industry appears to understand the notion of sensitive data. The *Wall Street Journal* found, "Among the top 10 finance apps in Apple's U.S. app store as of Thursday, none appeared to send sensitive information to Facebook, and only two sent any information at all."

Facebook's response to this is remarkably blasé. I've saved it for the end because its Orwellian "nothing to see here, move along" tone deafness will do more to scare you off the platform than any snarky comment I could conjure. "It's common for developers to share information with a wide range of platforms for advertising and analytics," Facebook said. "We require the other app developers to be clear with their users about the information they are sharing with us, and we prohibit app developers from sending us sensitive data. We also take steps to detect and remove data that should not be shared with us."

37

AMERICANS PAY BILLIONS TO LARGE CORPORATIONS TO NOT HIRE U.S. CITIZENS

Some of America's most prosperous companies—many of them in the tech industry—hire foreign college undergraduate and graduate students on F-1 visas, saving these mega-corporations hundreds of millions of dollars in Social Security, Medicare, and Unemployment Insurance Program taxes, which they don't have to pay for foreign workers.

Thanks to a little-known Department of Homeland Security program called Optional Practical Training (OPT), wealthy companies like Disney, Amazon, Facebook, and Google avoid paying some $2 billion a year into cash-strapped poverty programs for the elderly and the poor.[1] It's no wonder then that the number of OPT permits hit a record high of 203,462 in the 2017–2018 academic year.[2]

In its passing of the Immigration and Nationality Act of 1952, Congress never addressed student visas or the issue of permanence for guest workers living in the United States. This left the door open for immigration law to be created out of thin air by bureaucratic fiat. Thus, a year later, the Justice Department began enacting regulations allowing non-citizens to work in a very limited training capacity for six months on something of an internship-equivalent status. A series of regulations continued to flow from the Justice Department over the next several decades, slowly tipping the scales of justice away from U.S.-born students and workers toward foreign laborers. The Justice Department confronted a precursor to OPT in 1964, only then allowing for a student to receive continued training at a qualified U.S. educational institution. There was no mention of whether that training could continue on a post-graduate basis. When the Justice Department took on practical training in 1977, the agency admitted that there was "no statute under which employment of nonimmigrant students for practical training is authorized." The idea at the time, however, for practical training, was to allow foreign-born "graduates to prepare themselves for entrance level positions in their chosen fields."[3]

Incredibly, in announcing its 1977 regulation allowing post-graduate practical training, the Justice Department acknowledged that the Department of Labor had warned "that employment of non-resident alien students presents unfair competition to U.S. resident workers because some applicants worked for less than prevailing wages during their training period." As a result, the Justice Department reduced its earlier requirement for student practical training from eighteen months to one year.

Sweeping changes reshaped America's student visa and guest worker agenda in July 1992, when the Justice Department officially created the Optional Practical Training program. A handful of regulations continued to come down for years from the Department of Labor, the Immigration and Naturalization Service, and the Justice Department. In 2008, the George W. Bush administration ushered in changes to student F-1 visas, which allowed foreign graduates to work in the U.S. for up to twelve months after graduation. Those students were also authorized to remain in the U.S. for seventeen additional months if their degrees were obtained in disciplines the Department of Homeland Security designates as science, technology, engineering, mathematics (STEM). Today, a STEM student can work and live in the United States for up to forty-two months.[4]

David North, an analyst at the Center for Immigration Studies, notes that the current OPT program brings big benefits for some 100 U.S. colleges and corporations at the expense of American taxpayers, many of whom have no idea they're being fleeced.

"The employers benefiting from the subsidies directly, and universities benefiting indirectly, know all about the program, which is all but unknown to the older Americans subsidizing it, and is similarly unknown to the young U.S. college grads who are hurt by it," North writes in his analysis of the practical training program.[5] "Given this twisted political dynamic, inertia, and the total silence of the media on this point, the program persists and grows each year."

There are currently no annual limits on the number of OPT permits issued. And America's mega-tech companies have long used OPT to the degree that it has reaped them millions in savings in taxes every year. The tech sector also relies heavily on H-1B visas—which are limited by a 65,000 annual cap and another 20,000 for special dispensations—to employ foreign workers.

Indeed, "between 2004 and 2016, nearly 1.5 million foreign graduates of U.S. colleges and universities obtained authorization to remain and work in the U.S. through the OPT," according to a Pew Research Center analysis of U.S. Immigration and Customs

Enforcement data. OPT permit approvals outpaced H-1B visas in recent years, with the majority of OPT applications being filled by people from Asia.[6]

Forty years after the Department of Labor warned of the risk of employing hordes of nonresident alien students and the inherently "unfair competition" posed because those students will accept lower wages than U.S. workers, a program produced by unelected bureaucrats is doing exactly that. Amazon, valued at over a trillion in market cap, made headlines in 2017 when it paid no income tax on $5.6 billion in profits that year. As it turns out, thanks to OPT, Amazon saved several more millions by not paying into Social Security and Medicare. The company employed 7,700 OPT students and recent graduates for an estimated tax subsidy of $27.6 million, according to DHS data.[7]

38

NEARLY THREE-QUARTERS OF SILICON VALLEY WORKERS ARE FOREIGN-BORN

About 71 percent of tech sector employees in Silicon Valley, California, are foreign-born, as are around 50 percent of the tech workers in the San Francisco-Oakland-Hayward region, according to U.S. Census data.[1]

One major factor behind this phenomenon is the surge in participation in a little-known federal foreign worker training program called Optional Practical Training (OPT). Nearly 1.5 million foreign graduates of U.S. colleges and universities obtained authorization to remain and work in the United States between 2004 and 2016 because they received OPT temporary work permits.[2] Three California cities hovered near the top of the list of cities that saw foreign college graduates working in OPT fields between 2004 and 2016. These cities are: San Jose (44,500 OPT permit holders), San Francisco (33,700), and Los Angeles (27,800). Many OPT recipients make those metros home after coming from other parts of the country. "The New York-Newark-Jersey City metro area had the largest cumulative population of OPT participants (218,400)," Pew research showed. "That was followed by the Los Angeles-Long

Beach-Anaheim (103,600) and Boston-Cambridge-Newton metro areas (73,000)."

Another major factor furthering foreign-born labor dominance in Silicon Valley is the continued increase of U.S. companies seeking high-skilled foreign workers through the H-1B visa program. A product of the Immigration Act of 1990, nearly 1.8 million H-1B visas were awarded between 2001 and 2015. More than half of the H-1B visas distributed over that span were given to Indian nationals, according to Pew. And in 2013 the top state, which saw its employers receive nearly 18 percent (45,000) of that year's H-1B visas, was California.[3]

Data from the National Foundation for American Policies showed that leading U.S. tech companies, including Amazon, Microsoft, Intel, and Google were among the top ten employers of approved H-1B applicants in fiscal year 2017.[4] Some Indian tech companies saw a slight decline in application approvals, but the demand for H-1B applicants was still strong. Technology employment in the United States expanded by nearly 200,000 jobs in 2017, to an estimated 11.5 million workers. At an estimated $1.6 trillion a year, the tech sector is one of the largest components of America's economy. Consequently, filling these high-paying, high-demand jobs has led to a surge in the recruitment of technology workers with specific skills.

There are more than 4 million American students seeking employment every year, many of them obtaining degrees in the highly coveted science, technology, engineering, and mathematics (STEM) fields. They are often outbid by foreign-born workers competing for the same jobs. Most major tech firms like Facebook, Google, and

Microsoft see several financial incentives for hiring non-citizens over their U.S.-born counterparts.

Ron Hira, a research associate at the Economic Policy Institute (EPI), a nonprofit, nonpartisan think tank, warned Congress in 2016 about how major U.S. employers abuse the nation's immigration system and its various visa programs to hire high-skilled foreign workers at a discount. Citing a study conducted by EPI, Hira told the Subcommittee on Immigration and the National Interest that wages of H-1B workers were at least $40,000 lower per worker— amounting to a 40 to 50 percent discount.[5]

Current labor laws state that companies can pay H-1B workers based on four skill levels, all with different salary ranges. According to the United States Department of Labor website, hiring foreign workers cannot adversely affect the wages and working conditions of U.S. workers who are comparably employed. To try to control this "the department's regulations require that the wages offered to a foreign worker must be the prevailing wage rate for the occupational classification in the area of employment."

According to Hira, companies, especially in the technology sector, often seek workarounds to these laws and routinely define an H-1B employee's role as the lowest skill level because it corresponds with the lowest salary. "About 40 percent of all H-1B applications are at Level 1 now, and another 40 percent are at Level 2," he told *IEEE Spectrum*.[6]

There have been numerous headline-making examples in which major U.S. companies have laid off hundreds of employees, callously replacing them with workers awarded H-1B visas. When 250 Disney employees were given pink slips in 2014, many of them were given a preposterous and fury-inducing ultimatum: They were forced to train their visa-holding replacements or lose their severance packages.[7] "I just couldn't believe they could fly people in to sit at our desks and take over our jobs exactly," said one American former Disney worker who saw his job filled by a foreign worker brought to the U.S. by an India-based outsourcing firm. "It was so humiliating to train somebody else to take over your job. I still can't grasp it." Several Disney employees sued the company and ultimately lost in court. In another case, 300 American workers at California-based Edison saw their jobs taken by foreign-born workers.

Major tech firms often lean heavily on labor recruitment agencies to obtain the thousands of foreign-born tech workers seeking employment in the United States under specialized visas. Tech companies like PayPal routinely contract foreign workers through outsourcing firms. To be clear, elite Silicon Valley corporations have spent years burying the full extent of their reliance on the outsourcing firms they have used to hire cheaper, foreign-born labor at the expense of hiring Americans to fill the same jobs. For instance, one study by *Bloomberg News* revealed that between 2015 and 2016 PayPal partnered with an outsourcing firm that applied for half of the foreign H-1B visas the tech giant was requesting. The other half were applied for directly by PayPal. At Microsoft Corporation's headquarters, 43 percent of the foreign H-1B visas were applied for through an outsourcing outfit, as were 29 percent at eBay and 12 percent at Facebook's respective home bases.[8]

To be clear, most major employers utilize the visa system to satisfy job posts that are sometimes hard to fill. The *New York Times,* which often publishes sympathetic reporting on foreign-born laborers losing their jobs to U.S.-born workers, for example, relies somewhat heavily on the H-1B program.[9] The paper sought 163 H-1B workers from 2014 to 2018.[10] As another example, Verizon outsourced 44,000 jobs, including at least 2,500 computer jobs to low-wage Indian visa-workers.[11]

In recent years bills have circulated through Congress, many of them meant to either mandate that H-1B compensation be determined by current market salary or to enact a more laborious process for hiring H-1B recipients.

39

BLACK AND HISPANIC UNEMPLOYMENT HIT RECORD LOWS UNDER TRUMP

What political expert would have guessed that the two demographic blocs who supported Donald Trump least on Election Night would turn out to be the biggest benefactors of his America First jobs agenda? Interestingly enough, that's precisely what happened.

The day Trump was sworn into office, black unemployment stood at 8.8 percent. Less than a year into his presidency that number fell to 6.8 percent, the lowest ever recorded. Similarly, Hispanic unemployment stood at 5.8 percent.[1] By January 2019, the number dropped to 4.4 percent, the lowest rate recorded since the federal government began tracking unemployment by race in 1972.

Unemployment for black Americans has historically and stubbornly soared far above the national average. The Great Recession drove black unemployment near Great Depression–era levels, reaching 16.8 percent in March 2010. The pain of the housing crisis pushed prominent black lawmakers to publicly blame President Obama for black America's economic morass. Congresswoman Maxine Waters called out Obama and declared the black unemployment rate "unconscionable." In a statement to *Politico* in August 2011, Waters said, "There are roughly three million African Americans out of work today, a number nearly equal to the entire population of Iowa. I would suggest that if the entire population of Iowa, a key state on the electoral map and a place that served as a stop on the president's jobs bus tour, were unemployed, they would be mentioned in the president's speech and be the beneficiary of targeted public policy . . . This evening, as the president speaks to the nation about his plan to create jobs, he must acknowledge the economic disaster in the African American community."[2]

Days later, Emanuel Cleaver, the chairman of the Congressional Black Caucus, told reporters, "If Bill Clinton had been in the White House and had failed to address this problem, we probably would be marching on the White House."[3]

America's first black president was being called on the carpet by black lawmakers for failing to lift his most ardent supporters out of their economic morass. After four years in office, little had changed for black voters. Black leaders, like 2013 NAACP president Ben Jealous, were still dead set on holding Obama's feet to the fire. "The country's back to pretty much where it was when this president started," Jealous said on MSNBC's *Meet the Press* in January 2013, when the black unemployment rate sat at 14 percent.[4] "White people in this country are doing a bit better. Black people are doing a full point worse." Jealous went on to endorse Hillary Clinton for president, telling the audience at the Democratic National Convention that her presidency would bring about a "better America for all our daughters and sons." Ironically, it was Clinton's opponent who delivered on that promise.

In a campaign speech in North Carolina in October 2016, then-candidate Trump offered a "new deal" to black Americans based on three pillars: "safe communities, great education, and high-paying jobs." Seven months into his tenure, the Trump economy began to deliver on that third pledge.

Unemployment among black Americans ages sixteen and over had fallen from a high of over 16 percent to 7.5 percent, its lowest level since December 2000. Under Barack Obama, black teen unemployment had hit Depression-era levels. In September 2010, 48.9 percent of black teens looking for work were unemployed. By June 2016, the rate was still a depressing 33 percent. By October 2018, black teen unemployment had fallen to 19 percent, an all-time low. Two months later, Hispanic unemployment hit an all-time low. Indeed, under President Trump black employment grew by an average of nearly 40,000 jobs each month, noted Trump advisor Jason D. Meister.[5] Wages and incomes for black Americans have boomed. Among Hispanics, black women, and all women— three groups that overwhelmingly supported Trump's opponent— employment hit the same kind of record-breaking lows by the summer of 2018 and continued into 2019. (This was even true for Hispanics, black women, and women overall who have only a high-school diploma.) The payoff politically for President Trump began to take form in the polls. A Harvard/Harris Poll found a 10 percent rise in approval for Trump among Hispanics. Trump's approval among blacks jumped from the 8 percent who voted for him in 2016 to nearly three times as high less than two years later.

40

VENEZUELA WAS THE WEALTHIEST COUNTRY IN LATIN AMERICA BEFORE SOCIALISM

In 2018, Venezuela looked like a country in the grip of civil war, but its economy was once Latin America's richest. For a time, an oil-rich Venezuela played host to thousands of refugees.

Now, the number of Venezuelans forced to leave their homes has grown, reaching 5,000 per day in recent months, according to the United Nations High Commissioner for Refugees (UNHCR). Growing hunger and violence are forcing desperate migrants to pour into neighboring countries, fueling the worst humanitarian crisis in the region.

The country's economy is estimated to have shrunk by 10 percent last year—worse even than Syria's. Venezuela's GDP shrank by 19 percent. Venezuela also has the world's worst inflation at over one million percent (compare that to second-place South Sudan at 106 percent), rendering its currency almost worthless. Crafty Venezuelans use bolivar bills as art canvases and weaving material for baskets and purses, items that are often sold as novelties across the border in Colombia.[1]

In a country with one of the world's largest proven oil reserves, the government is forced to import 300,000 barrels of oil a
day.[2] Food had grown so scarce that three in four citizens reported
involuntary weight loss, averaging 24 pounds in a year.[3] The basic
medications the World Health Organization (WHO) deems necessary to run a functional health-care system do not exist. Doctors
request that patients bring their own medicine to hospitals if they
are lucky enough to have a relative abroad mail it in.[4]

Nearly twenty years of the Bolivarian Socialist Revolution has
sapped the South America nation. The evolution from "Saudi Venezuela" to a country where 15 percent of people need to scavenge
through garbage for food took long enough that the world saw it
coming.

Venezuela's decline is the inevitable result of socialism, told by
the deterioration of its streets, the abuse of its opposition politicians,
and the use of the military to maim and kill Venezuelan children as
young as fourteen.

Before 1999, the year military dictator Hugo Chávez took over
the country and vowed to ensure the rich would no longer enjoy
it, the cities of Venezuela were a marvel, built with oil profits and
maintained by pro-business governments. The Spanish newspaper
El País notes that between 1940 and 1980, Venezuela had the
highest economic growth rate of any country on earth.[5] Sand-
wiched between the Cuban Revolution to its east and the Revolu-
tionary Armed Forces of Colombia (FARC) terrorists to the west,
and stuck in a perilous political situation by the end of 1958, the
men who inherited Venezuela from fleeing military dictator Mar-
cos Pérez Jiménez made the opposite choice of their analogues in
Havana: They sat down and wrote a pact to hold elections.

The Puntofijo Pact of 1958 between three political parties—the Democratic Action Party (AD), the Social Christian Party (COPEI), and the Democratic Republican Union—made the parties agree to hold free and fair elections, accept the result of those elections, and share power as the people wished.[6] At the time, *power* primarily meant control of the nation's oil wealth and *the people* meant the urban or landed classes, but the pact nonetheless ensured political stability and economic growth for decades. It notably excluded the violent Venezuelan Communist Party from participating in any elections or political decisions.

The Democratic Republican Union eventually fell out of favor and left the country in the hands of AD and COPEI, who abided by the pact and traded power back and forth until the late 1990s. The stability allowed for great economic growth, albeit in an exclusionary way; Venezuela's rural and Amazon regions never quite shared in the economic boom, a national weakness Chávez would later exploit to great effect.[7]

The year was 1970 when Venezuela became Latin America's wealthiest country. For Cuba, 1970 was the year Fidel Castro promised a record-breaking harvest of ten million tons of sugar, cultivated in part through forced labor used to torture Christians, LGBT Cubans, and known dissidents. That year's harvest never came close.

Venezuela's refugee population, largely of Colombian descent, grew in the 1970s as the FARC tortured, killed, and disappeared tens of thousands in the name of communism. Between 1970 and 1979, nearly 170,000 Colombians migrated to Venezuela; by the next decade, another 207,000 came.[8]

"We would return to Colombia for vacation, but never with the idea of staying. Everyone lived so well in Venezuela that it was a country nobody wanted to leave," Alejandro Medina, a Colombian-born Venezuelan, told *El País* in 2017. Notably, he was being interviewed in Bogotá, his birthplace, not Caracas, his adopted home.[9]

The 1970s were not as kind to Venezuela as the sixties—nor were the eighties as kind as the seventies—yet even through the "rough" economic times during the AD/COPEI era, Venezuela's GDP grew. Between 1988 and 1998, for example, GDP grew by 23 percent.

"We had everything. The markets were enormous—not because we were wasteful, but because it was possible to buy in bulk. We would enjoy the beaches safely, we lived in paradise," Medina recalled.

What happened? After decades of hammering the Venezuelan government for being exclusionary, the leftist forces that had struggled to destabilize Colombia, Brazil, Argentina, and Peru had some facts on their side: AD and COPEI kept power tightly between themselves; the establishment governments failed to invest significantly in education, infrastructure, or social programs for the poor, particularly in the inland Amazon areas. Oil prices fell in the late 1980s, triggering violent protests. In 1992, Lt. Col. Hugo Chávez Frías led a failed *coup d'etat* against President Carlos Andrés Pérez. While failing to take power on that occasion, he became a surprise front-runner in the 1998 presidential elections, enticing lower-class voters fatigued with the establishment by offering to spend the nation's oil profits on social programs for the poor instead of reinvesting it into the country's corporate entities.

Some saw through Chávez's charade. "The people want a profound and radical change . . . if they make this mistake, we will sink even deeper than the circumstances we are in now," Pérez warned in

1998, predicting that Chávez would indeed win the election because of "the great rage, the great frustration" with the nation's elite. With Chávez at the helm, he predicted, "the prisons will open their doors to those not in agreement with the government."

Chávez rapidly went to work establishing a socialist economy. He nationalized billions in oil investments, forcing corporations like ExxonMobil and ConocoPhillips out of the country, taxing oil sales up to 60 percent, enacting sweeping agriculture land grabs (reminiscent of those in Zimbabwe), and shutting down small banks. Petróleos de Venezuela (PDVSA), the state-run oil company, became Chávez's "piggy bank" to buy off voters and friends alike.

Then came the political persecution. Dozens of radio stations, television networks, and newspapers succumbed to the new government while Chávez performed song covers and interviewed socialist celebrities like Sean Penn on his TV program *Aló Presidente*. El Helicoide—intended as a sprawling shopping mall complex when it was built in the 1950s, became home to the Experimental Security University. Chávez's successor, Nicolás Maduro, would turn it into the most brutal political prison known to operate in the country.

The poor who voted for Chávez never saw the billions in expropriations he took in in their name. Most of that profit went to Cuba, a parasitic regime that proved unable to survive on its own following the collapse of the Soviet Union in the early 1990s. In exchange for the oil, Cuba infected Venezuela with its toxic political model, sending nearly 100,000 government agents flooding into Venezuela's halls of power.[10]

Not coincidentally, twentieth-century Venezuela ceased to exist.

Foreign Policy ranked Caracas, once the crown jewel of Latin America, the murder capital of the world in 2008.[11] It has since consistently been counted in the top five of the world's most dangerous peacetime cities, jockeying for first place with drug-trafficking enclaves in Mexico and Honduras.

The now "free" health-care system began running out of everything from ibuprofen to birth control to cancer medications. Since Chávez's passing in 2013, Maduro—a former bus driver turned president—has implemented chaotic economic policies like replacing the worthless bolivar with cryptocurrency he has branded the *petro*.

Lacking the popularity that kept the poor loyal to Chávez, Maduro has failed to stop years of daily riots, protests calling for his resignation, and lootings of restaurants, as well as mass migration of millions. Facing more opposition than ever, Maduro has turned to the military to imprison, beat, and torture dissidents and political rivals; to control (and let rot) the little food the nation has left; and to run the sinking PDVSA.

Venezuelans have turned to desperate means to survive, now that most cannot afford to buy three meals' worth of food a day, or find it in supermarkets. (Taking photos of empty supermarket shelves can result in prison time.)[12] Since 2016, Venezuelan women have taken to selling their hair to make wigs to be sold in Colombia.[13] Prostitution and human trafficking are rampant. Opposition newspapers have conveniently run out of paper to print news.[14] Garbage, dog food, and stray animals have become common meals.[15]

The situation is so dire that Maduro brought in officials from North Korea to offer financial advice in 2017.[16]

Maduro has blamed a litany of culprits for this disaster: Presidents Donald Trump and Barack Obama, unspecified "capitalists," "coup plotters" organized by Colombia to overthrow the government, and every major opposition leader remaining in the country. Notably absent from his explanations—and those of many American mainstream media outlets—is socialism, a system that has failed with deadly results every time it has been tried.

41

AMERICAN CITIES WITH THE LARGEST HOMELESS POPULATIONS ARE ALL DEMOCRAT-RUN ENCLAVES

Some of America's most opulent city centers house nearly half the country's homeless population. Of the roughly 555,000 people who were homeless or unsheltered at some point in 2017, over a third of them, 192,526,[1] dwelled in Democrat-run cities.[2]

Whole swaths of San Francisco serve as a den of depravity and squalor to the thousands of often drug-addicted and mentally ill beggars who inhabit the city's excrement-filled sidewalk encampments. It's a great American city where there are more drug addicts than students enrolled in its public high schools, according to the city Health Department.[3] Complaints about discarded needles lying on city streets, some mere steps away from where children play, have more than doubled in just a few years, from fewer than 3,000 in 2015 to more than 7,500 as of October 2018. Complaints about human waste have increased twentyfold, from just over 1,700 in 2008 to more than 20,000 in 2018.[4]

Indeed, the incredible contrast between America's uber-wealthy and its poor is perhaps made no more startlingly clear than along the San Francisco–San Jose corridor. A painfully familiar sight outside the windows where tech titans reshape the social order—in many cases before their fortieth birthday—are the homeless, some sleeping in their own waste. Within mere miles of Mountain View, the suburban city where Google built its billion-dollar corporate hub, are long lines of rickety, run-down RVs, where some families of four and five live crammed, across the street from $3,000- and $4,000-a-month high-rise condominiums. Hiding in the shadow of Facebook's million-plus-square-foot Menlo Park property are the hundreds of frayed paupers crammed in squalid encampments.[5] The billion-dollar-plus campus and its neighboring small tent city of homeless people epitomize the depressing daily juxtaposition between Silicon Valley's breathtaking affluence and its gut-wrenching despair.

San Jose was once home to some 300 homeless living in a 65-plus-acre encampment, infamously known as The Jungle.[6] The massive, Depression-era shantytown—equivalent in size to more than fifty football fields—was neighbor to the plush offices of Silicon Valley moguls and was the largest homeless camp in the United States. The median home price in the San Jose region was nearly $700,000 in 2014 when city officials finally decided to destroy The Jungle.[7] A few years later, those property values had increased to nearly $800,000, as did the overall homeless population, by almost a thousand from 2015 to 2017.[8]

San Jose has never elected a Democratic mayor since the sprawling city began popularly electing mayors in 1967. The last Republican mayor of San Francisco was elected three years before that. Houston's last Republican mayor left office eighty years ago, but that city, while not without its wretched tracts of vagrancy, has managed to keep its homeless population among the lowest in the nation. San Francisco, in fact, has nearly twice the homeless population (7,499)[9] as Houston, Texas, (4,143) which has nearly three times more people (2.3 million) living within its city limits.[10] Houston, the fourth largest city in America, cut its homeless population in half between 2011 and 2017.[11] An eight percent increase in 2018 was largely attributed to the widespread destruction of housing by floods from Hurricane Harvey. Still, the city's political leaders working hand-in-hand with community partners to pare its homeless population cuts through the ascendant gospel that the homeless need only housing and handouts to escape their circumstances. But the gap is wide between elected officials serving as agents of positive change and those whose lofty promises have missed the mark and have managed to make the homeless epidemic in their respective cities much worse. By all accounts, New York City mayor Bill de Blasio inherited a homelessness crisis when he took office in 2013. His predecessor, Michael Bloomberg, cut funding for a federal program that helped poor people transition out of shelters to subsidized long-term housing units. Advocacy groups had long argued against Bloomberg's expansion of the city's for-profit shelters—which include hotels, shoddy motels, and so-called cluster site shelter units—in which tax dollars flow to private landlords who house the homeless, in most cases making more money than they would renting rooms to middle-class consumers.

In the decade since Bloomberg took office in 2002, the number of people sleeping in shelters rose 69 percent, according to the advocacy group Coalition for the Homeless; 52,000 New Yorkers were living in city shelters in 2012.[12] That number ballooned to 89,500 in 2016, under de Blasio. In 2018, startling statistics showed that there were 254,866 homeless New Yorkers at some point in 2018, a figure larger than the population of every city in the Empire State except Buffalo and New York City. Consequently, the *New York Daily News* dubbed de Blasio's homeless New York population "the third largest city in the state: Homelessville, N.Y."[13]

Indeed, a decades-old link exists between the mentally ill and homelessness. A study by the National Institute of Mental Health found that approximately 6 percent of Americans are severely mentally ill, compared to the 20 to 25 percent of the homeless population that suffers from some form of severe mental illness.[14] Another 45 percent of the homeless population show a history of mental illness diagnoses. A majority are either convicts, alcoholics, or drug-addicted.

Percentage of San Francisco's homeless who are black: 34[15]

Percentage of the city's overall population who are black: 6

Percentage of Los Angeles's homeless who are black: 39[16]

Percentage of the city's overall population who are black: 9

Percentage of New York City's homeless shelter residents who are black: 58[17]

Percentage who are Latino: 31

A survey, mandated by the federal government, found 6,904 homeless people in Washington, DC. While the figure represented a two-year decline for the city, which has never elected a Republican mayor, it was still larger than the homeless population of 6,865 in 2013.[18]

In 2018 the number of people living on the streets of Philadelphia increased by 10 percent from the prior year, despite the city increasing its budget for social welfare programs to help the homeless. A report by the Boston Foundation found that homelessness in Massachusetts has almost doubled over the past nine years, one of the largest increases in the country. Seattle's homelessness crisis, the *Seattle Times* reported, is, "by scale, worse than New York City or Los Angeles."[19]

"Seattle does not want to become San Francisco, a fate that has come to refer exclusively to the city's worst traits: its $5,000-a-month rents, its homeless encampments and the ever-present dissonance between those two," Emily Badger writes in the *New York Times*.[20] Nevertheless, progressive cities are looking to tax businesses to beget long-term solutions to their homeless problems. A San Francisco ballot initiative easily passed in November 2018, increasing taxes on businesses to fund the city's homelessness programs. The tax is expected to hit the tech-heavy industry in Silicon Valley the hardest, where over 1,000 businesses earn more than $50 million a year. The elite tech titans overwhelmingly opposed the tax, which is expected to raise about $300 million a year.[21]

42

MUSLIMS ACCOUNT FOR 1 PERCENT OF THE U.S. POPULATION, BUT RADICAL ISLAMIST EXTREMISTS ACCOUNTED FOR MORE THAN 50 PERCENT OF DEATHS BY EXTREMISTS

In April 2017, the Government Accountability Office (GAO) released a study titled, "Countering Violent Extremism: Actions Needed to Define Strategy and Assess Progress of Federal Efforts." The report set out to identify violent extremism in the United States and understand techniques to counter terrorism of all stripes. The topic is of prime importance to the DHS, FBI, CIA, and practically every other three-letter agency.[1]

The GAO studied every instance of violent extremism from September 12, 2001, through December 31, 2016. Isn't it funny that every study of terrorism seems to kick in *right after* 9/11?

The mainstream media and politicians love to crow about one of the statistics that came out of the GAO's report. The government had proven, in the opinion of the left, that Islam truly was the religion of peace! Out of 85 attacks by violent extremists that resulted in fatalities, 62 were perpetrated by *right-wing extremists*. Radical Islamists perpetrated only a comparatively modest 23 fatal attacks. Left-wing terrorists did not kill anyone in this period, according to the GAO.

As it were, the left reacted with glee. Right-wing extremists are the bad guys and Islam only gets associated with terror because *racism*. This logic only holds up to the barest level of scrutiny.

The first way this leftist spin on terror attacks falls apart is in the magnitude of extremist attacks on American soil. The 62 recorded fatal attacks by right-wing extremists resulted in the deaths of 106 innocent people. But the 23 fatal attacks associated with radical Islam killed 119 victims. Although fewer in number, Islamist terror attacks accounted for more than half of terror deaths. And if the study includes data from just one day earlier, the body count is a much starker contrast.

The second way the leftist spin fails here is if we consider the populations that produce extremists. America has a population of roughly 329 million people, as of 2019. That creates a relatively large pool of potential extremists on the right and the left, merely based on the size of the overall population. But extremist Muslims are a subset of a subset, as by definition they are members of the Muslim faith.

Muslims are just over 1 percent of the population according to Pew Research Center.[2] Not only are their attacks deadlier in magnitude, but Muslim extremists come from a disproportionately smaller pool of Americans—a population of fewer than 3.5 million people.

One way to confirm that deadly extremism is intimately tied to

Islam is to examine if other countries follow the same trend. In this case, they do. In 2016, 75 percent of all terror attacks in the world took place in ten countries.[3] You can probably name most of them if you tried—nine of the ten are Muslim-majority countries: Iraq, Afghanistan, India, Pakistan, the Philippines, Somalia, Turkey, Nigeria, Yemen, and Syria. Although the Philippines is not a majority-Muslim country, its Moro region is home to a large Muslim population.

What about the UK, one of our closest allies and home to an ever-expanding Muslim population? Well, terror offenses are at an all-time high, up nearly 60 percent from 2016 to 2017.[4] This information came from the left-wing *The Guardian* newspaper, not a right-wing source. The Muslim population in England's prison system has increased by 50 percent over the past decade as well. Not all of those are prisoners are incarcerated for terror-related crimes, but it is indicative of a larger cultural problem.

43

CHINA IS HOLDING TWO MILLION MUSLIMS IN INTERNMENT CAMP SWEATSHOPS

In modern-day America, the war on Islamophobia—the persecution and discrimination of people based on their Islamic faith—has become a cornerstone of the left's interpretation of twenty-first-century civil rights. From World Hijab Day to the presence of Palestinian support groups in Black Lives Matter protests and LGBT pride parades, the world's social justice warriors have spoken: Discrimination against Muslims will not be tolerated.

Yet in a political climate so loudly hostile toward Muslim persecution, a nation engaging in what its victims call "cultural genocide" against its Islamic population has largely escaped leftist condemnation. In China, the Communist Party has established camps to financially exploit, indoctrinate, torture, and kill Chinese Muslims.

The Chinese Communist Party refers to the camps by the Orwellian term "vocational training centers" or "boarding schools," claiming that its inhabitants are underprivileged members of the

nation's Uighur minority who are learning marketable job skills.[1]
The survivors of these camps use much more transparent terms.
These are internment or concentration camps, where the government
indoctrinates Muslims to abandon their faith and obey the Communist Party.

Reports from human rights advocacy groups, news organizations like Reuters, and the U.S. State Department concur that China
has established between 44 and 1,200 of these camps in Xinjiang,
the westernmost and largest province of China by area. Xinjiang is
home to most of the nation's ten million ethnic Uighurs—a Turkic,
majority-Muslim people with little in common with China's ruling
Han ethnic majority. Reports suggest that most prisoners in the
Xinjiang internment camps are Uighurs, but other Muslim eth-
nics, most notably Kazakhs and Kyrgyz, also populate the factory-
prisons.

The development of internment camps to torture Muslims into
abandoning their faith is the culmination of a policy known as sinicization, which was adopted after Xi Jinping assumed the leadership of the Communist Party in 2013. Sinicization is making all
aspects of life in China more "Chinese." The government defines
"Chinese" as a combination of traditional Han culture and atheist
communism, so the policy has largely consisted of targeting and
destroying anything that does not fit those parameters, including
religion, minority ethnic identity, and Western-style human-rights
norms. Chinese state media have admitted Beijing is working not
only to eradicate Islam, but also to replace the existing religion with
"a branch of Islam . . . fitting Chinese culture."[2]

The Uighurs have endured a tense relationship with China's

east for centuries. "Xinjiang" roughly translates to "new territories," meaning China's Wild West, where emperor after emperor failed to erase the local culture. Xi Jinping holds three executive titles under the Chinese constitution: head of the Communist Party, commander-in-chief of the People's Liberation Army (PLA), and president. The latter is the weakest of the three. As early as the thirteenth century, emperors like Kublai Khan used coercive measures like banning halal food preparation and circumcision to curb the spread of Islam. Where the Yuan dynasty succeeded in controlling Xinjiang, subsequent dynasties, notably the nearly three-century-long Qing dynasty, failed. Xinjiang officially became a province of China for good in 1884, after the near collapse of the Qing during the Taiping Rebellion.

The most recent attempt to replace Uighur with Han culture before today occurred under the Nationalist government of Chiang Kai-shek, who sought to erase ethnic barriers between Chinese minorities and the Han. That attempt triggered a violent backlash destining it to failure. The Communists, under Mao Zedong, learned the lessons of their Nationalist predecessors and, prior to Xi Jinping, granted Xinjiang special privileges, excluding it from the nation's brutal one-child policy and permitting widespread use of the Uighur language.

The Communists did not leave the Uighurs alone forever, though. The Mao-era Party clearly preferred a subdued Uighur Xinjiang to a Han Xinjiang. By the turn of the twenty-first century, Chinese officials had lost their patience. Many in Xinjiang, in turn, had become separatists, rejecting what was, in practice, the colonization of their territory by a faraway empire.

The years before Xi Jinping's ascent to power were rough ones in the province. The United States designated the East Turkestan Islamic Movement (ETIM), a Uighur jihadist separatist group, a terrorist organization in 2002 due to reports that it had ties to Osama bin Laden in neighboring Afghanistan. By 2009, Uighur separatists were engaging in deadly attacks on the minority Han representing the government. That year, Urumqi, the capital of Xinjiang, saw the deadliest protests in the country since the 1989 Tiananmen Square uprising. The riots killed over 150 people, according to the Chinese government, though the secretive nature of the Communist Party's information arms makes it impossible to know how many died for certain, or who killed them.[3]

Uighur separatists welcomed Xi Jinping's takeover of the Communist Party in 2013 with a series of knife attacks and bombings in Urumqi, with the worst of the assaults occurring in 2014. Xi's regime blamed violent "religious" sentiment for the attacks and launched a "people's war on terrorism" in January 2015. The Taiping Rebellion, which resulted in an estimated 20 million deaths, occurred roughly at the same time as the American Civil War and was triggered by the attempted establishment of a Christian state in the heart of central China.[4] The Chinese government used the rise of the Islamic State as an excuse for its repressive campaign not only against Uighurs but against Buddhists in Tibet and Christians nationwide. Any enemy of the Communist Party, including the Dalai Lama, was branded an "Islamic State sympathizer."

The "war" rapidly took a shape reminiscent of Kublai Khan's rule: city officials in Urumqi banned burqas, officials made it illegal to use public transportation while wearing "irregular beards" or Islamic clothing, and public fasting during Ramadan attracted police action. Han officials forced shops in Xinjiang to sell multiple brands of alcohol and cigarettes—haram items—to "weaken" religion. In 2017, Communist Party officials began assigning ethnic Uighurs to marry Han partners in an effort known as the "Uyghur-Han Marriage and Family Incentive Strategy."

Then came the camps.

Radio Free Asia (RFA), an investigative journalism outlet home to many Uighur reporters, began reporting in early 2018 that locals in major Uighur cities were getting arrested and disappearing into "re-education centers." Xinjiang "increas[ed] the security budget by more than 300 percent and advertis[ed] more than 90,800 security-related jobs" in 2017, shortly before the disappearances began, according to the State Department.[5] "Crimes" such as refusing to watch state propaganda, "religious activity," and teaching children a minority language could land a Xinjiang resident in the camps. By April 2018, the State Department reported that the Communist Party had detained "as many as one million" people of various ethnic minorities in the camps. The internments, at first, were temporary—allowing survivors to escape and tell their stories. Anonymous survivors began testifying that the government was forcing Muslims to eat pork, learn Mandarin (the dominant Han language), and enthusiastically perform Communist Party anthems.

Some said they were forced to endure a *Clockwork Orange*–style torture, strapped down with headphones on and forced to listen to communist propaganda for as long as 24 hours. Others described much more brutal treatment. "The authorities put a helmet-like thing on my head, and each time I was electrocuted, my whole body would shake violently, and I would feel the pain in my veins," Mihrigul Tursun, a twenty-nine-year-old Uighur survivor, told the National Press Club in November 2018. Officials killed one of her infant triplets during her internment. "They made me wear what they called iron clothes, a suit made of metal that weighed over 50 pounds," Kayrat Samarkand, an ethnic Kazakh survivor, told NPR.

The Chinese government launched a harassment campaign against the relatives of Radio Free Asia reporters still in Xinjiang in 2017 that same month.[6] "It forced my arms and legs into an outstretched position. I couldn't move at all, and my back was in terrible pain," recalled Samarkand. In December, the Associated Press revealed a new feature of the camps: slavery.[7] Chinese officials had begun building factories at the internment camps, teaching prisoners how to manufacture cheap goods. The regime insists the slave work is a necessary and obvious feature of its "vocational centers"—how else will these people learn skills to compete in the job market?—but the large number of doctors, business executives, and other highly skilled individuals interned makes this a dubious claim.

The Communist Party has reacted with vitriol at the international backlash, mostly coming from the administration of U.S. president Donald Trump.

"I don't know why they are worrying about Xinjiang situation. Why did they make this kind of request that puts pressure on China?" Hua Chunying, a Chinese Foreign Ministry spokeswoman, asked in November 2018. "I think this kind of action is very unreasonable." A few months prior, Hua curtly ordered the Trump administration to "mind its own business."

Hua's attempts to stifle the story have met with mixed results in the Muslim world. Most Islamic countries have remained silent in the face of this assault on fellow believers. Nations like Pakistan, which have bet high on Chinese investment in their economy, have shunned the topic. Saudi Arabia, the government responsible for the safekeeping of the holiest sites in Islam, has actually defended the camps.[8]

The United States is the most vocal state actor calling for freedom in Xinjiang.

"We've been speaking out recently about the challenges in China to religious freedom—not just the Uighurs but even more broadly than that. The absence of religious freedom there is of historic proportions," Secretary of State Mike Pompeo told Congress in April 2019.[9] The State Department was among the first to expose the camps in its annual religious freedom report.

The pressure has had only one noted effect on the behavior of the Chinese regime: Rather than release prisoners and end the internment program, the government has begun preparing its camps for international inspections, making them appear more like educational institutions—but the treatment of prisoners shows no signs of changing.[10]

44

LARGE-SCALE MINIMUM WAGE HIKES HAVE LED TO LAYOFFS, DECREASED HOURS, AND FEWER JOBS

As millions of Americans enjoyed the growing economy under President Donald Trump, leftists' push for minimum wage hikes intensified despite scores of studies and recent real-life examples proving that artificially raising wage rates only hurts workers or employers.

In January 2019, self-described Democratic Socialist senator Bernie Sanders (I-VT) introduced the Raise the Wage Act along with Representative Bobby Scott (D-VA). Their proposal would raise the federal minimum wage to $15 per hour by 2024 and index the minimum wage to median wage growth.

"Just a few short years ago, we were told that raising the minimum wage to $15 an hour was 'radical.' But a grassroots movement of millions of workers throughout this country refused to take 'no' for an answer," Sanders said in a statement. "It is not a radical idea to say a job should lift you out of poverty, not keep you in it. The current $7.25 an hour federal minimum wage is a starvation wage. It must be increased to a living wage of $15 an hour."

WAGE AND SALARY WORKERS PAID HOURLY RATES WITH EARNINGS AT OR BELOW PREVAILING FEDERAL MINIMUM WAGE, BY GENDER, 1979-2017 ANNUAL AVERAGES [NUMBERS IN THOUSANDS]

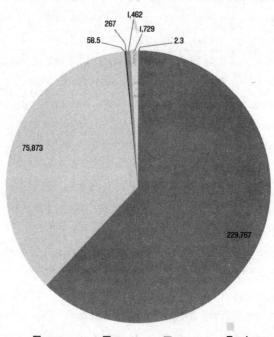

- Total wage and salary workers
- Total workers paid per hourly rate
- Percentage of total wage and salary workers
- At prevailing federal minimum wage[1]
- Below prevailing federal minimum wage[1]
- Total at or below prevailing federal minimum wage
- Percentage of hourly paid workers at or below prevailing federal minimum wage

[1] Data for 1990-1991, 1996-1997, and 2007-2009 reflect changes in the minimum wage that took place in those years.

Note: The comparability of historical labor force data has been affected at various times by methodological and conceptual changes in the Current Population Survey (CPS). Information about historical comparability is available at https://www.bls.gov/cps/documentation.htm#comp.Source: U.S. Bureau of Labor Statistics.

Source: https://www.bls.gov/opub/reports/minimum-wage/2017/home.htm

The legislation featured broad Democratic support in both chambers of Congress. The Senate version had the backing of over 30 Democratic senators while the House version saw over 180 lawmakers co-sponsoring the bill, including House Speaker Nancy Pelosi (D-CA). Despite the fervent Democratic support for a minimum wage hike, Jobs Creators Network president Alfredo Ortiz said in January that roughly three-tenths of one percent Americans over the age of 25 make the federal minimum wage.[1]

Indeed, of the roughly 78 million workers paid at an hourly wage, just 1.8 of them make the $7.25 federal minimum wage or less than that—which represents about 2.3 percent of all hourly paid workers. [2]

Beyond the fact that so few Americans would benefit from a federally mandated wage increase, such hikes have been disastrous when implemented on a local level.

A University of Washington study found that when Seattle, Washington, raised the minimum wage to $15 per hour, workers' hourly salary was lowered by $125 per month. "Employers who can't absorb the additional labor cost have no choice but to reduce hours for employees," said Ortiz in a January 2019 press conference. "It was very predictable, and the same thing will happen on a national scale if this bill passes."

One study by the American Action Forum (AAF) suggested that minimum-wage hikes across the country would eliminate 261,000 jobs in the short term and kill 1.7 million jobs over the long term.[3] Across the country, there's no shortage of evidence and wreckage left in the wake whenever a handful of well-intentioned lawmakers enacted a harsh minimum wage hike. The increases sounded good in theory but caused people pain and led to reduced salaries and fewer hours. Both private business and whole cities suffer the same pitiful fate if they jack up hourly wages. Amazon, a multibillion-dollar megacorporation, provides a perfect example of how substantially raising wages can harm workers. New York City's $15 minimum wage shows how it can slash restaurant jobs across an entire city.

In response to the backlash over Amazon's relatively low salaries and horrid working environments, Amazon enacted a $15 minimum wage for all its employees in 2019, which includes thousands of Whole Foods workers, since it acquired Whole Foods' more than 400 grocery stores in 2017. Whole Foods employees who made less than $15 per hour saw their wages increase to at least the new corporate minimum, while other workers saw an increase of at least $1 per hour, and team leaders saw an increase of at least $2 per hour. Many Whole Foods employees, however, saw decreases in their hourly working schedules, which negated the increase in salary.

"My hours went from 30 to 20 a week," one Whole Foods employee in Illinois said. The worker said that once Amazon enacted the $15 minimum wage, part-time employees saw their weekly hours cut from 30 to 21 hours per week, and full-time employees saw their average hours lowered from 37.5 hours to 34.5 hours. "We just have to work faster to meet the same goals in less time," the worker explained.

"This hours cut makes that raise pointless as people are losing more than they gained and we rely on working full shifts," a Whole Foods worker in Maryland said.

"At my store, all full-time team members are 36 to 38 hours per week now," a Whole Foods employee in Oregon said.[4] "So, what workers do if they want a full 40 hours is take a little bit of their paid time off each week to fill their hours to 40. Doing the same thing myself."

One worker in California said the increased minimum wage led to understaffing issues. "Things that have made it more noticeable are the long lines, the need to call for cashier and bagging assistance, and customers not being able to find help in certain departments because not enough are scheduled, and we are a big store," the employee said. "Just about every person on our team has complained about their hours being cut. Some have had to look for other jobs as they can't make ends meet."

The liberal paradise of New York wasn't spared the economic reality of arbitrarily raising worker wages as it experienced a significant jobs "recession" due to its enactment of a $15 minimum wage. In four years, New York City increased its minimum wage for businesses with more than ten workers from $10.50 to $15, which amounted to a 43 percent increase. Starting in 2020, New York employers will have to pay their workers $15 per hour. This may serve as a victory for some leftists to virtue signal about how they continue to help New York workers; however, the Bureau of Labor Statistics (BLS) found that in the early months of 2019, 4,000 workers lost jobs at full-service restaurants.[5] The BLS also concluded that there were fewer restaurant workers in the Big Apple compared to November 2016, even though overall employment had increased in New York City by more than 163,000.

A New York City Hospitality Alliance survey found that 47 percent of full-service restaurants expect to cut workers with the largest minimum wage hike.

Even during the Great Recession following the 2008 financial crisis, reluctant workers did not suffer as much as they did a decade later; during the December 2007 to June 2009 recession, the number of New York City restaurant jobs increased by 1,800.

Economist Mark Perry explained, "It usually takes an economic recession to cause year-over-year job losses at NYC's full-service restaurants. It's likely that this is a 'restaurant recession' tied to the annual series of minimum-wage hikes that brought the city's minimum wage to $15 an hour at the end of last year."[6]

"Though the new regulations are intended to benefit employees, some restaurateurs and staffers say that take-home pay *ends up being less* due to fewer hours—or that employees face more work because there are fewer staffers per shift," Tara Crowl said in an article on Eater New York.

Meanwhile, under President Donald Trump, American wages have risen at the fastest pace since 2008, even outpacing inflation. The U.S. Department of Labor found that American workers' wages rose by 2.8 percent.

45

ECONOMISTS PREDICTED A TRUMP VICTORY WOULD CRASH THE STOCK MARKET. INSTEAD IT HIT A RECORD HIGH THE WEEK AFTER HE WAS ELECTED

"For three quarters in a row, the growth rate of the economy has hovered around a mere 1%," read a *New York Times* description of President Obama's abysmal economy in August 2016. "In the last quarter of 2015 and the first quarter of 2016, the economy expanded at feeble annual rates of 0.9 percent and 0.8 percent, respectively."

In January 2017, the month Trump took office, the government reported that GDP growth for 2016 was a mere 1.6 percent—the weakest in five years. Days later, the nonpartisan Congressional Budget Office forecast growth for the year would be just 1.9 percent. By February 2017, CNBC had reported that the prolonged economic stagnation of the Obama years had led "many economists to worry that the country has entered a prolonged period where any expansion will be weaker than it has been in the past."

Indeed, stocks had flatlined in 2016, with major indexes trending down. Real median household income had also dropped. Signs of constant stagnation and warnings of sluggish growth going forward were everywhere. This was happening years after the Great Recession had ended. But in August 2018, *New York Times* reporter Patricia Cohen contradicted her own paper's reporting and declared that the economy "is following the upward trajectory begun under President Barack Obama." Under the headline "An Economic Upturn Begun Under Obama Is Now Trump's to Tout," Cohen wrote that "by nearly every standard measure, the American economy is doing well."[1] Again, Cohen's employer contended in August 2016 that, "the underlying reality of low growth will haunt whoever wins the White House." There simply was no "economic upturn" to speak of when Obama left office.

The economy under Trump—spurred by pro-growth trade policies, deregulation, and tax cuts—resurrected the U.S. economy, which grew by 2.3 percent in 2017. The U.S. GDP increased by 4.1 percent from the first quarter of 2018 to the second quarter of 2018. By the summer of 2018, several polls had begun to show that American voters were crediting Trump for the country's economic turnaround.

The *New York Times* didn't predict the Trump recovery—it recognized it in retrospect, when vision is 20/20. But the fact is, no one on the left predicted it—quite the opposite. In fact, bank executives, billionaires, lawmakers, economists, and media members predicted that the economy would collapse and the stock market would implode if Trump won the election.[2]

Shark Tank star and NBA Mavericks owner Mark Cuban declared in September 2016 that the stock market would crash if Trump won. "If the polls look like there's a decent chance that Donald could win, I'll put a huge hedge on that's over 100 percent of my equity positions . . . that protects me just in case he wins," Cuban said.[3]

Investor's Business Daily (IBD) gathered together some of the greatest quotes in an article published at the end of 2017, as the Trump economy was picking up major steam.[4] *IBD*'s selection includes:

> "It really does now look like President Donald J. Trump, and markets are plunging. When might we expect them to recover? A first-pass answer is never. . . . So we are very probably looking at a global recession, with no end in sight."
>
> —Paul Krugman of the *New York Times* the day after the election

> "His domestic policies would lead to recession."
>
> —Mitt Romney at the University of Utah's Hinckley Institute of Politics Forum, March 2016

> "Under Trump, I would expect a protracted recession to begin within 18 months. The damage would be felt far beyond the United States."
>
> —Former Clinton and Obama chief economist Larry Summers, June 2016

> "Trump would likely cause the stock market to crash and plunge the world into recession."
>
> —Simon Johnson, MIT economics professor, in the *New York Times*, November 2016

It wasn't just the leftist big brains in the government and academia that put out apocalyptic predictions of doom and gloom. Citigroup, one of the largest banks in the world, predicted a global recession in August 2016 if Trump were elected.[5] This was based in part on the certainty that Trump would have the world on the brink of war.

Indeed, the market never once flirted with anything close to a crash. All three major stock indexes—the Dow Jones Industrial Average, the Nasdaq, and the S&P 500—took off like rockets on the day after the election. The hysteria had been proven to be nothing more than fearmongering from vacuous elites. The stock market set a record, hitting 86 new record highs in Trump's first year in office. The Dow hit five 1,000-point milestones in one year. It had never been done in the 120-year existence of the exchange.[6]

President Obama certainly didn't believe Donald Trump could fix the economy, and he never dreamed that Trump could bring back jobs. In the mind of globalist elites like Obama, the good-paying jobs are long gone and cheap foreign labor can do everything Americans can. Their usual answer to the American worker is "learn to code," as if H-1B visa holders and eventually artificial intelligence (AI) won't take over all coding jobs in the future.

It's worth bringing up Obama's famous (or infamous) comments on Trump's promise to bring manufacturing jobs back to these shores. Obama said during a PBS town hall, "Well, how exactly are you going to do that? What exactly are you going to do? There's no answer to it." He continued, "He just says, 'Well, I'm going to negotiate a better deal.' Well, what, how exactly are you going to negotiate that? What magic wand do you have? And usually the answer is, he doesn't have an answer."[7]

Obama believed it would take a magic wand, maybe a wizard as powerful as Harry Potter, to put America back to work. But the *New York Times* somehow thinks the Trump economic boom is the result of Obama's policies?

Trump's economy borders on the miraculous. It isn't just blacks who have benefited. Hispanic unemployment is setting records, plummeting in January 2019 to a historic low. Women are setting employment and pay records. The female unemployment rate reached its lowest level in 65 years. Tons of people have traded McDonald's uniforms for the uniforms of skilled manufacturing workers. This is indicated by increases in wages seen throughout the economy.

Trump doesn't have a magic wand but he has an arsenal that includes strong pro-American trade policies, advisers with real-world experience, and a willingness to bully American companies that try to ship jobs overseas or to Mexico. Trump's pro-jobs blitz has resulted in American business creating 5.3 million jobs since Election Night in 2016. That's 5.3 million people creating wealth and opportunity, thanks to President Trump, despite what Barack Obama, Hillary Clinton, or the entire cast of swamp creatures in Washington warned.

46

FAMILY SEPARATION AND DETENTION OF ILLEGAL ALIENS AT THE BORDER EXPLODED UNDER PRESIDENT OBAMA AND DHS SECRETARY JEH JOHNSON

The Trump administration's zero-tolerance policy of apprehending, detaining, separating minors from adults, and prosecuting every person who illegally crosses the U.S.-Mexico border kicked off a burning media-induced hysteria. The press routinely overlooked the fact that the Obama administration detained thousands of illegals at the border, often separating family members and children from adults.

Actual figures for those children who were separated from their parents under Obama are not known because the Obama DHS didn't keep those records, *Politico*'s White House Correspondent and Associate Editor Anita Kumar and McClatchy's White House correspondent Franco Ordoñez reported in June 2018. "Leon Fresco, a deputy assistant attorney general under Obama, who defended

that administration's use of family detention in court, acknowledged that some fathers were separated from children," Kumar and
Ordoñez wrote, adding, "Most fathers and children were released
together, often times with an ankle bracelet. Fresco said there were
cases where the administration held fathers who were carrying
drugs or caught with other contraband who had to be separated
from their children. . . . ICE could not devise a safe way where men
and children could be in detention together in one facility," Fresco
said, according to Kumar and Ordoñez. "It was deemed too much
of a security risk."[1] "If there's any suspicion that they're not really
truly related to those people, then they will be separated for their
own safety," a chief border agent said at the time of children who
are routinely recycled by smugglers to sneak adults into the United
States.[2]

In most cases, the children were usually detained in separate
facilities. Department of Health and Human Services (HHS) officials
would administer medical care, and then the children were sent to
a shelter where they were later placed with a relative or a foster
family. Within weeks of the implementation of President Trump's
zero-tolerance policy—which ended a month after a Trump executive order started it—roughly 2,000 child border crossers had been
separated from the adults they crossed the border with. Many of
the adults were the parents of the child they were apprehended with
at the border. In an unknown number of cases, the children were
pawns of craven child traffickers smuggling minors across the border to gain entry into the United States to request asylum status.
Indeed, the number of adult illegal border crossers arriving at the
U.S.-Mexico border with a minor had increased more than 300 per-

cent from May 2017 to May 2018, according to White House senior adviser Stephen Miller said.

The ground on which the Trump administration's zero-tolerance policy stood had long been plowed by presidents going as far back as Bill Clinton. Clinton signed the Illegal Immigration Reform and Immigrant Responsibility Act (IIRIRA) into law in 1996. The legislation, which went into action in April 1997, was meant to address what was widely recognized as an exploding illegal immigration problem in the United States. Citing his administration's determination to "swiftly reverse the course of a decade of failed immigration policies," Clinton wrote in a February 1995 memorandum on "Deterring Illegal Immigration" that his White House would "devise a National Detention, Transportation, and Removal Policy" that would "focus on strong border deterrence backed up by effective worksite enforcement, removal of criminal and other deportable aliens and assistance to states" and that would "protect the security of our borders, our jobs and our communities for all Americans—citizens and legal immigrants alike."

Fast-forward nearly two decades later, and the Obama White House had inherited two dynamics. First, the media that couldn't care less about reporting the many instances in which children were separated from adults at the border, which didn't fit neatly into their narrative. Second, a full-fledged mass invasion of adults and minors flooded the U.S.-Mexico border. In 2014, the Border Patrol reported 486,651 apprehensions nationwide.[3] That number was up compared to the 420,789 apprehensions from just a year prior. "The increase is largely attributable to the influx in unaccompanied children and family units in South Texas last summer,"

DHS said in an end-of-year report. Many of the apprehensions, the report stated, "were of individuals from Mexico, El Salvador, Guatemala, and Honduras."[4] In tens of thousands of those cases, adults were separated from minors. But the media didn't manufacture white-hot headlines condemning President Obama and his Border Patrol of carrying out Holocaust-level atrocities.

Most in the media ignored Obama's border-separation tactics, even though separating children from adults had become a more widespread policy.

"Political journalism needs a bit of housecleaning on this child border crisis. I'll start. It was going on during the Obama years in large numbers. I never wrote about it. Was completely unaware, in large part because few reporters were interested enough to create critical mass," the *Daily Mail's* political editor David Martosko acknowledged during the news media–instigated rancor over Trump's adult separation enforcement. "To my colleagues out there chasing Pulitzers over this: Why didn't today's critical mass form when we were looking at unaccompanied minors by the tens of thousands in 2014. Why didn't those kids matter as much as these? Few of us chased those stories down with any vigor."[5]

In reality, the Obama administration enforced a far more punitive policy, known as the Alien Transfer Exit Program (ATEP) or Lateral Repatriation, which saw detained male migrants who were caught crossing into the United States from Mexico shipped across the country and then escorted back across the U.S.-Mexico border at another border sector—thousands of miles from their original border sector of illegal entry. The tactic was one of a few key efforts enforced by the DHS to disrupt smuggling networks. In many cases, women were separated from the men they were apprehended with and were deported separately, according to a study conducted by the *Journal on Migration and Human Security*. The policy, which went into effect in February 2008, was ramped up under Obama. "ATEP was initiated in the San Diego, Yuma and El Centro Sectors in February 2008 and has since expanded to the Tucson and El Paso Sectors," said Michael J. Fisher, chief of the U.S. Border Patrol, before the House Committee on Homeland Security, Subcommittee on Border and Maritime Security. "In FY11, as of February 2, 18,257 apprehensions have been transferred as part of ATEP, and only 3,558 subjects have been encountered after illegally re-entering the United States."[6]

ATEP was called "a form of cruel and unusual punishment" by one Arizona-based illegal immigration advocacy group. "ATEP routinely broke up families migrating together, and it made it a logistical nightmare for a couple to find each other again. Imagine a weeks- or months-long ordeal in which you didn't know where your husband was, and he didn't know where you and your children were," said Mary Small, policy director of Detention Watch Network.[7]

What's more, Obama-era detention centers were "tortuous," according to Angelo Guisado, a staff attorney with the Center for Constitutional Rights. "Policies include banning mothers and children from sleeping together and turning lights on and off every hour to ensure this . . . guaranteeing sleep deprivation," Guisado said of the conditions detained aliens faced under Obama.[8] The number of "family detention beds" spiked from a few hundred when Obama took office to more than 3,600 in 2014.[9] In December 2014, the liberal American Civil Liberties Union sued the Obama administration over its "policy of locking up asylum-seeking mothers and children to intimidate others from coming to the United States." Illegal border crossers went from sleeping on cold cement floors covered with wool blankets to receiving warm beds, hot meals, clothing, education, recreation, medical care, and counseling under Trump. That's far from "ethnic cleansing," as New York Democratic Socialist Alexandria Ocasio-Cortez described Trump's immigration policy.

47

ILLEGAL IMMIGRATION MAY HAVE COST BLACK AMERICANS MORE THAN I MILLION JOBS

"The number of immigrants added to the labor force every year is of a magnitude not seen in this country for over a century," Barack Obama said in his book *The Audacity of Hope*. Obama's warning continued, "If this huge influx of mostly low-skill workers provides some benefits to the economy as a whole—especially by keeping our workforce young, it also threatens to depress further the wages of blue-collar Americans and put strains on an already overburdened safety net."

The dirty little secret about illegal immigration is that it directly harms the employment prospects for black Americans and legal immigrants, who badly need work in low-skill occupations not only to provide for their families, but also to gain the experience necessary to capitalize on better employment opportunities. That's the American Dream. And black Americans have dreams, too, dreams that are crushed when their potential prospects for work are wrecked by unfettered illegal immigration.

The fact that illegal immigration negatively impacts black Americans' job opportunities and wages isn't a secret. It's widely known but not often acknowledged. In many ways, acknowledging the pain illegal immigration inflicts on black workers has become a sort of litmus test to determine the courage of black political leaders. Are they willing to break rank with the lockstep Democratic mantra of open borders? Or will they "go along to get along" even if illegals take money out of the hands of black workers, thus driving up black unemployment?

Peter Kirsanow is an attorney and has been a member of the U.S. Commission on Civil Rights (USCCR) for the past fifteen years, where he has been warning about the disastrous effects of illegal immigration on black workers. Kirsanow explained the problem clearly in a 2017 letter to Congress that describes a USCCR hearing in 2008: "All the witnesses acknowledged that illegal immigration has a negative impact on black employment, both in terms of employment opportunities and wages. The witnesses differed somewhat on the precise extent of that impact, but every witness agreed that illegal immigration has a discernible negative effect on black employment."[1]

Our country's experts have known about the effects of illegal immigration on the black community for decades, but haven't done anything about it.

According to Kirsanow, competition with illegal aliens accounts for as much as 40 percent of the drop in employment suffered by black Americans during the Obama years. Roughly a million black workers lost jobs to illegals based on this calculation. And those who kept jobs saw their wages decreased by this same competition.

Illegal immigrants causing depressed wages for legal immigrants and black Americans in the hospitality industry, for example, cost these workers $1,500 a year.

> "The country's persistent economic stagnation between 2008–2016 disproportionately harmed African-Americans, especially those with little education. Eight years into the economic recovery, African-Americans still faced particular difficulty obtaining employment. According to the Bureau of Labor Statistics, the December 2017 unemployment rate for all black Americans—not just those with few skills—was 6.8 percent, nearly twice the white unemployment rate of 3.7 percent. The economy has a glut of low-skilled workers, not a shortage. The unemployment rate for black teens is nearly 23 percent. The black labor force participation rate remains 62.1 percent. In addition, black median household income was stagnant for years."
>
> —Peter Kirsanow, in a 2018 letter to Congress[2]

The left often blames low-skilled black workers' chronic stagnation on the tired argument that "illegal aliens do the jobs Americans won't do." I've devoted a whole chapter in this book to dispelling that myth because Americans will do any job, no matter how dirty, if they are paid for it. However, it's worth revisiting this cockeyed argument because it's used to explain away illegal workers' siphoning employment opportunities away from blacks and legal immigrants.

The Center for Immigration Studies, a think tank dedicated to examining the impact of mass immigration, conducted a study on hundreds of occupations, looking at what percentage of workers were immigrant versus native-born Americans, while also estimating the percentage of illegal immigrants in the field and the native-born unemployment rate.

In a few examples, the percentage of immigrant workers is high, but the percentage of illegals is low, while the percentage of unemployed native-born workers is close to the national average across occupations. For example, for "appearance workers," 59 percent of all people employed are immigrants, but only about 10 percent are illegal immigrants.[3] The unemployment for native-born Americans is at the national average.

But in other cases, where the percentage of illegal workers is higher, the unemployment rate for native-born workers is dramatically higher. For example, "Helpers, construction trades" is only 34 percent immigrant overall, but more than 20 percent are illegal immigrants. The native-born unemployment rate is 32 percent. Construction helpers are not Yale graduates, folks. They are unskilled black, white, and Hispanic Americans, probably raised in a poor family. This type of position also serves as a crucial gateway into the workforce, providing on-the-job learning that results in higher-skill work, like eventually becoming a plumber or equipment operator.

Other great jobs for black Americans are in similar circumstances, such as roofers, drywall workers, production helpers, and paving crewmembers. Wouldn't we all be better off if America's low-skilled workers were filling these jobs instead of illegals? This would benefit the black community and America overall in so many ways that it's hard to count. Not the least of which would be a lessening of the dependence on social programs and a falling crime rate—after all, idle hands do the devil's work.

Some members of the clergy, like Bishop Aubrey Shines, have also seen the light on this issue. Shines is the founder of G2G Ministries as well as a pastor, author, and evangelist. Writing for Real-ClearPolitics, Shines shared his perspective on the problems caused in the black community by illegal immigration, and also gave advice for white Americans witnessing the results of leftist immigration policies: "Blacks are being adversely impacted by the failed policies of the men and women that they have unwisely elected. Often, instead of hearing the clarion call of Dr. Martin Luther King to never judge an individual by the color of their skin but by the content of their character, they continue to elect individuals whose only interest is to keep them on the plantation called ignorance, while they cloak themselves in the garments of emancipators."[4]

48

THERE HAVE BEEN MORE THAN 630 EXAMPLES OF LEFT-WING POLITICAL VIOLENCE AND THREATS AGAINST TRUMP SUPPORTERS

As of this writing, there have been more than 630 instances of violent attacks, threats, vandalism, and menacing against supporters of President Donald Trump since he took office in January 2017.[1] That's nearly one act of violence a day. Many of them involve women, the elderly, and even children—including intimidation tactics and slurs hurled at kids in school by teachers and other school district employees. The barrage of beatdowns, bullying, and intimidation has come exclusively from frenzied and unforgiving "liberals" hellbent on brutalizing anyone who dares to publicly support Trump.

The level of incivility toward Americans over their political views has rarely been so toxic.

Most Americans are repulsed by the level of abhorrent behavior displayed by rabid leftists, despite the mainstream media, led by CNN, constantly feeding millions of viewers a steady stream of stories about Trump supporters being racist, sexist, fascist, and all-around deplorable. But the facts show that Trump supporters are regularly on the receiving end of politically motivated threats and violence. And I'm not talking about the Jussie Smollett made-for-TV beat down.

The violence, threats, and invective toward President Trump's supporters didn't start with his inauguration. One of the earliest reported attacks dates back to September 2015, when a Texas teenager was assaulted at a bus stop for the crime of supporting candidate Trump. Neither the victim nor his attacker was old enough to vote in the 2016 election.

Throughout the election cycle, Trump supporters faced attacks, especially on the West Coast. One high-profile attack at a Trump rally in Anaheim, California, involved five Trump supporters, including a senior man, women, and children, being pepper-sprayed by a leftist agitator.[2] And if you think these violent attacks and threats ended after Trump's inauguration, which included antifa riots in Washington, DC, and elsewhere, you'd be sadly mistaken.

Consider UC Berkeley. Berkeley, like many colleges around the country, has shifted from being a battleground of ideas and free speech to being an old-fashioned battleground. In February 2019, an activist training student members of the conservative organization Turning Point USA on how to recruit new members was confronted by a leftist who punched him multiple times in the face with no provocation. The attack left the student with a black eye. UC Berkeley took several days to condemn the attack, which was allegedly perpetrated by a Berkeley resident who was briefly employed by the college.

The obvious question at this point is "Why?" Why is the toxicity toward Trump supporters so noxious and the restraint on violent tendencies nearly nonexistent? One obvious answer is that Democratic leaders and the mainstream media have done their best to whip the left into a horde of unhinged hysterics when it comes to Trump.

Here are just a few examples of prominent Democratic lawmakers and leaders instigating violence with revolting language.

- **Representative Maxine Waters called on Trump's cabinet, and by extension his supporters, to be harassed in public: "I want to tell you, these members of his cabinet who remain and try to defend him, they won't be able to go to a restaurant, they won't be able to stop at a gas station, they're not going to be able to shop at a department store. The people are going to turn on them. They're going to protest. They're absolutely going to harass them until they decide that they're going to tell the president, 'No, I can't hang with you.'"**
- **Former attorney general Eric Holder modified Michelle Obama's famous quote: "It is time for us as Democrats to be as tough as they are, to be as dedicated as they are, to be as committed as they are. Michelle says, 'When they go low, we go high.' No. No. When they go low, we kick 'em."**

- **Failed presidential candidate Hillary Clinton gave her supporters the green light to harass and attack Trump supporters: "You cannot be civil with a political party that wants to destroy what you stand for, what you care about."**
- **2020 hopeful Joe Biden told us specifically what he would do to President Trump: "They asked me would I like to debate this gentleman, and I said no. I said, 'If we were in high school, I'd take him behind the gym and beat the hell out of him.'" (Biden didn't comment on what he'd do to the first lady, probably prudent given the troubles he's had for being too hands-on with women and girls.)**

The mainstream media has marched in lockstep with these politicians. For example, in the three weeks before an antifa attack on the home of Tucker Carlson—in which the group Smash Racism DC attempted to break down his front door, terrorizing his wife and children—CNN ran a half dozen attack articles on Carlson, in what one onlooker called a "campaign of personal demonization."[3]

CNN's attacks on Carlson included calling him part of a movement of "white anxiety" and that he is "laying the groundwork for an authoritarian agenda."[4] The media shouldn't be shocked when its viewers, whom it has conditioned to only consider their own political point of view, take their words literally, take to the streets, and attack commentators like Carlson.

The attack on Carlson isn't the only example of leftists being provoked by the mainstream media to commit violence. It also happens to people who are not famous cable news anchors. One of the biggest controversies in the early days of 2019 was the Covington Catholic hate hoax, in which the mainstream media, Internet pundits, and Hollywood celebrities used a deceptive video and false news reporting designed to frame innocent Catholic high school students attending a March for Life event in Washington, DC, as racist supporters of the president.[5]

The threats were flying hot and heavy. Verified Twitter leftists threatened violence against the teenagers without repercussion from the tech platform, including CNN's Reza Aslan, who posted a picture of high schooler Nick Sandmann with the comment, "Honest question. Have you ever seen a more punchable face than this kid's?" Comedian Kathy Griffin chimed in, "Ps. The reply from the school was pathetic and impotent. Name these kids. I want NAMES. Shame them. If you think these fuckers wouldn't dox you in a heartbeat, think again."

The situation got much more serious when CNN and the *Washington Post*, among dozens of other mainstream outlets, jumped into the fray, basically calling the Kentucky high school kids the biggest bigots on the planet.

Sandmann, perhaps taking cues from Trump, did not cower and beg for forgiveness—he stood up for himself. The teenagers were completely exonerated by an uncut video depicting the entire incident. The full video showed that the teens were not provoking a confrontation, despite the lie being tweeted and repeatedly reported about them. You try standing still and smiling while an old guy beats a drum in your face—it ain't easy!

Although multiple mainstream media outlets issued corrections on their stories about the Covington Catholic hate hoax, Sandmann's attorney, L. Lin Wood, has filed multiple defamation lawsuits and warnings. CNN and *Washington Post* are reportedly being sued for more than $250 million for defaming the teen, which also affected his school and his entire community.[6]

A video produced by Wood's law office provides a true level of clarity to the media's role in whipping up the left to attack, threaten, and harass Trump supporters. According to the video: "The *Washington Post*, owned by the richest man in the world, led the print media's false attacks against Nicholas' reputation. CNN led the broadcast media's charge against Nicholas. Both recklessly spread lies about a minor to advance their own financial and political agendas." The video continued, "Despite raw video debunking the false narrative, the *Post* and CNN doubled down on their reckless lies. Lies that will forever haunt and endanger the life of an innocent young man, lies that further divided our nation."

49

DICK'S SPORTING GOODS' ANTI-GUN POLICY RESULTED IN A $150 MILLION LOSS FOR THE COMPANY, BUT THE LEFT'S APPROVAL IS WORTH MORE

Corporations across an array of industries are attempting to subvert your freedoms with a zeal not seen in our lifetime. If it was limited to just one industry, such as the Silicon Valley tech masters, it might be easier to see and grapple with. But under the guise of moral management, the U.S. economy has become a battlefield of corporate fascism and conservative-minded Americans being caught dead in the crosshairs.

Consider the case of Dick's Sporting Goods. The company, founded in 1984, quickly became a popular one-stop shop for hunters and gun enthusiasts. But following the tragic Parkland school shooting, Dick's joined the corporate fascism crusade to usurp Americans' Second Amendment rights. Dick's immediately announced sweeping changes to its gun sales. The chain announced it would stop selling "assault rifles," the media's buzzword for semiautomatic rifles. It also cut sales of "high-capacity" magazines. Most important, it unilaterally decided not to sell guns to customers under the age of twenty-one—ignoring the rights of eighteen- to twenty-year-olds.[1]

Dick's didn't stop there. Eventually, the company announced a plan to pull all guns from 125 of its stores, along with hunting gear and other gun-related items.

American consumers responded to Dick's by taking their dollars elsewhere. The company's CEO admitted that "some gun enthusiasts have stopped shopping at the chain." The new policy resulted in a $150 million loss for the company, but there's been no sign that Dick's will reverse course.

Dick's Sporting Goods isn't alone in its corporate gun-control campaign. Levi Strauss, of all companies, has dedicated a million dollars toward advancing gun control.[2] Big banks have spearheaded much more malicious opposition to the Second Amendment. In March 2018, Citigroup announced that it would no longer do business with gun shops that sold guns to Americans under age 21.[3] The bank also put restrictions on magazine capacities. Bank of America announced it would no longer provide loans to companies in the gun industry that produce "military-style firearms."[4]

The days of financial institutions in the business of keeping our money safe in accounts, facilitating transactions when we want that money, and lending capital to businesses and individuals have come to an end. No. Now banks and financial institutions are in the dubious business of picking and choosing, based on an opaque moral code or the ever-changing political climate, who is worthy of a loan to start or finance their business.

The Electronic Freedom Frontier Foundation (EFF), a liberal non-profit devoted to free expression and privacy on the Internet, thinks banks and payment processors are the biggest censors and political bullies. A spokesperson for the EFF said, "I'm deeply concerned that we're letting banks and payment processors turn into de facto Internet censors."

Banks, payment processors, and other financial companies can censor Internet content that they don't like by restricting organizations from accepting credit cards for use on their websites. For example, Mastercard pushed several payment processors into cutting off service to Jihad Watch and its founder, Richard Spencer.[5] Mastercard decided that Jihad Watch and its content is too dangerous for Americans to be exposed to, so it attacked Spencer's organization the best way it knew how—by cutting its funding.

PayPal, one of the most popular online payment services, is also one of the worst offenders in the corporate fascism war. The company pulled out of a planned investment in North Carolina after the state passed a law in 2016 requiring people to use the bathroom of their biological sex.[6] CEO Dan Schulman said at the time, "I think North Carolina was probably the moment that was the most visible, where we basically said this violates our core value and we need to make a very public stand on it."

PayPal has gone on a rampage against voices on the right, black-listing content creators on the right from receiving PayPal payments, to stifle their voices. A short list, compiled by Breitbart, includes: Infowars, conservative commentator and Vice co-founder Gavin McInnes, political activist Tommy Robinson, investigative journalist Laura Loomer, blogger Roosh V, free speech social network Gab, YouTube alternative BitChute, and a black metal music label.

Silicon Valley is full of companies willing to blacklist conservatives from their platforms, but one of the most recent and most alarming examples is a tech company *not* in the valley, e-commerce giant Amazon.

After conquering the book industry, Amazon has begun banning books with the wrong politics from its platform. Many of the books banned come from wingnuts on the far right and deal with white nationalism, but these are books Amazon has had no trouble selling for years.[7] For example, Jared Taylor's *White Identity* has been on sale since 2011.

These books were banned[8] while Jeff Bezos's company happily sells the Unabomber's manifesto, *The Anarchist's Cookbook*, and books by renowned anti-Semite Louis Farrakhan.[9] A clear rebuke of Amazon's censorship came from an unlikely source. They wrote: "it is censorship not to sell certain books simply because we or others believe their message is objectionable." The unlikely source? Amazon itself. That is a 2010 quote from an Amazon spokesman, who added, "Amazon does not support or promote hatred or criminal acts, however, we do support the right of every individual to make their own purchasing decisions."[10]

Talk about a 180! Amazon has now joined its Big Tech brethren and massive corporations across the country in attempting to control what you buy, read, and think.

50

CHRISTIANITY IS THE WORLD'S MOST PERSECUTED RELIGION

There is a global war on Christianity occurring as the mainstream media looks the other way. It's not the type of war on Christianity you're used to hearing about—a cold war, consisting of Starbucks coffee cups and people saying "Happy Holidays" instead of "Merry Christmas."

No, I'm talking about a hot war—mass murder, bible-banning, and church burnings.

One of the hot zones in the global war on Christianity is Nigeria, an African country split evenly between Christians and Muslims. An Islamic extremist group known as the Fulani Jihadists killed 120 Christians over the course of three weeks in February and March 2019. This event went practically unreported in the West.[1]

Breitbart News' Thomas Williams, one of the few in the Western media to report the atrocity, described the final attack, which killed 50 Christians: The assailants reportedly split into three groups, the first of which fired upon the people, the second set fire to buildings, and the third chased down people fleeing from the scene. Victims of the assault included women and children.[2]

Fulani Jihadists are not the only Muslim terrorist group Nigerian Christians have to deal with. They are also attacked by Boko Haram, the group made infamous by their kidnapping of a group of more than 200 schoolgirls. Boko Haram is alive and well—and raiding Christian towns. Here is how one resident described the terrorists' March 2019 raid of a Christian town named Michika: "I can confirm to you that many people were killed last night and many were injured as well," said a man named Bala. "I may not know all of those who lost their lives but I am sure of four persons whom I know personally, that were killed in the attack. My aunt's husband and their daughter were killed. I also know of a retired soldier and local businessman that were killed in front of their houses."[3]

This begs the question: Why isn't the Western media reporting these atrocities? Where is the BBC? You know they love putting on pith helmets and trekking across Africa in Land Rovers. One expert, Dede Laugesen, the director of Save the Persecuted Christians, explained in a recent *Breitbart News Sunday* radio interview that the mainstream media has an "anti-Christian bias" that results in its downplaying the murder of Christians by Islamic extremists because it doesn't fit the global narrative the media is attempting to push.[4]

Laugesen explained:

> People don't believe that Christians can be persecuted, that they could be slaughtered. Here in the United States, we just have a different sense of who Christians are, but out in the greater world, Christians are viewed as a threat to control and power. What you have operating in Nigeria,

which is Africa's most populous country—200 million people living there with 50 percent Christians, 50 percent Muslims—you have two of the world's most dangerous terrorist groups operating . . . Fulani militants and Boko Haram, now affiliated with ISIS Islamic State in West Africa—and they are driven by radical Sharia supremacist ideology, seeking to spread Sharia across the entire country of Nigeria.[5]

There is significant evidence that Laugesen is right about the media. Left-wing fact-check site Snopes, which has a tenuous relationship with the truth at best, recently fact-checked Breitbart's article on the Nigeria attacks. It rated the article and several related pieces a "mixture" of truth and lies. Snopes agrees that 120+ Christians were slaughtered by Muslims in a several-week period, but claims the lie is that it has anything to do with religion. To Snopes, a weeks-long mass murder campaign of Christians by Muslims in Nigeria is a dispute between farmers fighting over fields.

But if attacks on Christians were limited to Nigeria or even the continent of Africa, we could hardly call it a global war on Christianity. Unfortunately, attacks against Christians and their religion have spread everywhere.

In India, persecution of Christians has jumped 57 percent when we compare January and February 2019 to the previous year.[6] This includes multiple murders. In one incident that thankfully did not reach the level of murder, police interrupted a Christian service and arrested four women and two men. The police beat the female pastor to unconsciousness, and then forced boiling tea into her mouth because they thought she was "faking it."

China is looking no better for Christians. A September 2018 report on the communist government of China's crackdown on religion included "piles of burning bibles" along with art and church pews.[7] Hundreds of churches have been reported closed in Henan Province alone.[8] At the same time, the Catholic Church is making deals with the communist party that many believe will see party officials replace priests in churches. Cardinal Joseph Zen wrote of this, "To us, a terrifying scenario is unfolding, the sellout of our church! There is no essential freedom but a semblance of freedom."[9]

Indonesia and its Aceh province, which observes Sharia law, is no better. In 2015 it demolished or burned ten churches, which the government claimed did not have the appropriate building permits.[10]

The war on Christianity has already spread to the West.

On New Year's Eve in 2017, a gang of at least 1,000 Muslim men in Dortmund launched fireworks into the German crowd, tangled with police, and eventually set fire to the roof of one of the oldest churches in Germany, St. Reinhold's Church.[11] Of course, they were chanting "Allahu Akbar" the whole time. The police reported the events of the night as "quiet." In 2018, an average of two Christian churches were desecrated in France *every day.*[12] In March 2019, twelve French churches were vandalized or desecrated in a single week.[13] These are not minor churches and the damage is not minor. The Church of Saint-Sulpice in Paris suffered an arson attack that will reportedly cost "several hundred million Euros" to repair.

A 2018 study by the University of Notre Dame's Center for Ethics and Culture, the Religious Freedom Institute, and Georgetown's Religious Freedom Research Project found that Christianity was the world's most persecuted religion. Despite this, the study found that "Christian responses to persecution are almost always nonviolent."[14]

ACKNOWLEDGMENTS

I would like to thank my editor, Eric Nelson, whose patience and wisdom truly helped make this a better book. I would also like to thank Wynton Hall, for whose endless counsel and support I will be forever grateful.

I thank my amazing colleagues at Breitbart News, and its leadership, Larry Solov, Jon Kahn, and Alexander Marlow, for having faith in me. And to Colin Madine, Frances Martel, Locus Nolan, Sean Moran, Katherine Rodriguez, and Dr. Susan Berry. Their expertise and assistance in the research and writing is found herein. To my family for their love and encouragement.

NOTES

I: FROM 2012 TO 2016, MORE BLACK WOMEN IN NEW YORK CITY HAD ABORTIONS THAN GAVE BIRTH

1. New York City Department of Health and Mental Hygiene, "Summary of Vital Statistics 2013: The City of New York Pregnancy Outcomes," February 2013, 25.
2. New York City Department of Health and Mental Hygiene, "Summary of Vital Statistics 2016: The City of New York," July 2018, 81, 98. Accessed April 2, 2019, https://www1.nyc.gov/assets/doh/downloads/pdf/vs/2016sum.pdf.
3. Tara C. Jatlaoui et al. "Abortion Surveillance—United States, 2015," *Morbidity and Mortality Weekly Report*, Surveillance Summaries 67(13), 2018, 1–45. Accessed May 2, 2019, https://www.cdc.gov/mmwr/volumes/67/ss/pdfs/ss6713a1-H.pdf.
4. Star Parker, "The Effects of Abortion on the Black Community" (Washington, DC; Center for Urban Renewal and Education, 2015).
5. Ibid.
6. Margaret Sanger, "Birth Control," *Britannica Book of the Year* 1944, 110–111, accessed online via the Margaret Sanger Papers Project. Accessed April 2, 2019, https://www.nyu.edu/projects/sanger/webedition/app/documents/show.php?sangerDoc=320975.xml.
7. Jamie Hall and Roger Severino, "Disentangling the Data on Planned Parenthood Affiliates' Abortion Services and Receipt of Taxpayer Funding," Heritage Foundation, November 30, 2015. Accessed April 2, 2019, https://www.heritage.org/health-care-reform/report/disentangling-the-data-planned-parenthood-affiliates-abortion-services.
8. "Grassley Refers Planned Parenthood, Fetal Tissue Procurement Organizations to FBI, Justice Dept. for Investigation | Chuck Grassley," press release, December 13, 2016. Accessed April 2, 2019, https://www.grassley.senate.gov/news/news-releases/grassley-refers-planned-parenthood-fetal-tissue-procurement-organizations-fbi.
9. Planned Parenthood, *2016–2017 Annual Report*. Accessed April 2, 2019, https://www.plannedparenthood.org/uploads/filer_public/71/53/7153464c-8f5d-4a26-bead-2a0dfe2b32ec/20171229_ar16–17_p01_lowres.pdf.
10. Rachael Larimore, "The Most Meaningless Abortion Statistic Ever," *Slate*, May 7, 2013. Accessed April 2, 2019, https://slate.com/human-interest/2013/05/3-percent-of-planned-parenthood-s-services-are-abortion-but-what-about-their-revenues.html.

11. Jeff Jacoby, "Chelsea Clinton's Twisted Argument About Abortion and Economic Growth," *Boston Globe*, August 21, 2018. Accessed April 2, 2019, https://www.bostonglobe.com/opinion/2018/08/22/chelsea-clinton-twisted -argument-about-abortion-and-economic-growth/6ajP713rANYAO izO3ohLeN/story.html.

12. "2019–02-YouGov-AUL-National-Survey.Pdf," accessed April 2, 2019, https://aul.org/wp-content/uploads/2019/02/2019–02-YouGov-AUL -National-Survey.pdf.

2: THE U.S. GOVERNMENT AWARDED 100 MILLION IN TAX DOLLARS FOR CONTRACTS TO THE ABORTED-BABY-TISSUE INDUSTRY

1. Federal Procurement Data System – Next Generation, "FPDS-NG ezSearch" (n.d.). Accessed April 3, 2019, https://www.fpds.gov/ezsearch/fpdsportal ?amp;templateName=1.4.4&q=advanced+bioscience+resources+ VENDOR_DUNS_NUMBER%3A%22786845982%22&sort By=SIGNED_DATE&s=FPDSNG.COM&indexName=award full&desc=Y&&templateName=1.5.1&indexName=awardfull.

2. Terence P. Jeffrey, "FDA Acquiring 'Fresh' Aborted Baby Parts to Make Mice with Human Immune Systems," *CNSNews*, August 7, 2018. Accessed May 3, 2019, https://www.cnsnews.com/news/article/terence-p-jeffrey/fda -acquiring-fresh-aborted-baby-parts-make-mice-human-immune-systems.

3. "Grassley Refers Planned Parenthood, Fetal Tissue Procurement Organiza- tions to FBI, Justice Dept. for Investigation | Chuck Grassley," press release, December 13, 2016. Accessed April 2, 2019, https://www.grassley.senate .gov/news/news-releases/grassley-refers-planned-parenthood-fetal-tissue -procurement-organizations-fbi.

4. Meredith Wadman and Jocelyn Kaiser, "NIH Chief Defends Use of Human Fetal Tissue as Opponents Decry It Before Congress," *Science*, December 13, 2018. Accessed April 6, 2019, https://www.sciencemag.org/news/2018/12 /nih-chief-defends-use-human-fetal-tissue-opponents-decry-it-congress.

5. National Institutes of Health, "NOT-OD-19–042: Notice of Intent to Publish Funding Opportunity Announcements for Research to Develop, Demon- strate, and Validate Experimental Human Tissue Models That Do Not Rely on Human Fetal Tissue," December 10, 2018. Accessed April 6, 2019, https://grants.nih.gov/grants/guide/notice-files/NOT-OD-19-042.html.

6. Tara Sander Lee, "Written Testimony of Tara Sander Lee, Ph.D., in Support of Ethical Alternatives to Aborted Fetal Tissue Research," Charlotte Lozier Institute, December 20, 2018. Accessed April 6, 2019, https://lozierinstitute .org/written-testimony-of-tara-sander-lee-ph-d-in-support-of-ethical -alternatives-to-aborted-fetal-tissue-research/.

7. Dave Andrusko, "Scientist Tells Congress: 'No Scientific' Reason to Use Aborted Baby Parts in Research," *LifeNews*, December 13, 2018, https://www.lifenews.com/2018/12/13/scientist-tells-congress-no-scientific-reason-to-use-aborted-baby-parts-in-research/.

3: BLACK AND HISPANIC STUDENTS ARE MORE UNDERREPRESENTED AT AMERICA'S TOP COLLEGES AND UNIVERSITIES THAN BEFORE AFFIRMATIVE ACTION

1. Jeremy Ashkenas, Haeyoun Park, and Adam Pierce, "Even with Affirmative Action, Blacks and Hispanics Are More Underrepresented at Top Colleges Than 35 Years Ago," *New York Times*, August 24, 3017. Accessed April 6, 2019, https://www.nytimes.com/interactive/2017/08/24/us/affirmative-action.html.
2. National Archives, "Order of Argument in the Case, Brown v. Board of Education," August 15, 2016. Accessed May 3, 2019, https://www.archives.gov/education/lessons/brown-case-order.
3. National Center for Education Statistics, "National Assessment of Adult Literacy (NAAL)," 1993. Accessed April 6, 2019, https://nces.ed.gov/naal/lit_history.asp#illiteracy.
4. Thomas Sowell, "Dunbar High School After 100 Years," Creators Syndicate, October 4, 2016. Accessed October 4, 2016, https://www.creators.com/read/thomas-sowell/10/16/dunbar-high-school-after-100-years.
5. Stuart Taylor Jr., "We Must Face Persistent Racial Gaps in Academic Performance," RealClear Politics, December 4, 2018. Accessed April 6, 2019, https://www.realclearpolitics.com/articles/2018/12/04/we_must_face_persistent_racial_gaps_in_academic_performance_138818.html.
6. U.S. Department of Labor, "The Negro Family: The Case for National Action," March 1965. Accessed April 6, 2019, https://www.dol.gov/general/aboutdol/history/webid-moynihan.
7. Wendy Leopold, "Study: Stark Differences in Media Use Between Minority, White Youth: Northwestern University News," Northwestern University press release, June 8, 2011. Accessed April 6, 2019, https://www.northwestern.edu/newscenter/stories/2011/06/media-usa-youth-wartella.html.
8. Coleman Hughes, "What the New Integrationists Fail to See," *City Journal*, July 2, 2018, https://www.city-journal.org/html/black-only-schools-16000.html.
9. National Assessment of Educational Progress, "NAEP Mathematics and Reading Highlights," Nation's Report Card, 2018. Accessed April 6, 2019, https://www.nationsreportcard.gov/reading_math_2017_highlights/.
10. Richard V. Reeves and Dimitrios Halikias, "Race Gaps in SAT Scores Highlight Inequality and Hinder Upward Mobility," *Brookings* (blog), Brookings

Institution, February 1, 2017, https://www.brookings.edu/research/race
-gaps-in-sat-scores-highlight-inequality-and-hinder-upward-mobility/.

11. "The Persisting Racial Scoring Gap on Graduate and Professional School
Admission Tests," *Journal of Blacks in Higher Education*, no. 38 (2002): 16–20,
JSTOR, www.jstor.org/stable/3134172.

12. Quote in Myron Magnet, *The Dream and the Nightmare: The Sixties' Legacy
to the Underclass* (New York: William Morrow), 1993.

4: AMERICA'S MOST DEADLY AND DANGEROUS CITIES ARE RUN BY DEMOCRATS

1. Robert Downen, "Houston Murders Drop 11 Percent in 2017," *Houston Chronicle*, January 5, 2018, https://www.houstonchronicle.com/news
/houston-texas/houston/article/Houston-murders-drop-11-percent-in
-2017-12477945.php.

2. Kevin Rector, "2017 Homicide Data Provide Insight into Baltimore's Gun
Wars, Police Say," *Baltimore Sun*, January 3, 2018. Accessed April 6, 2019,
https://www.baltimoresun.com/news/maryland/crime/bs-md-ci-2017
-homicide-data-breakdown-20180103-story.html.

3. "The 30 Cities with the Highest Murder Rates in the US," *Bismarck Tribune*,
April 15, 2019. Accessed May 3, 2019, https://bismarcktribune.com/news
/national/the-cities-with-the-highest-murder-rates-in-the-us/collection
_85921a38-c5e1-5cdc-82b9-d1246c065352.html#28.

4. Philadelphia Police Department, "Crime Maps & Stats," PhillyPolice.com,
n.d. Accessed April 6, 2019, https://www.phillypolice.com/crime-maps
-stats/index.html.

5. Oralandar Brand-Williams, "Detroit Grapples with 'Devastating' Impact of
Black Male Homicides," *Detroit News*, October 21, 2018.

6. Ryan Marx, "Chicago Homicide Data Since 1957," *Chicago Tribune*, March 2,
2016. Accessed April 6, 2019, https://www.chicagotribune.com/news/local
/breaking/ct-chicago-homicides-data-since-1957-20160302-htmlstory.html.

7. ICasualties, "Iraq Fatalities" and "Afghanistan Fatalities," ICasualties.org,
n.d. Accessed April 6, 2019, http://icasualties.org/.

8. Kimberly Kindy et al., "Police Fatally Shoot Nearly 1,000 People in 2015,"
Washington Post, December 26, 2015. Accessed April 6, 2019, https://www
.washingtonpost.com/sf/investigative/2015/12/26/a-year-of-reckoning
-police-fatally-shoot-nearly-1000/?utm_term=.e254694e2921.

9. #Black Lives Matter #LBC, "Demands," Black Lives Matter LBC website.
Accessed April 6, 2019, https://blacklivesmatterlbc.wordpress.com/demands/.

10. Rob Arthur and Jeff Asher, "Gun Violence Spiked—and Arrests Declined—
in Chicago Right After the Laquan McDonald Video Release," *FiveThirty-
Eight*, April 11, 2016. Accessed April 6, 2019, https://fivethirtyeight.com

/features/gun-violence-spiked-and-arrests-declined-in-chicago-right
-after-the-laquan-mcdonald-video-release/.

11. Violence Policy Center, "Black Homicide Victimization in the United States:
An Analysis of 2015 Homicide Data," April 2018. Accessed April 6, 2019,
http://www.vpc.org/studies/blackhomicide18.pdf.

5: THE OBAMA ADMINISTRATION KNEW THAT UP TO TWO-THIRDS OF AMERICANS MIGHT NOT BE ABLE TO KEEP THEIR HEALTH CARE PLANS UNDER OBAMACARE

1. Assistant Secretary for Public Affairs (ASPA), "HHS REPORT: Average
Health Insurance Premiums Doubled Since 2013," HHS.gov press release,
May 23, 2017, https://www.hhs.gov/about/news/2017/05/23/hhs-report
-average-health-insurance-premiums-doubled-2013.html.

2. The White House, "Remember All of Obamacare's Broken Promises?"
White House website, June 30, 2017, https://www.whitehouse.gov/articles
/remember-obamacares-broken-promises/.

3. J. B. Wogan, "The Obameter: Cut the Cost of a Typical Family's Health
Insurance Premium by up to $2,500 a Year," *PolitiFact*, August 31, 2012. Accessed April 6, 2019, https://www.politifact.com/truth-o-meter/promises
/obameter/promise/521/cut-cost-typical-familys-health-insurance
-premium/.

4. Angie Drobnic Holan, "Lie of the Year: 'If You like Your Health Care Plan,
You Can Keep It,'" *PolitiFact*, December 12, 2013. Accessed April 6, 2019,
https://www.politifact.com/truth-o-meter/article/2013/dec/12/lie-year-if
-you-like-your-health-care-plan-keep-it/.

5. NBC News, "Watch Chuck Todd's Full Interview with President Obama,"
November 7, 2013. Accessed April 6, 2019, http://www.nbcnews.com/video
/nbc-news/53492840.

6. Lisa Myers and Hannah Rappleye, "Obama Admin. Knew Millions Could
Not Keep Their Health Insurance," NBC News website, October 28, 2013. Accessed April 6, 2019, http://www.nbcnews.com/news/world/obama-admin
-knew-millions-could-not-keep-their-health-insurance-flna8C11484394.

7. Ibid.

8. Sean Moran, "Obamacare Continues to Collapse by Design, Not Because of
President Trump," Breitbart News, August 19, 2017, https://www.breitbart
.com/politics/2017/08/18/obamacare-continues-to-collapse-by-design-not
-because-of-president-trump/.

9. Centers for Medicare & Medicaid Services, "Data on 2019 Individual
Health Insurance Market Conditions," October 11, 2018. Accessed April
6, 2019, https://www.cms.gov/newsroom/fact-sheets/data-2019-individual
-health-insurance-market-conditions.

10. Yusra Murad, "Majority of Voters Say Obama, Not Trump, Responsible for State of Health Care, ACA," *Morning Consult* (blog), October 26, 2018, https://morningconsult.com/2018/10/26/majority-of-voters-say-obama-not-trump-responsible-for-state-of-health-care-aca/.

6: SINCE 1950, 97.8 PERCENT OF MASS SHOOTINGS HAVE OCCURRED IN "GUN-FREE ZONES"

1. Crime Prevention Research Center, "UPDATED: Mass Public Shootings Keep Occurring in Gun-Free Zones: 97.8% of Attacks Since 1950," June 15, 2018, https://crimeresearch.org/2018/06/more-misleading-information-from-bloombergs-everytown-for-gun-safety-on-guns-analysis-of-recent-mass-shootings/.
2. David Sherfinski, "Gun-Free Zones for School Safety a Tough Debate to Settle," *Washington Times*, August 19, 2018. Accessed April 6, 2019, https://m.washingtontimes.com/news/2018/aug/19/gun-free-zones-school-safety-tough-debate-settle/.
3. John Lott Jr., "How Gun-Free Zones Invite Mass Shootings," *Chicago Tribune*, November 20, 2018. Accessed April 6, 2019, https://www.chicagotribune.com/news/opinion/commentary/ct-perspec-mass-shooters-russia-public-shootings-thousand-oaks-mercy-hospital-chicago-1121-story.html.
4. National Research Council, Institute of Medicine et al. *Priorities for Research to Reduce the Threat of Firearm-Related Violence*, (Washington, DC: National Academies Press), 2013, https://doi.org/10.17226/18319.

7: DRUG OVERDOSES KILL MORE AMERICANS THAN GUN VIOLENCE

1. Associated Press, "In Puerto Rico, Growing Opioid Crisis Adds to Island's Post-Hurricane Issues," January 7, 2019. Accessed April 6, 2019, https://www.nbcnews.com/news/latino/puerto-rico-growing-opioid-crisis-adds-island-s-post-hurricane-n955726.
2. Edwin Mora, "U.S. Opioid Crisis Deadlier Than Global Terrorism in 2017, Say Feds," Breitbart, August 16, 2018, https://www.breitbart.com/border/2018/08/16/u-s-opioid-crisis-deadlier-than-global-terrorism-in-2017-say-feds/.
3. Centers for Disease Control and Prevention, "HIV in the United States and Dependent Areas," January 29, 2019, https://www.cdc.gov/hiv/statistics/overview/ataglance.html.
4. Beth Macy, *Dopesick: Dealers, Doctors, and the Drug Company That Addicted America*, New York: Little, Brown, 2018.
5. Edwin Mora, "White House on Opioids: U.S. 'Enduring a Death Toll Equal to' 9/11 'Every 3 Weeks,'" Breitbart, August 1, 2017, https://www.breitbart

.com/national-security/2017/08/01/white-house-on-opioids-overdoses-u-s
-enduring-a-death-toll-equal-to-911-every-3-weeks/.

6. "Watchdog: Taliban Replacing Bombed Heroin Labs in 'Three to Four . . .,'"
   n.d., accessed April 12, 2019, https://www.breitbart.com/national-security
   /2018/01/30/watchdog-taliban-replacing-bombed-heroin-labs-three-four-days/.

7. United Nations Office on Drugs and Crime, "The Opiate Market," World
   Drug Report, 2017. Accessed April 6, 2019, https://www.unodc.org/wdr
   2017/field/Booklet_3_Opiate_market.pdf.

8. James Fredrick, "On the Hunt for Poppies in Mexico—America's Biggest
   Heroin Supplier," *Morning Edition*, January 14, 2018. Accessed April 6, 2019,
   https://www.npr.org/sections/parallels/2018/01/14/571184153/on-the
   -hunt-for-poppies-in-mexico-americas-biggest-heroin-supplier.

9. Chriss W. Street, "Mexico Drug Cartel Super-Labs Help Drive Overdose
   Deaths in California," Breitbart, November 22, 2017. Accessed April 12, 2019,
   https://www.breitbart.com/local/2017/11/22/cal-combo-of-street-drug
   -purity-legal-prescriptions-to-drive-overdose-deaths/.

10. Blythe Bernhard, "First It Was Painkillers, Then Heroin. Now It's Fentanyl
    Driving Record Overdose Deaths in St. Louis Area," *St. Louis Post-Dispatch*,
    November 26, 2018. Accessed April 6, 2019, https://www.stltoday.com
    /news/local/metro/first-it-was-painkillers-then-heroin-now-it-s-fentanyl
    /article_b4b88bad-dbb0-53b9-ae2c-4425bc4fe002.html.

11. Ai Jun, "Harsh Punishment Helps China's Anti-Drug Campaign," *Global
    Times*, December 27, 2018. Accessed April 6, 2019, http://www.globaltimes
    .cn/content/1133859.shtml.

12. Del Quentin Wilber, "Fentanyl Smuggled from China Is Killing Thou-
    sands of Americans," *Los Angeles Times*, October 19, 2018. Accessed April 12,
    2019, https://www.latimes.com/politics/la-na-pol-china-fentanyl-20181019
    -story.html.

13. Michael Martina, "U.S. Welcomes China's Expanded Clampdown on Fen-
    tanyl," Reuters, March 31, 2019. Accessed April 12, 2019, https://www
    .reuters.com/article/us-usa-trade-china-fentanyl-idUSKCN1RD137.

14. Jade Scipioni, "Demi Lovato's Overdose Sparked Massive Interest in Narcan,
    President Says," FoxBusiness, September 28, 2018, https://www.foxbusiness
    .com/features/demi-lovatos-overdose-sparked-narcan-maker-to-launch
    -awareness-campaign.

15. Ibid.

8: FALLING AND THE FLU ARE FAR DEADLIER THAN MASS SHOOTINGS

1. Editorial Board, "On an Average Day, 96 Americans Die by Firearms,"
   New York Times, June 10, 2018, https://www.nytimes.com/interactive
   /2018/06/10/opinion/editorials/gun-violence-pulse-orlando.html.

2. Deanna Pan, "US Mass Shootings, 1982–2019: Data from Mother Jones' Investigation," *Mother Jones*, February 15, 2019. Accessed April 6, 2019, https://www.motherjones.com/politics/2012/12/mass-shootings-mother-jones-full-data/.

3. Centers for Disease Control and Prevention, "National Press Conference Kicks Off 2018–2019 Flu Vaccination Campaign," February 24, 2019, https://www.cdc.gov/flu/spotlights/press-conference-2018-19.htm.

4. Elizabeth Burns and Ramakrishna Kakara, "Deaths from Falls Among Persons Aged ≥65 Years—United States, 2007–2016," *Morbidity and Mortality Weekly Report* 67(18), May 11, 2018, https://doi.org/10.15585/mmwr.mm6718a1.

5. Federal Bureau of Investigation, "Quick Look: 250 Active Shooter Incidents in the United States from 2000 to 2017," Office of Partner Engagement, n.d. Accessed April 6, 2019, https://www.fbi.gov/about/partnerships/office-of-partner-engagement/active-shooter-incidents-graphics.

6. Institute of Medicine and National Research Council of the National Academies, *Priorities for Research to Reduce the Threat of Firearm-Related Violence* (Washington, DC: National Academies Press), 2010, https://www.nap.edu/read/18319/chapter/1.

7. CBS Miami, "School Hires Combat Vets With Rifles To 'Put Down' Active Shooters," February 13, 2019. Accessed April 6, 2019, https://miami.cbslocal.com/2019/02/13/school-hires-combat-vets-with-rifles-to-put-down-active-shooters/.

9: THE U.S. RESETTLED MORE REFUGEES IN 2018 THAN ANY OTHER NATION

1. Refugee Processing Center, "Snapshot." Accessed April 6, 2019, https://www.wrapsnet.org/archives.

2. Phillip Connor and Jens Manuel Krogstad, "US Resettled Fewer Refugees Than Rest of World in 2017 for First Time," Pew Research Center FactTank (blog), July 5, 2018. Accessed April 6, 2019, https://www.pewresearch.org/fact-tank/2018/07/05/for-the-first-time-u-s-resettles-fewer-refugees-than-the-rest-of-the-world/.

3. Josh Rogin, "White House Refugee Plan Overwhelmed by Syrian Exodus," *Bloomberg Opinion*, September 16, 2015, https://www.bloomberg.com/opinion/articles/2015-09-16/white-house-refugee-plan-overwhelmed-by-syrian-exodus.

4. Pew Research Center, "Mixed Views of Initial U.S. Response to Europe's Migrant Crisis," September 29, 2015, https://www.people-press.org/2015/09/29/mixed-views-of-initial-u-s-response-to-europes-migrant-crisis/.

5. Jennifer Rankin, "EU Declares Migration Crisis over as It Hits Out at 'Fake News,'" *The Guardian*, March 6, 2019, https://www.theguardian.com

/world/2019/mar/06/eu-declares-migration-crisis-over-hits-out-fake-news
-european-commission.

10: EIGHTY PERCENT OF CENTRAL AMERICAN WOMEN AND GIRLS ARE RAPED WHILE CROSSING INTO THE U.S. ILLEGALLY

1. Deborah Bonello and Erin Siegal McIntyre, "Is Rape the Price to Pay for Migrant Women Chasing the American Dream?," *Splinter*, July 24, 2017, https://splinternews.com/is-rape-the-price-to-pay-for-migrant-women -chasing-the-1793842446.
2. Manny Fernandez, "'You Have to Pay With Your Body': The Hidden Night-mare of Sexual Violence on the Border," *New York Times*, March 3, 2019, https://www.nytimes.com/2019/03/03/us/border-rapes-migrant-women .html.
3. Neil Munro, "Study: 103,000 Migrant Women Will Be Raped on Way to U.S. This Year," Breitbart, March 7, 2019, https://www.breitbart.com /immigration/2019/03/06/forecast-expect-2600-murders-103000-rapes -migrants-2019/.
4. National Human Trafficking Hotline, "Hotline Statistics," n.d. Accessed April 15, 2019, https://humantraffickinghotline.org/states.
5. Timothy Ballard, "I've Fought Sex Trafficking as a DHS Special Agent— We Need to Build the Wall for the Children," Fox News, January 29, 2019. Accessed April 15, 2019, https://www.foxnews.com/opinion/ive-fought -sex-trafficking-as-a-dhs-special-agent-we-need-to-build-the-wall-for-the -children.
6. Ibid.

11: OBAMA DEPORTED MORE PEOPLE THAN ANY OTHER PRESIDENT

1. "Yearbook of Immigration Statistics," Department of Homeland Security, September 13, 2018, https://www.dhs.gov/immigration-statistics/yearbook.
2. Devin Dwyer, "Obama Warns Central Americans: 'Do Not Send Your Children to the Borders," June 26, 2014. Accessed April 15, 2019, https:// abcnews.go.com/Politics/obama-warns-central-americans-send-children -borders/story?id=24320063.
3. Jorge Rivas, "Here Are Some of the Democrats Who Paved the Way for Family Separation Crisis," *Splinter*, June 20, 2018, https://splinternews.com /here-are-some-of-the-democrats-who-paved-the-way-for-th-1826963453.
4. Department of Homeland Security, "Statement by Secretary Jeh C. Johnson on Southwest Border Security," September 21, 2018, https://www.dhs.gov /news/2016/01/04/statement-secretary-jeh-c-johnson-southwest-border -security#wcm-survey-target-id.

5. #Not1More, "BREAKING: Atlanta Blocks Road to Immigration, Demands Moratorium Now," June 27, 2016. Accessed April 15, 2019, http://www .notonemoredeportation.com/2016/06/27/atl-moratorium/.

6. Alfonso Chardy, "Record Number of Deportations Took Place on Obama's Watch," *Miami Herald*, December 25, 2016, https://www.miamiherald.com /news/local/immigration/article122715474.html.

12: THE IRS DOCUMENTED 1.2 MILLION IDENTITY THEFTS COMMITTED BY ILLEGAL ALIENS IN 2017

1. NumbersUSA, "IRS: 1.2 Million Illegal Aliens Committed Identity Theft in FY 2017," March 19, 2018, https://www.numbersusa.com/news/irs-12-million -illegal-aliens-committed-identity-theft-fy-2017.

2. LifeLock, "How Common Is Identity Theft? (Updated 2018) The Latest Stats," n.d. Accessed April 6, 2019, https://www.lifelock.com/learn-identity -theft-resources-how-common-is-identity-theft.html

3. U.S. Immigration and Customs Enforcement, "Identity and Benefit Fraud," July 11, 2018. Accessed April 6, 2019, https://www.ice.gov/identity-benefit -fraud.

4. "Itin_report-Tigta-September_1999.Pdf." Accessed April 6, 2019, https://cdn .cnsnews.com/attachments/itin_report-tigta-september_1999.pdf.

5. Terence P. Jeffrey, "IRS Documented 1.3M Identity Thefts by Illegal Aliens; Can't Say It Referred Any for Prosecution," *CNS News*, March 16, 2018. Accessed April 6, 2019, https://www.cnsnews.com/news/article/terence-p -jeffrey/irs-documented-13m-identity-thefts-illegal-aliens-cant-say-it.

6. Immigration Reform Law Institute, "39 MILLION: IRLI Investigation Reveals Massive Identity Fraud by Illegal Aliens," IRLI, September 11, 2018. Accessed April 6, 2019, https://www.irli.org/single-post/2018/09/11/39 -MILLION-IRLI-Investigation-Reveals-Massive-Identity-Fraud-by -Illegal-Aliens.

7. Joel Rose, "The Latest Immigration Crackdown May Be Fake Social Security Numbers," *Morning Edition*, March 29, 2019. Accessed April 6, 2019, https:// www.npr.org/2019/03/29/707931619/social-security-administration -plans-to-revive-no-match-letters.

13: THERE ARE NO JOBS AMERICANS WON'T DO

1. Steven A. Camarota, Jason Richwine, and Karen Zeigler, "There Are No Jobs Americans Won't Do," Center for Immigration Studies, August 26, 2018. Accessed April 6, 2019, https://cis.org/Report/There-Are-No-Jobs -Americans-Wont-Do.

2. Editorial Board, "Swift Raids," *New York Times*, December 18, 2006, https://www.nytimes.com/2006/12/18/opinion/18mon1.html.

14: FOR EVERY $1 A NETFLIX EMPLOYEE DONATES TO A REPUBLICAN, $141 GETS DONATED TO DEMOCRATS

1. Ari Levy, "Apple, Netflix Workers Contributing More to Democrats Than Republicans," CNBC.com, October 25, 2018, https://www.cnbc.com/2018/10/25/apple-netflix-workers-contributing-more-to-democrats-than-republicans.html.
2. Matt Rosoff, "Reed Hastings Confronted Peter Thiel on Facebook Board over Trump," CNBC.com, August 9, 2017, https://www.cnbc.com/2017/08/08/reed-hastings-confronted-peter-thiel-on-facebook-board-over-trump.html.
3. Matthew Kazin, "Netflix Names Susan Rice, Former Obama Official, to Board," Fox Business, March 28, 2018, https://www.foxbusiness.com/features/netflix-names-susan-rice-former-obama-official-to-board.
4. Rick Porter, "Obamas Option Michael Lewis' 'The Fifth Risk' for Netflix," *Hollywood Reporter*, October 31, 2018. Accessed April 7, 2019, https://www.hollywoodreporter.com/live-feed/obamas-option-michael-lewis-fifth-risk-netflix-1156733.
5. Chelsea Handler, "Tonight I Start Shooting My Documentary for #netflix on White Privilege. Starting with My Own Privilege and My Own Whiteness. To Learn More About What It's like to Be a Person Who Isn't White in This Country. Please Message Me Your Questions on the Topic and I Will Incorporate." @chelseahandler, Twitter, October 1, 2018, https://twitter.com/chelseahandler/status/1046941770586578945?lang=en.
6. Amnesty International, "Netflix Comedy Show Censored in Saudi Arabia," 2019. Accessed April 7, 2019, https://www.amnesty.org/en/latest/news/2019/01/saudi-arabia-censorship-of-netflix-is-latest-proof-of-crackdown-on-freedom-of-expression/.

15: HALF OF FEDERAL ARRESTS ARE RELATED TO IMMIGRATION

1. John Gramlich and Kristen Bialik, "Immigration Offenses Make Up a Growing Share of Federal Arests," Pew Research Center, April 10, 2017. Accessed April 7, 2019, https://www.pewresearch.org/fact-tank/2017/04/10/immigration-offenses-make-up-a-growing-share-of-federal-arrests/.
2. Mark Motivans, "Federal Justice Statistics, 2015–2016, "U.S. Department of Justice, January 2019. Accessed April 7, 2019, https://www.bjs.gov/content/pub/pdf/fjs1516.pdf.

3. U.S. Government Accountability Office, "Criminal Alien Statistics: Information on Incarcerations, Arrests, Convictions, Costs, and Removals," GAO-18-433 (August 16, 2018), https://www.gao.gov/products/GAO-18-433.

16: AMAZON PAID $0 IN TAXES ON $11.2 BILLION IN PROFITS IN 2018

1. Bruce Murphy, "Wisconsin's $4.1 Billion Foxconn Factory Boondoggle," *The Verge*, October 29, 2018, https://www.theverge.com/2018/10/29/18027032/foxconn-wisconsin-plant-jobs-deal-subsidy-governor-scott-walker.
2. Reuters, "Apple to Build Iowa Data Center, Get $207.8 Million in Incentives," August 24, 2017. Accessed April 7, 2019, https://www.reuters.com/article/us-apple-iowa/apple-to-build-iowa-data-center-get-207-8-million-in-incentives-idUSKCN1B422L.
3. Danielle Paquette, "Why Iowa Is Giving Apple $208 Million for a Project That Will Create 50 Full-Time Jobs," *Chicago Tribune*, August 24, 2017. Accessed April 7, 2019, https://www.chicagotribune.com/bluesky/technology/ct-iowa-apple-data-center-20170824-story.html.
4. Todd Wallack, "Jobs Program Lost Its Way—and Tax Money," Boston.Com, March 14, 2010, http://archive.boston.com/business/articles/2010/03/14/jobs_program_lost_its_way__and_tax_money/?page=full.
5. Greg LeRoy and Maryann Feldman, "Cities Need to Stop Selling Out to Big Tech Companies. There's a Better Way," *The Guardian*, July 3, 2018, https://www.theguardian.com/cities/2018/jul/03/cities-need-to-stop-selling-out-to-big-tech-companies-theres-a-better-way.
6. Stephen Cohen, "Amazon Paid No US Income Taxes for 2017," *SFGate*, February 27, 2018. Accessed April 7, 2019, https://www.sfgate.com/business/tech/article/Amazon-paid-no-US-income-taxes-for-2017-12713961.php.
7. Joel Shannon, "Amazon Pays No 2018 Federal Income Tax, Report Says," *USA Today*, February 15, 2019. Accessed April 7, 2019, https://www.usatoday.com/story/money/2019/02/15/amazon-pays-no-2018-federal-income-tax-report-says/2886639002/.
8. Jerry Hirsch, "Elon Musk's Growing Empire Is Fueled by $4.9 Billion in Government Subsidies," *Los Angeles Times*, May 30, 2015. Accessed April 7, 2019, https://www.latimes.com/business/la-fi-hy-musk-subsidies-20150531-story.html.
9. Bob Sechler, "Progress Slow at SpaceX's Planned Spaceport," *Atlanta Journal-Constitution*, November 22, 2017. Accessed April 7, 2019, https://www.ajc.com/news/national/progress-slow-spacex-planned-spaceport/M8M9cPsrxXsM83TaN8Id3L/.
10. Lucas Nolan, "SpaceX Claims It Can't Test Fire Rocket Due to Government Shutdown Despite Billions in Taxpayer Funding," Breitbart, January 22, 2018,

https://www.breitbart.com/tech/2018/01/22/spacex-claims-it-cant-test-fire
-rocket-due-to-government-shutdown-despite-billions-in-taxpayer-funding/.

11. "Did Elon Musk Forget About Buffalo?," Bloomberg, November 20, 2018, https://www.bloomberg.com/news/features/2018-11-20/inside-elon-musk-s-forgotten-gigafactory-2-in-buffalo.

12. Jake Swearingen, "Tesla's Car Business Is Booming. Unfortunately, It's Not Just a Car Company," *New York*, February 9, 2019, http://nymag.com/intelligencer/2019/02/teslas-solar-power-business-may-stall-out-its-car-ambitions.html.

13. Good Jobs First, "Information Technology Summary," n.d. Accessed April 7, 2019, https://subsidytracker.goodjobsfirst.org/industry/information%20technology.

17: AMERICA HAS SPENT $22 TRILLION FIGHTING THE WAR ON POVERTY

1. Rachel Sheffield, "The War on Poverty After 50 Years," Heritage Foundation, n.d. Accessed April 7, 2019, https://www.heritage.org/poverty-and-inequality/report/the-war-poverty-after-50-years.

2. Lyndon B. Johnson, "State of the Union January 8, 1964." Accessed April 7, 2019, http://www.let.rug.nl/usa/presidents/lyndon-baines-johnson/state-of-the-union-1964.php.

3. Louis Woodhill, "The War on Poverty Wasn't a Failure—It Was a Catastrophe," *Forbes*, March 19, 2014. Accessed April 7, 2019, https://www.forbes.com/sites/louiswoodhill/2014/03/19/the-war-on-poverty-wasnt-a-failure-it-was-a-catastrophe/#3804e536f49d.

4. Walter E. Williams, "The Welfare State's Legacy," Creators Syndicate, September 20, 2017. Accessed April 7, 2019, https://www.creators.com/read/walter-williams/09/17/the-welfare-states-legacy.

5. Thomas Sowell, "Liberalism Versus Blacks," January 15, 2013, https://www.creators.com/read/thomas-sowell/01/13/liberalism-versus-blacks.

18: AMERICA'S TRADE DEFICIT GREW 600 PERCENT AFTER NAFTA

1. Eric D. Gould, "Torn Apart? The Impact of Manufacturing Employment," IZA Institute of Labor Economics, June 2018. Accessed April 7, 2019, http://ftp.iza.org/dp11614.pdf.

2. Replace Nafta, "NAFTA at 25: Promises Versus Reality," *Public Citizen's NAFTA 2.0 Analysis* (blog), January 1, 2019. Accessed April 7, 2019, http://infographic.replacenafta.org/nafta-at-25-promises-vs-reality/.

3. "Where Donald Trump Is King: Inside the West Virginia Steel Town Destroyed by Nafta—Where 94% of Jobs Vanished," *Belfast Telegraph*. Accessed

April 7, 2019, https://www.belfasttelegraph.co.uk/news/world-news/where
-donald-trump-is-king-inside-the-west-virginia-steel-town-destroyed-by
-nafta-where-94-of-jobs-vanished-35180721.html.

4. Chadwick Moore, "Chadwick Moore—Left for Dead in Danville: How Globalism Is Killing Working Class America," Breitbart, July 12, 2018, https://
www.breitbart.com/politics/2018/07/12/chadwick-moore-left-for-dead
-in-danville-how-globalism-is-killing-working-class-america/.

5. Rebecca Savransky, "Obama to Trump: 'What Magic Wand Do You Have?,'"
The Hill, June 1, 2016, https://thehill.com/blogs/blog-briefing-room/news
/281936-obama-to-trump-what-magic-wand-do-you-have.

19: TAXPAYERS DOLED OUT $2.6 BILLION IN FOOD STAMPS TO DEAD PEOPLE

1. Office of Inspector General, "Detecting Potential SNAP Trafficking Using
Data Analysis," U.S. Department of Agriculture, January 2017. Accessed
April 7, 2019, https://www.usda.gov/oig/webdocs/27901-0002-13.pdf.

2. Food and Nutrition Service, "Am I Eligible for SNAP?," U.S. Department
of Agriculture, n.d. Accessed April 7, 2019, https://www.fns.usda.gov/snap
/eligibility.

3. Nicole Galloway, "Supplemental Nutrition Assistance Program (SNAP) Data
Analytics Program," Office of Missouri State Auditor, June 2018. Accessed
April 7, 2019, https://app.auditor.mo.gov/Repository/Press/2018032266672
.pdf?_ga=2.226394200.378221354.1528218578–1529149781.1528218578.

4. Government Accountability Institute, "EBTerrorism," 2018. Accessed April
7, 2019, http://g-a-i.org/wp-content/uploads/2018/10/2018_GAI_SNAP
_FRAUD_TERROR.pdf.

5. Peter Schweizer, "JP Morgan's Food Stamp Empire," *Daily Beast*, October 1,
2012. Accessed April 12, 2019, https://www.thedailybeast.com/jp-morgans
-food-stamp-empire.

6. Cheryl K. Chumley, "Food Stamp President: Enrollment up 70 Percent
Under Obama," *Washington Times*, March 28, 2013. Accessed April 7,
2019, https://www.washingtontimes.com/news/2013/mar/28/food-stamp
-president-enrollment-70-percent-under-o/.

7. Ned Resnikoff, "President Obama Signs $8.7 Billion Food Stamp Cut into
Law," MSNBC.com, August 25, 2014, http://www.msnbc.com/msnbc
/obama-signs-food-stamp-cut.

8. Lindsay Tice, "LePage Administration Wants Adults Without Children to
Work to Get Food Stamps," *Sun Journal*, July 23, 2014. Accessed April 7, 2019,
https://bangordailynews.com/2014/07/23/politics/state-house/lepage
-administration-wants-adults-without-children-to-work-to-get-food
-stamps/.

9. Ibid.

10. John Binder, "Food Stamp Usage by Newly Arrived Immigrants Drops 10 Percent," Breitbart, November 21, 2018. Accessed April 7, 2019, https://www.breitbart.com/politics/2018/11/21/food-stamp-usage-immigrants-drops-10-percent-immigration-controls/.

20: WORLD LEADERS FLEW TO DAVOS IN A FLEET OF 1,700 PRIVATE JETS TO DISCUSS THE IMPACT OF GLOBAL WARMING

1. Jaime Fuller, "1,700 Private Jets Descend upon Davos . . . and Jon Stewart Shakes His Head," *Washington Post*, January 23, 2015. Accessed April 7, 2019, https://www.washingtonpost.com/news/the-fix/wp/2015/01/23/1700-private-jets-descend-upon-davos-and-jon-stewart-shakes-his-head/.

2. Norwich University Online, "10 Largest Air to Air Battles in Military History," n.d. Accessed April 7, 2019, https://online.norwich.edu/academic-programs/masters/military-history/resources/infographics/10-largest-air-to-air-battles-in-military-history.

3. Harry Bradford, "Top Ideas on Climate Change from 2014's Davos," *Huffington Post*, January 17, 2015, https://www.huffpost.com/entry/climate-change-davos_n_6462992.

4. Matthew G. Miller, "Billionaire Greene Bets on U.S. While Bemoaning Jobs," *Bloomberg News*, January 22, 2015. Accessed April 7, 2019, https://www.bloomberg.com/news/articles/2015-01-22/billionaire-greene-bets-on-u-s-while-bemoaning-jobs.

5. Quentin Fottrell and Passy Jacob, "How Many Private Jets Are Expected to Land in Davos This Week?," MarketWatch, January 22, 2019. Accessed April 7, 2019, https://www.marketwatch.com/story/1500-private-jets-expected-at-davos-despite-global-warming-being-a-major-concern-2019-01-22.

6. Dante Chinni and Sally Bronston, "Polling: Consensus Emerges in Climate Change Debate," *Meet the Press*, December 30, 2018. Accessed April 7, 2019, https://www.nbcnews.com/politics/meet-the-press/consensus-emerges-climate-change-debate-n950646.

7. Nick Gass, "Bill Nye Flies with Obama on Everglades Trip, Loves Smell of Jet Fuel," *Politico*, April 2015. Accessed April 7, 2019, https://www.politico.com/story/2015/04/bill-nye-obama-everglades-trip-117235.html.

8. Bill Nye, "Heading down to DC to Catch an #EarthDay Flight on Air Force One Tomorrow with the President. We're Going to #ActOnClimate.," @BillNye, Twitter April 21, 2015, https://twitter.com/BillNye/status/590661734102409217?ref_src=twsrc%5Etfw%7Ctwcamp%5Etweetembed%7Ctwterm%5E590661734102409217&ref_url=https%3A%2F%2Fwww.politico.com%2Fstory%2F2015%2F04%2Fbill-nye-obama-everglades-trip-117235.

9. Ekin Karasin and Ariel Zilber, "Barack Obama Flew to Milan on Private Jet," *Daily Mail*, May 11, 2017. Accessed April 7, 2019, https://www.daily mail.co.uk/news/article-4493930/Obama-used-private-jet-14-car-convoy -attend-summit.html.

10. Ezra Klein, "Al Gore Explains Why He's Optimistic About Stopping Global Warming," *Washington Post*, August 21, 2013. Accessed April 7, 2019, https://www.washingtonpost.com/news/wonk/wp/2013/08/21/al-gore -explains-why-hes-optimistic-about-stopping-global-warming/.

11. Drew Johnson, "Al Gore's Inconvenient Reality: The Former Vice President's Home Energy Use Surges Up to 34 Times the National Average Despite Costly Green Renovations," National Center for Public Policy Research, August 1, 2017, https://nationalcenter.org/ncppr/2017/08/01/al -gores-inconvenient-reality-the-former-vice-presidents-home-energy -use-surges-up-to-34-times-the-national-average-despite-costly-green -renovations-by-drew-johnso/.

12. Anthony Adragna and Zack Colman, "'The Existential Threat of Our Time': Pelosi Elevates Climate Change on Day One," *Politico*, January 3, 2019. Accessed April 7, 2019, https://www.politico.com/story/2019/01/03/nancy -pelosi-climate-change-congress-1059148.

13. Judicial Watch, "Weekly Update: Air Pelosi Exposed," January 25, 2019. Accessed April 7, 2019, https://www.judicialwatch.org/press-room/weekly -updates/weekly-update-air-pelosi-exposed/.

14. Bernie Sanders, Facebook post, September 22, 2018. Accessed April 7, 2019, https://www.facebook.com/berniesanders/posts/1941045619283766.

15. Isabel Vincent and Melissa Klein, "Gas-Guzzling Car Rides Expose AOC's Hypocrisy amid Green New Deal Pledge," *New York Post*, March 2, 2019. Accessed April 7, 2019, https://nypost.com/2019/03/02/gas-guzzling-car -rides-expose-aocs-hypocrisy-amid-green-new-deal-pledge/.

21: NINETY PERCENT OF PLASTIC WASTE COMES FROM ASIA AND AFRICA

1. Niall McCarthy, "The World's Oceans Are Infested with Over 5 Trillion Pieces of Plastic [Infographic]," *Forbes*, March 21, 2017. Accessed April 7, 2019, https://www.forbes.com/sites/niallmccarthy/2017/03/21/the-worlds -oceans-are-infested-with-over-5-trillion-pieces-of-plastic-infographic/.

2. Hannah Leung, "Five Asian Countries Dump More Plastic Into Oceans Than Anyone Else Combined: How You Can Help," *Forbes*, April 21, 2018. Accessed April 7, 2019, https://www.forbes.com/sites/hannahleung/2018/04/21/five -asian-countries-dump-more-plastic-than-anyone-else-combined-how-you -can-help/.

3. Shivali Best, "95% of Plastic in Oceans Comes from Just Ten Rivers," *Daily*

Mail, October 11, 2017. Accessed April 7, 2019, https://www.dailymail .co.uk/sciencetech/article-4970214/95-plastic-oceans-comes-just-TEN -rivers.html.

4. Christian Schmidt, Tobias Krauth, and Stephan Wagner, "Export of Plastic Debris by Rivers into the Sea," *Environmental Science & Technology* 51(21), November 7, 2017: 12246–53, https://doi.org/10.1021/acs.est.7b02368.

5. Roland Geyer, Jenna R. Jambeck, and Kara Lavender Law, "Production, Use, and Fate of All Plastics Ever Made," *Science Advances* 3(7), July 1, 2017: e1700782, https://doi.org/10.1126/sciadv.1700782.

6. Brian Clark Howard et al. "A Running List of Action on Plastic Pollution," *National Geographic*, July 2018. Accessed April 7, 2019, https://www .nationalgeographic.com/environment/2018/07/ocean-plastic-pollution -solutions/.

7. Roger Harrabin, "Ocean Plastic a 'Planetary Crisis'-UN," BBC News, December 5, 2017, https://www.bbc.com/news/science-environment-42225915.

8. Olivia Rosane, "UN Launches First-Ever Global Plastics Report on World Environment Day," *EcoWatch*, June 5, 2018, https://www.ecowatch.com /global-plastics-report-united-nations-2575329817.html.

22: NEARLY 70 PERCENT OF MUSLIMS (1.2 BILLION) SUPPORT SHARIA LAW

1. Michael Lipka, "Muslims and Islam: Key Findings in the U.S. and Around the World," Pew Research Center Fact Tank, October 9, 2017. Accessed April 8, 2019, https://www.pewresearch.org/fact-tank/2017/08/09/muslims -and-islam-key-findings-in-the-u-s-and-around-the-world/.

2. "Rabia Kazan: President Trump Breaking 'Silence' on Abuse of Women Under Sharia Law," JWPlatform.com, n.d. Accessed April 8, 2019, https:// content.jwplatform.com/previews/gGA8nWGZ-o73dHpYz.

3. Emma Day, "Charges Dropped Against Rania Youssef over Dress," *Vogue Arabia*, November 5, 2018. Accessed April 13, 2019, https://en.vogue.me/fashion /news/charges-dropped-egyptian-actress-rania-youssef-revealing-dress/.

4. Associated Press, "Gang-Raped Indonesian Woman May Be Caned for Violating Islamic Law," CBSNews.com, May 7, 2014. Accessed April 8, 2019, https://www.cbsnews.com/news/gang-raped-indonesia-woman-may-be -caned-for-violating-islamic-law/.

5. Steve Mollman, "A 60-Year-Old Christian Woman Was Caned in Indonesia for Breaking Sharia Law," *Quartz*, April 13, 2016. Accessed April 8, 2019, https://qz.com/660994/a-60-year-old-christian-woman-was-caned-in -indonesia-for-breaking-sharia-law/.

6. Lee Roden, "Swedish Assault Case Thrown out Because Man 'Seemed to Come from a Good Family,'" TheLocal.se, March 2, 2018, https://www

.thelocal.se/20180302/swedish-assault-case-thrown-out-because-man
-seemed-to-come-from-a-good-family.

7. Jim Edwards, "In Britain, Police Arrest Twitter and Facebook Users If They Make Anti-Muslim Statements," *Business Insider*, May 2013. Accessed April 8, 2019, https://www.businessinsider.com/in-britain -police-arrest-twitter-and-facebook-users-if-they-make-anti-muslim -statements-2013–5.

8. Roger Scruton, "Why Did British Police Ignore Pakistani Gangs Abusing 1,400 Rotherham Children? Political Correctness," *Forbes*, August 30, 2014. Accessed April 8, 2019, https://www.forbes.com/sites/roger scruton/2014/08/30/why-did-british-police-ignore-pakistani-gangs-raping -rotherham-children-political-correctness/.

9. Charlie Nash, "Twitter Warns Michelle Malkin for Violating Pakistan's Sharia Law on Platform," Breitbart News, February 28, 2019. Accessed April 8, 2019, https://www.breitbart.com/tech/2019/02/28/twitter-warns -michelle-malkin-for-violating-pakistans-sharia-law-on-platform/.

23: JIHADISTS FROM IRAN, PALESTINE, AND SYRIA TOOK HOME BILLIONS IN U.S. MONEY AND WEAPONS DURING THE OBAMA ERA

1. U.S. Central Command, "Reports of New Syrian Force Equipment Being Provided to Al Nusra Front," September 25, 2015. Accessed April 8, 2019, https://www.centcom.mil/MEDIA/PRESS-RELEASES/Press-Release -View/Article/904036/sept-25-reports-of-new-syrian-force-equipment -being-provided-to-al-nusra-front/

2. White House, "Remarks by the President at Cairo University," June 4, 2009." Accessed April 8, 2019, https://obamawhitehouse.archives.gov/the-press -office/remarks-president-cairo-university-6-04-09

3. Barack Obama. "Full Text of President Obama's Speech in Ramallah," Haaretz.com. Accessed April 8, 2019, https://www.haaretz.com/the-full -text-of-president-obama-s-speech-in-ramallah-1.5235192.

4. Jim Zanotti, "U.S. Foreign Aid to the Palestinians," n.d., 33.

5. Anna Lekas Miller, "Obama Releases Aid to Palestinian Authority," Daily Beast, March 28, 2013, https://www.thedailybeast.com/articles/2013/03/28 /obama-releases-aid-to-palestinian-authority.

6. Avi Issacharoff, "Palestinians Say Obama's Last-Minute $221 Million Payout Frozen by Trump," Associated Press, January 25, 2017. Accessed April 8, 2019, http://www.timesofisrael.com/palestinians-say-trump-freezes -obamas-last-minute-221-million-payout/.

7. Rabbi Shmuley Boteach, "Do American Taxpayers Know They're Funding Palestinian Terrorists?," *The Hill*, May 2, 2017, https://thehill.com

/blogs/pundits-blog/international-affairs/331470-do-american-taxpayers
-know-theyre-funding.

8. Julian Borger, "President Barack Obama Willing to Negotiate with Iran 'without Preconditions,'" *The Guardian*, January 21, 2009, https://www.theguardian.com/world/2009/jan/21/barack-obama-iran-negotiations.

9. White House, "Remarks by Deputy National Security Advisor Ben Rhodes at the Iran Project," WhiteHouse.gov, June 16, 2016, https://obamawhitehouse.archives.gov/the-press-office/2016/06/16/remarks-deputy-national-security-advisor-ben-rhodes-iran-project.

10. Fredrik Dahl, "Iran Has $100 Billion Abroad, Can Draw $4.2 Billion: U.S. Official," Reuters, January 17, 2014. Accessed April 8, 2019, https://www.reuters.com/article/us-iran-assets-usa/iran-has-100-billion-abroad-can-draw-4-2-billion-u-s-official-idUSBREA0G0LR20140117.

11. Jeffrey Goldberg, "'Look . . . It's My Name on This': Obama Defends the Iran Nuclear Deal," *The Atlantic*, May 21, 2015, https://www.theatlantic.com/international/archive/2015/05/obama-interview-iran-isis-israel/393782/.

12. Al Arabiya English, "Protests Continue in at Least a Dozen Cities Throughout Iran," accessed April 8, 2019, http://english.alarabiya.net/en/News/gulf/2017/12/29/Protests-continue-in-Iran-as-cleric-urges-tough-action.html.

13. Raf Sanchez, Richard Spencer, and Damien McElroy, "Barack Obama 'Red Line' Warning over Chemical Weapons in Syria," *The Telegraph*, August 20, 2012, https://www.telegraph.co.uk/news/worldnews/middleeast/syria/9488314/Barack-Obama-red-line-warning-over-chemical-weapons-in-Syria.html.

14. Karen DeYoung, "Obama Backs U.S. Military Training for Syrian Rebels," *Washington Post*, June 26, 2014. Accessed April 8, 2019, https://www.washingtonpost.com/world/national-security/obama-backs-us-military-training-for-syrian-rebels/2014/06/26/ead59104-fd62-11e3-932c-0a55b81f48ce_story.html.

15. Austin Wright, "Price Tag for Syrian Rebels: $4 Million Each," *Politico*, July 2015. Accessed April 8, 2019, https://www.politico.com/story/2015/07/price-for-syrian-rebels-4-million-each-119858.

16. Diyar Güldoğan, "Turkish Forces, Free Syrian Army Capture Afrin Village," Anadolu Agency, May 2, 2018. Accessed April 8, 2019, https://www.aa.com.tr/en/middle-east/turkish-forces-free-syrian-army-capture-afrin-village/1055097.

17. Ben Kesling, "Powerful Antitank Missiles Put U.S. Forces in Middle East at Risk," *Wall Street Journal*, January 2, 2019, https://www.wsj.com/articles/powerful-antitank-missiles-put-u-s-forces-in-middle-east-at-risk-11546347600.

24: THE TAXPAYER COST OF ILLEGAL IMMIGRATION WILL EXCEED $1 TRILLION BY 2028

1. Matt O'Brien and Spencer Raley, "The Cost of Illegal Immigration to US Taxpayers," FAIR, September 27, 2017, https://fairus.org/issue/publications -resources/fiscal-burden-illegal-immigration-united-states-taxpayers.

25: AMERICA PROTECTS AND FOOTS THE BILL FOR BORDER WALLS AROUND THE WORLD

1. Tucker Carlson, "Democrats Say Border Walls Are Immoral, Don't Work. What about Israel?," Fox News, December 13, 2018, https://www.foxnews .com/opinion/tucker-carlson-democrats-say-border-walls-are-immoral -dont-work-what-about-israel.
2. "BILLS-115SAHR1625-RCP115–66.Pdf," accessed April 9, 2019, https:// docs.house.gov/billsthisweek/20180319/BILLS-115SAHR1625 -RCP115–66.pdf.
3. William M. Arkin, "The Great Wall of Jordan: How the US Wants to Keep the Islamic State Out," Vice News, February 24, 2016, https://news.vice .com/en_us/article/pa4vqz/the-great-wall-of-jordan-how-the-us-wants-to -keep-the-islamic-state-out.
4. Joanne McEvoy and Brendan O'Leary, *Power Sharing in Deeply Divided Places* (Philadelphia: University of Pennsylvania Press, 2013).
5. Benjamin Netanyahu, "President Trump Is Right. I Built a Wall along Israel's Southern Border. It Stopped All Illegal Immigration. Great Success. Great Idea." Tweet, @netanyahu (blog), January 28, 2017, https://twitter .com/netanyahu/status/825371795972825089.
6. "Devin Sper, "Build Trump's Border Wall? Learn from Israel First," *AZ Central*, September 20, 2017. Accessed April 14, 2019, https://www.azcentral .com/story/opinion/op-ed/2017/09/20/build-trump-border-wall-learn -israel-first/678600001/.

26: U.S. GREENHOUSE GAS EMISSIONS HAVE PLUMMETED FOR DECADES WITHOUT FEDERAL LAWS OR A MASSIVE CARBON TAX

1. Matthew Robinson, "Sun-Dimming Aerosols Could Curb Global Warming—CNN," November 23, 2018. Accessed April 9, 2019, https://www.cnn .com/2018/11/23/health/sun-dimming-aerosols-global-warming-intl-scli /index.html.
2. David Morgan, "Republican Introduces Bill Calling for Carbon Tax," Reuters, July 23, 2018. Accessed April 9, 2019, https://www.reuters.com

/article/us-usa-tax-carbon/u-s-republican-unveils-bill-calling-for-carbon
-tax-idUSKBN1KD21Q.

3. "CO₂ Emissions | Energy Economics | Home," BP global, accessed April 9, 2019, https://www.bp.com/en/global/corporate/energy-economics/statistical
-review-of-world-energy/co2-emissions.html.

4. "CO2 emissions," BP p.l.c., https://www.bp.com/en/global/corporate/energy
-economics/statistical-review-of-world-energy/co2-emissions.html.

5. Alexei Koseff, "California Approves Goal for 100% Carbon-Free Electricity by 2045," *Sacramento Bee*, September 10, 2018. Accessed April 9, 2019, https://www.sacbee.com/news/politics-government/capitol-alert/article 218128485.html.

6. Peter Shawn Taylor, "B.C.'s Carbon Tax: Revenue Neutrality Couldn't Survive Exposure to Politics," *Globe and Mail*, October 4, 2017. Accessed April 9, 2019, https://www.theglobeandmail.com/report-on-business/rob-commentary /bcs-carbon-tax-revenue-neutrality-couldnt-survive-exposure-to-politics /article36488526/.

7. "The British Columbia Carbon Tax: A Failed Experiment in Market-Based Solutions to Climate Change," Food & Water Watch, October 24, 2016, https://www.foodandwaterwatch.org/insight/british-columbia-carbon
-tax-failed-experiment-market-based-solutions-climate-change.

8. David Flemming, "Canada's Carbon Tax Failure, Eh?," Ethan Allen Institute, August 15, 2018, http://ethanallen.org/canadas-carbon-tax-failure-eh/.

9. Jonathan A. Lesser, "Flaw in UN Climate Report: China, India Will Never Impose Carbon Tax on Themselves," *The Hill*, October 26, 2018. Accessed April 14, 2019, https://thehill.com/opinion/energy-environment/413394 -flaw-in-un-climate-report-china-india-will-never-impose-carbon-tax.

27: HILLARY CLINTON SUPPORTED A "STRONG, COMPETENT, PROSPEROUS, STABLE RUSSIA" BEFORE BLAMING IT FOR HER ELECTION LOSS

1. U.S. Department of State, "Interview with Vladimir Pozner of First Channel Television." Accessed April 9, 2019, https://2009-2017.state.gov/secretary /20092013clinton/rm/2010/03/138712.htm.

2. U.S. Department of State, "Russia," 2009. Accessed April 9, 2019, http:// www.state.gov/j/drl/rls/hrrpt/2009/eur/136054.htm.

3. Karen Robes Meeks, "Hillary Clinton Compares Vladimir Putin's Actions in Ukraine to Adolf Hitler's in Nazi Germany," *Press Telegram*, March 5, 2014, http://www.presstelegram.com/general-news/20140304/hillary-clinton -compares-vladimir-putins-actions-in-ukraine-to-adolf-hitlers-in-nazi-germany.

4. Haley Britzky, "16 Things Hillary Clinton Blames for Her Election Loss," *Axios*, September 17, 2016. Accessed April 9, 2019, https://www.axios.com

/16-things-hillary-clinton-blames-for-her-election-loss-1513305545
-cf6505a6-76a8-49a0-989a-1be67190d4ed.html.

28: HILLARY AND BILL CLINTON MADE MILLIONS AND RUSSIA GOT 20 PERCENT OF ALL U.S. URANIUM

1. Jo Becker and Mike McIntire, "Cash Flowed to Clinton Foundation Amid Russian Uranium Deal," *New York Times*, January 19, 2018, https://www.nytimes.com/2015/04/24/us/cash-flowed-to-clinton-foundation-as-russians-pressed-for-control-of-uranium-company.html.
2. Peter Schweitzer, *Clinton Cash* (New York: Harper, 2015).
3. John Solomon and Alison Spann, "FBI Uncovered Russian Bribery Plot Before Obama Administration Approved Controversial Nuclear Deal with Moscow," *The Hill*, October 17, 2017. Accessed April 9, 2019, https://thehill.com/policy/national-security/355749-fbi-uncovered-russian-bribery-plot-before-obama-administration.
4. Frank E. Lockwood, "Money to Clintons' Nonprofit Tapers for Third Year in Row," *Arkansas Democrat Gazette*, November 11, 2018, https:// www.arkansasonline.com/news/2018/nov/11/money-to-clintons-nonprofit-tapering-20/.
5. Peter Schweizer, "Trump vs. Clintons' Russia Ties (Guess Who Always Got a Free Pass)," Fox News, March 3, 2017, https://www.foxnews.com/opinion/peter-schweizer-trump-vs-clintons-russia-ties-guess-who-always-got-a-free-pass.

29: PRESIDENT OBAMA AND HILLARY CLINTON ENCOURAGED U.S. INVESTORS TO FUND TECH RESEARCH USED BY RUSSIA'S MILITARY

1. U.S. Department of State, "Interview with Vladimir Pozner of First Channel Television," 2010. Accessed April 9, 2019, https://2009–2017.state.gov/secretary/20092013clinton/rm/2010/03/138712.htm.
2. Jackie Calmes, "Obama and Medvedev Meet Yet Again," *New York Times*, June 24, 2010, https://www.nytimes.com/2010/06/25/world/europe/25prexy.html.
3. Cisco, "Cisco Commits to Sustainable Development of Russian Technology Innovation Agenda Through $1B Multi-Year Investment," press release, n.d. Accessed April 9, 2019, https://newsroom.cisco.com/press-release-content?type=webcontent&articleId=5582254.
4. "From Russia with Money: Hillary Clinton, the Russian Reset, and Cronyism" (Washington, DC: Government Accountability Institute), July 7, 2016, 56, https://www.g-a-i.org/wp-content/uploads/2016/08/Report-Skolkvovo-08012016.pdf.
5. Peter Schweizer, "The Clinton Foundation, State and Kremlin Connections,"

Wall Street Journal, July 31, 2016, https://www.wsj.com/articles/the-clinton
-foundation-state-and-kremlin-connections-1469997195.

6. BetaBoston, "FBI Says Russians out to Steal Technology from Boston
Firms," *Boston Globe*, April 7, 2014. Accessed April 9, 2019, https://www
.bostonglobe.com/2014/04/07/fbi-says-russians-out-steal-technology
-from-boston-firms/MoOrWJeexWHCNq6iODLgRI/story.html.

7. Lucia Ziobro, "FBI's Boston Office Warns Businesses of Venture Capital
Scams," *Boston Business Journal*, April 4, 2014, https://www.bizjournals
.com/boston/blog/startups/2014/04/fbis-boston-office-warns-businesses
-of-venture.html.

8. Gregory Feifer, "Russia's Skolkovo Innovation Center Part 1: Summary,
Key Findings, and Policy Implications," 2013. Accessed April 9, 2019,
https://webcache.googleusercontent.com/search?q=cache:LZDnVUqImC
4J:https://community.apan.org/cfs-file/__key/docpreview-s/00-00-00
-84-84/20130805-Allen-_2D00_-Russias-Skolkovo-Innovation-Center
.pdf+&cd=1&hl=en&ct=clnk&gl=us&client=safari.

9. "Russia's Silicon Valley Dreams May Threaten Cybersecurity," Radio Free
Europe, accessed April 9, 2019, https://www.rferl.org/a/Russias_Silicon
_Valley_Dreams_May_Threaten_Cybersecurity/2219756.html.

10. Maxim Tucker, "Russia Launches Next Deadly Phase of Hybrid War on
Ukraine," *Newsweek*, April 10, 2015. Accessed April 9, 2019, https://www
.newsweek.com/2015/04/10/russia-launches-next-deadly-phase-hybrid
-war-ukraine-318218.html.

30: TOP DEMOCRATS BLAMED OBAMA FOR DOING LITTLE TO STOP RUSSIA'S 2016 ELECTION MEDDLING

1. President Obama: "I'd Invite Mr. Trump to Stop Whining . . ." C-SPAN,
2016. Accessed April 10, 2019, https://www.youtube.com/watch?v=L3mQa
HTj7ow.

2. Mike Memoli, "Top Democrat Says Obama Shares Responsibility for
Russia's Meddling," NBC News, February 16, 2018. Accessed April
10, 2019, https://www.nbcnews.com/politics/politics-news/top-democrat
-says-obama-shares-responsibility-russia-s-meddling-n848661.

3. Aaron Blake, "'I Feel like We Sort of Choked': Obama's No-Drama Approach to Russian Hacking Isn't Sitting Well," *Washington Post*, June 24,
2017. Accessed April 10, 2019, http://wapo.st/2sYHfmF?tid=ss_mail&utm
_term-.3f99d61aa76b.

4. Eugene Scott, "Trump: Obama 'Did Nothing' about Russia Election Meddling," CNN, June 23, 2017. Accessed April 10, 2019, https://www.cnn
.com/2017/06/23/politics/vladmir-putin-russia-election/index.html.

5. Evan Perez and Shimon Prokupecz, "How Russians Hacked the White

House," CNN, April 7, 2015. Accessed April 10, 2019, https://www.cnn
.com/2015/04/07/politics/how-russians-hacked-the-wh/index.html.

6. Elise Viebeck, "Russians Hacked DOD's Unclassified Networks," *The Hill*,
April 23, 2015, https://thehill.com/policy/cybersecurity/239893-russians
-hacked-dods-unclassified-networks.

7. Noah Shachtman, "General: Russia Is 'Existential Threat,'" *Daily Beast*, July
24, 2015, https://www.thedailybeast.com/cheats/2015/07/24/top-general
-russia-existential-threat-to-u-s.

8. "'Russia Presents the Greatest Threat to Our National Security,'" C-SPAN,
n.d. Accessed April 10, 2019, https://www.c-span.org/video/?c4543566
/russia-presents-greatest-threat-national-security.

9. Nancy A. Youssef, "Russians Hacked Joint Chiefs of Staff," *Daily Beast*, August 6, 2015, https://www.thedailybeast.com/cheats/2015/08/06/russians
-hacked-joint-chiefs-of-staff.

10. Brian Barrett, "DNC Lawsuit Reveals Key Details About Devastating 2016
Hack," *Wired*, April 20, 2018, https://www.wired.com/story/dnc-lawsuit
-reveals-key-details-2016-hack/.

11. GRIZZLY STEPPE—Russian Malicious Cyber Activity, NCCIC/FBI Report
JAR-16-20296A, December 29, 2016 Accessed April 10, 2019, https://www
.us-cert.gov/sites/default/files/publications/JAR_16-20296A_GRIZZLY
%20STEPPE-2016-1229.pdf.

12. "Joint Statement from the Department Of Homeland Security and Office of the Director of National Intelligence on Election Security," Department of Homeland Security, October 7, 2016, https://www.dhs.gov
/news/2016/10/07/joint-statement-department-homeland-security-and
-office-director-national.

13. "Obama Intel Chiefs Gave Russia a Pass, and Now Blame—Donald . . .,"
The Hill, accessed April 14, 2019, https://thehill.com/opinion/white
-house/398299-obama-intel-chiefs-gave-russia-a-pass-and-now-blame
-donald-trump.

31: DONALD TRUMP WON THE 2016 ELECTION BY WINNING MICHIGAN, A STATE RUSSIA DIDN'T ATTEMPT TO HACK

1. Erin V. Kelly, "Senate Report: No Evidence That Russians Changed Vote
Tallies in 2016," *USA Today*, May 8, 2018. Accessed April 10, 2019, https://
www.usatoday.com/story/news/politics/2018/05/08/senate-report-no
-evidence-russians-changed-vote-tallies-2016/592978002/.

2. RealClearPolitics, "Election 2016-General Election: Trump vs. Clinton,"
2016. Accessed April 10, 2019, https://www.realclearpolitics.com/epolls
/2016/president/us/general_election_trump_vs_clinton-5491.html.

3. Brendan Nyhan and Yusaku Horiuchi, "Homegrown 'Fake News' Is a Bigger

Problem Than Russian Propaganda. Here's a Way to Make Falsehoods More Costly for Politicians.," *Washington Post*, October 23, 2017. Accessed April 10, 2019, https://www.washingtonpost.com/news/monkey-cage/wp/2017/10/23/homegrown-fake-news-is-a-bigger-problem-than-russian-propaganda-heres-a-way-to-make-falsehoods-more-costly-for-politicians/.

4. Gregory Krieg, "Reliving the Day Hillary Clinton Says Cost Her the Election—One Year Later," CNN, October 28, 2017. Accessed April 10, 2019, https://www.cnn.com/2017/10/28/politics/james-comey-clinton-letter-one-year/index.html.

5. Lucan Ahmad Way and Adam Casey, "Russia Has Been Meddling in Foreign Elections for Decades. Has It Made a Difference?" *Washington Post*, Accessed April 10, 2019, https://www.washingtonpost.com/news/monkey-cage/wp/2018/01/05/russia-has-been-meddling-in-foreign-elections-for-decades-has-it-made-a-difference/?utm_term=.2fd79a140218.

6. Freedom House, "The Rise of Digital Authoritarianism: Fake News, Data Collection and the Challenge to Democracy," November 1, 2018, https://freedomhouse.org/article/rise-digital-authoritarianism-fake-news-data-collection-and-challenge-democracy.

32: GOOGLE COULD SWING AN ELECTION BY SECRETLY ADJUSTING ITS SEARCH ALGORITHM, AND WE WOULD HAVE NO WAY OF KNOWING

1. "Robert Epstein's Midterm Warning: Big Tech Can 'Shift Upwards of 12 Million Votes,'" Breitbart News, August 24, 2018. Accessed April 10, 2019, https://www.breitbart.com/tech/2018/08/24/robert-epsteins-midterm-warning-big-tech-can-shift-upwards-of-12-million-votes-in-november/.

2. Robert Epstein, "How Google Could Rig the 2016 Election," *Politico*, August 19, 2015. Accessed April 10, 2019, https://www.politico.com/magazine/story/2015/08/how-google-could-rig-the-2016-election-121548.html.

3. Jack Nicas, "Alphabet's Eric Schmidt Gave Advice to Clinton Campaign, Leaked Emails Show," *Wall Street Journal*, November 2, 2016. Accessed April 10, 2019, https://www.wsj.com/articles/alphabets-eric-schmidt-gave-advice-to-clinton-campaign-leaked-emails-show-1478111270.

4. JW Platform, "Leaked Video Shows Google Leadership In Dismay at 2016 Election," n.d. Accessed April 10, 2019, https://content.jwplatform.com/previews/TYgVGuSC-o73dHpYz.

5. Allum Bokhari, "Research: Google Search Bias Flipped Seats for Democrats in Midterms," Breitbart News, March 22, 2019. Accessed April 10, 2019, https://www.breitbart.com/tech/2019/03/22/research-google-search-bias-flipped-seats-for-democrats-in-midterms/.

6. Allum Bokhari, "EXCLUSIVE—Research: Google Search Manipulation Can Swing Nearly 80 Percent of Undecided Voters," Breitbart News, April 24,

2018. Accessed April 10, 2019, https://www.breitbart.com/tech/2018/04/24
/exclusive-research-google-search-manipulation-can-swing-nearly-80
-percent-undecided-voters/.

33: GOOGLE WORKS WITH THE OPPRESSIVE CHINESE GOVERNMENT TO BUILD A CENSORIAL SEARCH ENGINE BUT REFUSES TO WORK WITH THE U.S. GOVERNMENT

1. Ryan Gallagher, "Google Plans to Launch Censored Search Engine in China, Leaked Documents Reveal," *The Intercept* (blog), August 1, 2018, https://theintercept.com/2018/08/01/google-china-search-engine-censorship/.

2. Christopher Bodeen, "Rights Groups to Google: No Censored Search in China," Associated Press, August 29, 2018, https://apnews.com/acff41c8e da8481da1063de010992c8d.

3. Kate Conger and Daisuke Wakabayashi, "Google Employees Protest Secret Work on Censored Search Engine for China," *New York Times*, September 10, 2018, https://www.nytimes.com/2018/08/16/technology/google-employees -protest-search-censored-china.html.

4. Ryan Gallagher, "Senior Google Scientist Resigns Over 'Forfeiture of Our Values' in China," *The Intercept* (blog), September 13, 2018, https://theintercept .com/2018/09/13/google-china-search-engine-employee-resigns/.

5. Reuters, "Pence Says Google Should Halt Dragonfly App Development," October 4, 2018. Accessed April 10, 2019, https://www.reuters.com/article /us-usa-china-pence-technology/pence-says-google-should-halt-dragonfly -app-development-idUSKCN1ME20H.

6. Jillian D'Onfro, "Google Dodges Questions about China during Senate Privacy Hearing," CNBC.com, September 26, 2018. Accessed April 10, 2019, https://www.cnbc.com/2018/09/26/google-keith-enright-dodges-china -questions-senate-privacy-hearing.html.

7. Dave Lee, "Ex-Google Employee Warns of 'Disturbing' China Plans," BBC News, September 26, 2018, https://www.bbc.com/news/technology -45653035.

8. Scott Shane and Daisuke Wakabayashi, "'The Business of War': Google Employees Protest Work for the Pentagon," *New York Times*, November 2, 2018, https://www.nytimes.com/2018/04/04/technology/google-letter-ceo-pentagon -project.html.

9. Kate Couger, "Tech Workers Ask Google, Microsoft, IBM, and Amazon to Not Pursue Pentagon Contracts," *Gizmodo*, accessed April 10, 2019, https://gizmodo.com/tech-workers-ask-google-microsoft-ibm-and-amazon -to-1825394821.

10. Yasmin Tadjdeh, "Algorithmic Warfare: Google Versus the Pentagon, The Fallout," *National Defense*, August 2, 2018. Accessed April 10, 2019,

http://www.nationaldefensemagazine.org/articles/2018/8/2/google-versus
-the-pentagon-the-fallout.

11. Ryan Gallagher, "Google Is Conducting a Secret 'Performance Review' of Its Censored China Search Project," *The Intercept* (blog), March 27, 2019, https://theintercept.com/2019/03/27/google-dragonfly-china-review/.

34: FACEBOOK CHANGED ITS ALGORITHM, LEADING TO A 45 PERCENT DROP IN USERS INTERACTING WITH PRESIDENT TRUMP

1. Jonah Engel Bromwich and Matthew Haag, "Facebook Is Changing. What Does That Mean for Your News Feed?," *New York Times*, January 14, 2018, https://www.nytimes.com/2018/01/12/technology/facebook-news-feed -changes.html.

2. "Facebook to Prioritize 'trustworthy' News Based on Surveys," Reuters, Accessed April 10, 2019, https://www.reuters.com/article/us-facebook-media /facebook-to-prioritize-trustworthy-news-based-on-surveys-idUSKBN 1F82M2.

3. Allum Bokhari, "EXCLUSIVE: Trump's Facebook Engagement Declined By 45 Percent Following Algorithm Change," Breitbart News, February 28, 2018. Accessed April 10, 2019, https://www.breitbart.com/tech/2018/02/28 /exclusive-trumps-facebook-engagement-declined-45-percent-following -algorithm-change/.

4. Adam Mosseri, "Bringing People Closer Together," Facebook Newsroom, January 2018. Accessed April 10, 2019, https://newsroom.fb.com /news/2018/01/news-feed-fyi-bringing-people-closer-together/.

5. Allum Bokhari, "Report: Establishment Media Soaring on Facebook, Conservative Media in Decline Following Algorithm Change," Breitbart News, April 9, 2018. Accessed April 10, 2019, https://www.breitbart.com /tech/2018/04/09/report-establishment-media-soaring-on-facebook -conservative-media-in-decline-following-algorithm-change/.

6. Adam Mosseri, "Helping Ensure News on Facebook Is From Trusted Sources," Facebook Newsroom, January 2018. Accessed April 10, 2019, https://newsroom.fb.com/news/2018/01/trusted-sources/.

7. Aja Romano, "Mark Zuckerberg Lays Out Facebook's 3-Pronged Approach to Fake News," *Vox*, April 3, 2018, https://www.vox.com/tech nology/2018/4/3/17188332/zuckerberg-kinds-of-fake-news-facebook-making -progress.

8. Allum Bokhari, "Western Journal: Facebook's Algorithm Change Disproportionately Hits Conservative Sites," Breitbart, March 15, 2018. Accessed April 10, 2019, https://www.breitbart.com/tech/2018/03/15/western-journal -facebooks-algorithm-change-disproportionately-hits-conservative-sites/.

9. Ellie Zolfagharifard, "Facebook's Attempt to Bring 'People Closer Together.'"

Makes People Feel Miserable, Study Reveals," *Daily Mail Online*, May 11, 2018. Accessed April 10, 2019, https://www.dailymail.co.uk/sciencetech /article-5718385/Facebooks-attempt-bring-people-closer-demoting-news -sites-makes-users-feel-MISERABLE.html.

10. Lucas Nolan, "Breitbart News Ranks in Top 10 Publishers on Facebook for October 2018," Breitbart News, November 10, 2018. Accessed April 10, 2019, https://www.breitbart.com/tech/2018/11/10/breitbart-news-ranks-in-top -10-publishers-on-facebook-for-october-2018/.

35: GOOGLE AND FACEBOOK ENLISTED BIASED "FAKE NEWS" FACT-CHECKERS WHO WERE OFTEN WRONG

1. "Will Hillary Explain Her Dream of 'Open Borders'?" *Chicago Tribune*, October 11, 2016. Accessed April 10, 2019, https://www.chicagotribune .com/news/columnists/kass/ct-hillary-clinton-open-borders-kass-1012 –20161011-column.html.

2. Amy Sherman, "Donald Trump Says Hillary Clinton Wants to Have Open Borders," *PolitiFact*, October 19, 2016. Accessed April 10, 2019, https:// www.politifact.com/truth-o-meter/statements/2016/oct/19/donald-trump /donald-trump-says-hillary-clinton-wants-have-open-/.

3. PolitiFact, "Trump Says Russia Has Added Nuclear Warheads, While US Hasn't," *PolitiFact*. Accessed April 10, 2019, https://www.politifact.com /truth-o-meter/statements/2016/oct/20/donald-trump/trump-says-russia -has-upped-its-nuclear-warheads-w/.

4. Bethania Palma, "Did 33 Republicans Who Voted to Repeal Obamacare Lose Their Congressional Seats?," *Snopes*, December 5, 2018. Accessed April 10, 2019, https://www.snopes.com/fact-check/gop-obamacare-repeal-election/.

5. Will Thorne, "ABC News Apologizes for Staged Crime-Scene Shot," *Variety*, November 4, 2016. Accessed April 10, 2019, https://variety.com/2016/tv /news/abc-news-staged-crime-scene-shot-apology-1201910160/.

6. Daily Caller, "Snopes, Which Will Be Fact-Checking For Facebook, Employs Leftists Almost Exclusively," December 16, 2016. Accessed April 10, 2019, https://dailycaller.com/2016/12/16/snopes-facebooks-new-fact -checker-employs-leftists-almost-exclusively/.

7. David Mikkelson, "Did CNN Purchase an Industrial-Sized Washing Machine to Spin News?," *Snopes*, March 1, 2018. Accessed April 10, 2019, https://www.snopes.com/fact-check/cnn-washing-machine/.

8. Tim Morris, "No, CNN Did Not Buy a Big Washing Machine to Spin the News," NOLA.com, March 6, 2018, https://www.nola.com/opinions /2018/03/cnn_washing_machine_spin_news.html.

9. Sam Levin, "'They Don't Care': Facebook Factchecking in Disarray as Journalists Push to Cut Ties," *The Guardian*, December 13, 2018, https://www

.theguardian.com/technology/2018/dec/13/they-dont-care-facebook-fact
-checking-in-disarray-as-journalists-push-to-cut-ties.

10. Daniel Funke, "Snopes Pulls Out of Its Fact-Checking Partnership with Facebook," Poynter, February 1, 2019. Accessed April 10, 2019, https://www .poynter.org/fact-checking/2019/snopes-pulls-out-of-its-fact-checking -partnership-with-facebook/.

11. CBS News, "Mueller's Office Disputes BuzzFeed Report That Trump Told Cohen to Lie," January 18, 2019. Accessed April 10, 2019, https://www .cbsnews.com/news/buzzfeed-cohen-story-special-counsel-robert-mueller -office-disputes-report-trump-told-michael-cohen-to-lie-2019–01–18/.

36: FACEBOOK RECEIVES YOUR MOST SENSITIVE PERSONAL INFO FROM YOUR PHONE'S OTHER APPS

1. Sam Schechner, "Eleven Popular Apps That Shared Data with Facebook," *Wall Street Journal*, February 25, 2019, https://www.wsj.com/articles/eleven -popular-apps-that-shared-data-with-facebook-11551055132.

37: AMERICANS PAY BILLIONS TO LARGE CORPORATIONS TO NOT HIRE U.S. CITIZENS

1. David North, "Feds Provide Almost $2 Billion in Subsidies to Hire Alien Grads Rather Than U.S. Grads," CIS.org, February 27, 2018. Accessed April 11, 2019, https://cis.org/North/Feds-Provide-Almost-2-Billion-Subsidies -Hire-Alien-Grads-Rather-US-Grads.

2. Pew Research Center, "Growth of OPT Foreign College Graduate Work Program Slowed in 2017," Pew Research Center (blog), July 25, 2018. Accessed April 11, 2019, https://www.pewresearch.org/fact-tank/2018/07/25 /number-of-foreign-college-graduates-staying-in-u-s-to-work-climbed -again-in-2017-but-growth-has-slowed/.

3. John Miano, "A History of the 'Optional Practical Training' Guestworker Program," CIS.org, September 18, 2017. Accessed April 11, 2019, https://cis .org/Report/History-Optional-Practical-Training-Guestworker-Program.

4. Federal Register, "Extending Period of Optional Practical Training by 17 Months for F-1 Nonimmigrant Students with STEM Degrees and Expand- ing Cap-Gap Relief for All F-1 Students with Pending H-1B Petitions," April 8, 2008, https://www.federalregister.gov/documents/2008/04/08 /E8–7427/extending-period-of-optional-practical-training-by-17-months -for-f-1-nonimmigrant-students-with-stem.

5. Miano, "A History of the 'Optional Practical Training' Guestworker Program."

6. Pew Research Center, "Nearly Three-Quarters of the 1.5 Million Graduates on OPT Came from Asia," May 10, 2018. Accessed April 11, 2019, https://

www.pewglobal.org/2018/05/10/number-of-foreign-college-students-staying-and-working-in-u-s-after-graduation-surges/pgmd_2018–05–10_foreign-student-graduate-workers-opt_0–01/.

7. David North, "Data Shows U.S. Gives Big Firms Oodles of Millions for *Not* Hiring Citizens," CIS.org, October 26, 2018. Accessed April 11, 2019, https://cis.org/North/Data-Shows-US-Gives-Big-Firms-Oodles-Millions-Not-Hiring-Citizens.

38: NEARLY THREE-QUARTERS OF SILICON VALLEY WORKERS ARE FOREIGN-BORN

1. "H-1B: Nearly Three-Quarters of Valley Techies Are Foreign," *Mercury News*, n.d., accessed April 14, 2019, https://www.mercurynews.com/2018/01/17/h-1b-foreign-citizens-make-up-nearly-three-quarters-of-silicon-valley-tech-workforce-report-says/.

2. Levin, "They Don't Care."

3. Pew Research Center, "Increase in Foreign Student Graduates Staying and Working in U.S." May 10, 2018, https://www.pewglobal.org/2018/05/10/number-of-foreign-college-students-staying-and-working-in-u-s-after-graduation-surges/.

4. Paayal Zaveri and Aditi Roy, "Big American Tech Companies Are Snapping Up H1-B Visas," April 20, 2018, https://www.cnbc.com/2018/04/20/big-american-tech-companies-are-snapping-up-h1-b-visas.html.

5. Ron Hira, "Congressional Testimony: The Impact of High-Skilled Immigration on U.S. Workers," Economic Policy Institute (blog), March 1, 2016. Accessed April 11, 2019, https://www.epi.org/publication/congressional-testimony-the-impact-of-high-skilled-immigration-on-u-s-workers-4/.

6. David North, "About 40% of H-1B Jobs Give Employers a Tidy $40,000/Year Discount," CIS.org, January 18, 2019. Accessed April 11, 2019, https://cis.org/North/About-40-H1B-Jobs-Give-Employers-Tidy-40000Year-Discount.

7. Beth Kassab, "Disney Turns Heads with Foreign Worker Program," *Orlando Sentinel*, June 8, 2016. Accessed April 11, 2019, https://www.orlandosentinel.com/opinion/os-disney-layoffs-visas-beth-kassab-20150608-column.html.

8. "The Secret Way Silicon Valley Uses the H-1B Program," *Bloomberg*, June 6, 2017. Accessed April 11, 2019, https://www.bloomberg.com/news/articles/2017–06–06/silicon-valley-s-h-1b-secret.

9. David North, "*New York Times* Urges Sympathy for H-1B Workers in Million-Dollar Homes," CIS.org, April 9, 2018. Accessed April 14, 2019, https://cis.org/North/New-York-Times-Urges-Sympathy-H1B-Workers-Million-Dollar-Homes.

10. David North, *"New York Times* Seeks 163 H-1B Workers over Five Years, Also 31 Green Cards," CIS.org, September 18, 2018. Accessed April 11, 2019, https://cis.org/North/New-York-Times-Seeks-163-H1B-Workers-over -Five-Years-Also-31-Green-Cards.

11. Neil Munro, "Verizon's Board Members Push Armies of H-1B Outsourcing Workers into Many U.S. Companies," Breitbart News, October 5, 2018, https://www.breitbart.com/politics/2018/10/04/verizons-board-members -push-armies-of-h-1b-outsourcing-workers-into-many-u-s-companies/.

39: BLACK AND HISPANIC UNEMPLOYMENT HIT RECORD LOWS UNDER TRUMP

1. John Carney, "Fact Check: Hispanic Unemployment Rate Hit Lowest Level Ever," Breitbart News, February 6, 2019, https://www.breitbart.com /economy/2019/02/05/fact-check-hispanic-unemployment-rate-hit-lowest -level-ever/.

2. Jonathan Allen, "Waters to Obama: Iowans or Blacks?," *Politico*, September 8, 2011. Accessed April 11, 2019, https://www.politico.com/news/stories /0911/62979.html.

3. "Cleaver: If Obama Wasn't President, We Would Be 'Marching on the White House'," *The Hill*. Accessed April 11, 2019, https://thehill.com/blogs/blog -briefing-room/news/182209-cbc-chairman-if-obama-wasnt-in-office-we -would-be-marching-on-white-house.

4. "NAACP President Ben Jealous: Black People "Are Doing Far Worse . . ." News One, n.d. Accessed April 11, 2019, https://newsone.com/2172703/ben -jealous-barack-obama/.

5. Investor's Business Daily, "The U.S.' Colorblind Jobs Boom Under Trump Continues", n.d. Accessed April 11, 2019. https://www.investors.com/politics /editorials/u-s-jobs-boom-colorblind/.

40: VENEZUELA WAS THE WEALTHIEST COUNTRY IN LATIN AMERICA BEFORE SOCIALISM

1. Katherine Koleski and Alec Blivas, "China's Engagement with Latin America and the Caribbean," October 17, 2018. Accessed April 14, 2019, https://www .uscc.gov/sites/default/files/Research/China%27s%20Engagement%20 with%20Latin%20America%20and%20the%20Caribbean_.pdf.

2. Ben Kew, "Oil-Rich Venezuela Importing 300,000 Barrels of Fuel a Day," Breitbart News, December 7, 2018. Accessed April 14, 2019, https://www .breitbart.com/latin-america/2018/12/07/oil-rich-venezuela-importing -300000-barrels-fuel-day/.

3. Reuters, "Venezuelans Report Big Weight Losses in 2017 As Hunger Hits-Reuters", n.d., Accessed April 14, 2019, https://www.reuters.com /article/us-venezuela-food/venezuelans-report-big-weight-losses-in-2017 -as-hunger-hits-idUSKCN1G52HA.

4. Maolis Castro, "La Emergencia de Los Hospitales En Venezuela," *El País*, July 26, 2016. Accessed April 14, 2019, https://elpais.com/internacional /2016/07/24/actualidad/1469375553_518332.html.

5. "Venezuela: Una economía Antes Poderosa, Hoy En Estado De Coma," *La República*, January 8, 2018. Accessed April 14, 2019, https://larepublica.pe /mundo/1168015-venezuela-una-economia-antes-poderosa-hoy-en-estado -de-coma.

6. "Document #22: 'Pact of Punto Fijo,' Acción Democrática, COPEI and Union Republicana Democrática (1958)," n.d., accessed April 14, 2019, https:// library.brown.edu/create/modernlatinamerica/chapters/chapter-8-venezuela /primary-documents-with-accompanying-discussion-questions/document -22-pact-of-punto-fijo-accion-democratica-copei-and-union-republicana -democratica-1958/.

7. "Venezuela: AD and COPEI Break down (Chapter 5)-Party Brands in . . .," n.d., accessed April 14, 2019, https://www.cambridge.org/core/books /party-brands-in-crisis/venezuela-ad-and-copei-break-down/60B2E 696029AB16D3D4C1CCED9178811.

8. Sally Palomino, "En Venezuela Se Vivía Tan Bien, Que Era Un país Del Que Nadie Se Quería ir," *El País*, April 1, 2017. Accessed April 14, 2019, https:// elpais.com/internacional/2017/04/01/colombia/1490999234_665682.html.

9. Ibid.

10. Edwin Mora, "General: Nearly 100,000 Cuban Regime Agents Have Run Venezuela Since 2010," Breitbart News, November 16, 2017. Accessed April 14, 2019, https://www.breitbart.com/national-security/2017/11/16/venezuela -gen-socialist-govt-employs-92700-cubans-to-bolster-castros-ill-fated -communism/.

11. Foreign Policy, "The List: Murder Capitals of the World," September 29, 2008. Accessed April 14, 2019, https://foreignpolicy.com/2008/09/29/the -list-murder-capitals-of-the-world/.

12. Ben Kew, "Report: 80 Percent of Venezuelans Short of Food," Breitbart News, November 20, 2018. Accessed April 14, 2019, https://www.breitbart.com /latin-america/2018/11/20/report-80-percent-venezuelans-short-food/.

13. "Las Siete Plagas Cuasibíblicas de Maduro Que los Medios del Estado No Pueden Ocultar," *Dolar Today*, January 7, 2015. Accessed April 14, 2019, https://dolartoday.com/las-siete-plagas-cuasibiblicas-de-maduro-que -la-censura-informativa-estatal-puede-ocultar/.

14. Frances Martel, "Venezuela's Last National Independent Newspaper Stops Printing", Breitbart News, December 18, 2018. Accessed April 14, 2019,

https://www.breitbart.com/the-media/2018/12/14/venezuela-el-nacional
-ends-print-run/.

15. Frances Martel, "Starving Venezuelans Abandon Dogs, Buy Dog Food for Themselves," Breitbart News, February 28, 2018. Accessed April 14, 2019, https://www.breitbart.com/national-security/2018/02/28/starving -venezuelans-abandon-dogs-buy-dog-food-themselves/.

16. Frances Martel, "North Korea Offers Venezuela Financial Advice at National Bank Meeting," Breitbart News, December 4, 2017. Accessed April 14, 2019, https://www.breitbart.com/national-security/2017/12/04/north-korea -lends-venezuela-financial-advice-at-national-bank-meeting/.

41: AMERICAN CITIES WITH THE LARGEST HOMELESS POPULATIONS ARE ALL DEMOCRAT-RUN ENCLAVES

1. Niall McCarthy, "The U.S. Cities With The Most Homeless People," Statista, December 20, 2018. Accessed April 14, 2019, https://www.statista .com/chart/6949/the-us-cities-with-the-most-homeless-people/.

2. "US Homeless Numbers Rise for the First Time In 7 Years—New . . .", New Frontier, December 6, 2017. Accessed April 14, 2019, https://newfrontier .news/2017/12/06/us-homeless-numbers-rise-for-the-first-time-in-7-years/.

3. Phil Matier, "San Francisco—Where Drug Addicts Outnumber High School Students," San Francisco Chronicle, January 30, 2019. Accessed April 15, 2019. https://www.sfchronicle.com/bayarea/philmatier/article/San-Francisco -where-street-addicts-outnumber-13571702.php.

4. Dan Simon, "The Impact Homelessness and the Opioid Crisis Are Having on San Francisco Streets," CNN, December 30, 2018, https://www.cnn .com/2018/12/27/health/drug-use-san-francisco-streets/index.html.

5. Alastair Gee, "Living Under a Tarp Next to Facebook HQ: 'I Don't Want People to See Me,'" The Guardian, March 31, 2017, https://www.theguardian .com/us-news/2017/mar/31/facebook-campus-homeless-tent-city-menlo -park-california.

6. Business Insider, "Silicon Valley's Massive Homeless Camp Is Being Shut Down for Good—Here's What We Saw When We Visited Last Year," December 4, 2014, https://www.businessinsider.com/the-jungle-largest -homeless-camp-in-us-2014-12.

7. Rong-Gong Lin II and Gale Holland, "San Jose Begins Closing Down 68-Acre Homeless Encampment," Los Angeles Times, December 4, 2014, https://www.latimes.com/local/lanow/la-me-ln-san-jose-homeless-camp -20141204-story.html.

8. Ibid.

9. Kevin Fagan, "The Situation on the Streets," San Francisco Chronicle, June 28, 2018, https://projects.sfchronicle.com/sf-homeless/2018-state-of-homelessness/.

10. Alyson Ward, "Homeless After Harvey: For Some, the Historic Flooding in Houston Washed Away Shelter and Security," *Houston Chronicle*, August 26, 2018, https://www.houstonchronicle.com/news/houston-weather/hurricaneharvey/article/Homeless-after-Harvey-For-some-the-historic-13171309.php.

11. Andrew Kragie, "Homelessness Down Slightly in Houston Area Since 2016," *Houston Chronicle*, May 16, 2017, https://www.chron.com/news/houston-texas/houston/article/houston-homeless-count-slightly-down-2017-11149868.php.

12. Patrick Markee, "State of the Homeless 2015," Coalition For the Homeless. Accessed April 15, 2019, https://www.coalitionforthehomeless.org/state-homeless-2015/.

13. Wes Parnell and Kenneth Lovett, "EXCLUSIVE: State Homeless Population Said to Be Larger Than Population in All but Two New York Cities," *New York Daily News*, December 12, 2018, https://www.nydailynews.com/news/politics/ny-pol-homeless-students-cuomo-hevesi-nortz-20181121-story.html.

14. Mingu Kim, "Mental Illness and Homelessness: Facts and Figures," SMHR, July 31, 2017. Accessed April 15, 2019, https://www.hcs.harvard.edu/~hcht/blog/homelessness-and-mental-health-facts.

15. Adam Brinklow, "San Francisco Has 7,499 Homeless Residents by Latest Count," *Curbed SF*, June 16, 2017, https://sf.curbed.com/2017/6/16/15818104/homeless-sf-count-2017.

16. City News Service, "A Report Finds One-Third of LA County's Homeless Are Black," NBC Southern California, February 25, 2019, https://www.nbclosangeles.com/news/local/Report-Finds-One-Third-of-LA-County-Homeless-Are-Black-506337151.html.

17. Coalition for the Homeless, "Basic Facts About Homelessness: New York City," n.d. Accessed April 15, 2019, https://www.coalitionforthehomeless.org/basic-facts-about-homelessness-new-york-city/.

18. Peter Jamison, "D.C. Homeless Population Drops for Second Straight Year, Report Finds," *Washington Post*, May 8, 2018, https://www.washingtonpost.com/local/dc-politics/dc-homeless-population-drops-for-second-straight-year-report-finds/2018/05/08/5505b828-5238-11e8-abd8-265bd07a9859_story.html.

19. Scott Greenstone, "Is Seattle's Homeless Crisis the Worst in the Country?," *Seattle Times*, April 26, 2018), https://www.seattletimes.com/seattle-news/homeless/is-seattles-homeless-crisis-the-worst-in-the-country/.

20. Emily Badger, "Happy New Year! May Your City Never Become San Francisco, New York or Seattle," *New York Times*, December 26, 2018, https://www.nytimes.com/2018/12/26/upshot/happy-new-year-may-your-city-never-become-san-francisco-new-york-or-seattle.html.

21. Nicole Karlis, "Tech Companies Spending Millions to Oppose San Francisco's 'Homelessness Tax,'" *Salon*, October 29, 2018, https://www.salon.com/2018/10/29/tech-companies-spending-millions-to-oppose-san-franciscos-homelessness-tax/.

42: MUSLIMS ACCOUNT FOR 1 PERCENT OF THE U.S. POPULATION, BUT RADICAL ISLAMIST EXTREMISTS ACCOUNTED FOR MORE THAN 50 PERCENT OF DEATHS BY EXTREMISTS

1. U.S. Government Accountability Office, "Countering Violent Extremism: Actions Needed to Define Strategy and Assess Progress of Federal Efforts." April 6, 2017, www.gao.gov/products/GAO-17-300.
2. Besheer Mohamed, "New Estimates Show U.S. Mulsim Population Continues to Grow," Pew Research Center, January 3, 2018, https://www.pewresearch.org/fact-tank/2018/01/03/new-estimates-show-u-s-muslim-population-continues-to-grow/.
3. Sophie Chou, "More Than 75% of Terror Attacks in 2016 Took Place in Just 10 Countries," *USA Today*, July 14, 2017, https://www.usatoday.com/story/news/world/2017/07/14/terrorist-attacks-2016-isis-10-countries/480336001/.
4. Alan Travis, "UK Terror-Related Arrests Rose Almost 60% to Record High in 2017," *The Gardian*, March 8, 2018, https://www.theguardian.com/uk-news/2018/mar/08/uk-terror-related-arrests-rose-almost-60-to-record-high-in-2017.

43: CHINA IS HOLDING TWO MILLION MUSLIMS IN INTERNMENT CAMP SWEATSHOPS

1. John Hayward, "China Calls Concentration Camps for Uighur Muslims 'Boarding Schools,'" Breitbart News, March 12, 2019, https://www.breitbart.com/national-security/2019/03/12/china-boarding-schools-for-uighur-muslims-may-gradually-disappear-when-society-does-not-need-them/.
2. Frances Martel, "State Media China Creating a Branch of Islam 'Fitting Chinese Culture,'" Breitbart News, April 8, 2019, https://www.breitbart.com/asia/2019/04/08/state-media-internment-camps-creating-a-branch-of-islam-fitting-chinese-culture/.
3. Kathleen E. McLaughlin, "What Really Happened in Urumqi?," *Foreign Policy*, June 24, 2010, https://foreignpolicy.com/2010/06/24/what-really-happened-in-urumqi/.
4. Jonathan Spence, *God's Chinese Son: The Taiping Heavenly Kingdom of Hong Xiuquan*, (New York: W. W. Norton, 1997).
5. U.S. Department of State, "Human Rights Report," March 13, 2019. Accessed

April 15, 2019, https://www.state.gov/j/drl/rls/hrrpt/humanrightsreport
/index.htm#wrapper.

6. Austin Ramzy, "After U.S.-Based Reporters Exposed Abuses, China Seized
Their Relatives," *New York Times*, March 1, 2018, https://www.nytimes
.com/2018/03/01/world/asia/china-xinjiang-rfa.html.

7. Dake Kang, Martha Mendoza, and Yanan Wang, "US Sportswear Traced
to Factory in China's Internment Camps," Associated Press, December
19, 2018, https://apnews.com/99016849cddb4b99a048b863b52c28cb?utm
_medium=AP&utm_source=Twitter&utm_campaign=SocialFlow.

8. John Hayward, "Saudi Prince Defends China's Re-Education Camps for Uighur Muslims," Breitbart News, February 24, 2019, https://www.breitbart
.com/national-security/2019/02/24/saudi-crown-prince-defends-chinas
-re-education-camps-for-uighur-muslims/.

9. Edwin Mora, "Pompeo: China's Oppression of Religion Reaches 'Historic
Proportions,'" Breitbart News, April 10, 2019, https://www.breitbart.com
/national-security/2019/04/10/pompeo-chinas-orwellian-oppression-muslims
-christians-reaches-historic-proportions/.

10. Frances Martel, "China Allows Cuban, Venezuelan Diplomats to Tour Muslim Internment Camps," Breitbart News, February 18, 2019, https://www
.breitbart.com/national-security/2019/02/18/china-allows-cuban-venezuelan
-diplomats-tour-muslim-internment-camps/.

44: LARGE-SCALE MINIMUM WAGE HIKES HAVE LED TO LAYOFFS, DECREASED HOURS, AND FEWER JOBS

1. Senator Bernie Sanders, "Top Democrats Introduce Bill Raising Minimum Wage to $15," January 16, 2019, https://www.sanders.senate.gov
/newsroom/press-releases/top-democrats-introduce-bill-raising-minimum
-wage-to-15.

2. U.S. Bureau of Labor Statistics, "Characteristics of Minimum Wage Workers,
2017: BLS Reports," March 1, 2018, https://www.bls.gov/opub/reports
/minimum-wage/2017/home.htm.

3. American Action Forum, "Recent State Minimum Wage Increase Will Result
in 1.7 Million Lost Jobs," AAF website, n.d. Accessed April 15, 2019, https://
www.americanactionforum.org/press-release/recent-state-minimum
-wage-increase-will-result-in-1-7-million-lost-jobs/.

4. Michael Sainato, "Whole Foods Cuts Workers' Hours After Amazon Introduces Minimum Wage," *The Guardian*, March 6, 2019, https://www
.theguardian.com/us-news/2019/mar/06/whole-foods-amazon-cuts
-minimum-wage-workers-hours-changes.

5. John Merline, "$15 Minimum Wages Sparks a Jobs Recession in New York,"

Investor's Business Daily, February 20, 2019, https://www.investors.com/politics/editorials/minimum-wage-new-york-jobs-recession/.

6. Ibid.

45: ECONOMISTS PREDICTED A TRUMP VICTORY WOULD CRASH THE STOCK MARKET. INSTEAD IT HIT A RECORD HIGH THE WEEK AFTER HE WAS ELECTED

1. Patricia Cohen, "An Economic Upturn Begun Under Obama Is Now Trump's to Tout," *New York Times*, August 10, 2018, https://www.nytimes.com/2018/08/10/business/economy/trump-economy-credit.html.
2. John Carney, "All the Experts Who Told Us Stocks Would Crash If Trump Won," Breitbart News, November 9, 2017, https://www.breitbart.com/politics/2017/11/08/all-the-experts-who-told-us-stocks-would-crash-if-trump-won/.
3. Chauncy L. Alcorn, "Mark Cuban Predicts Stock Market Mayhem If Trump Wins the White House," *Fortune*, September 7, 2016. Accessed April 15, 2019, http://fortune.com/2016/09/07/mark-cuban-criticizes-trump/.
4. Terry Jones, "And the Hits Just Kept Coming: The Greatest (False) Predictions of 2017," *Investor's Business Daily*, December 28, 2017, https://www.investors.com/politics/columnists/and-the-hits-just-kept-coming-the-greatest-false-predictions-of-2017/.
5. Luke Kawa, "Citigroup: A Trump Victory in November Could Cause a Global Recession," *Bloomberg News*, August 25, 2016. Accessed April 15, 2019, https://www.bloomberg.com/news/articles/2016-08-25/citigroup-a-trump-victory-in-november-could-cause-a-global-recession.
6. Marmor Shaw and Terrence Horan, "All of the Important Dow Milestones in One Chart," *MarketWatch*, January 5, 2018, https://www.marketwatch.com/story/all-of-the-important-dow-milestones-in-one-chart-2016-12-28.
7. Sylvan Lane, "Trump Hits Obama for 2016 'Magic Wand' Comment About Economy," *The Hill*, September 10, 2018, https://thehill.com/policy/finance/405878-trump-bashes-obama-for-2016-magic-wand-comment-about-economy.

46: FAMILY SEPARATION AND DETENTION OF ILLEGAL ALIENS AT THE BORDER EXPLODED UNDER PRESIDENT OBAMA AND DHS SECRETARY JEH JOHNSON

1. Franco Ordonez and Anita Kumar, "Yes, Obama Separated Families at the Border, Too," McClatchy Washington Bureau, April 9, 2019, https://www.mcclatchydc.com/news/politics-government/white-house/article213525764.html.

2. Politico, "'If there's any suspicion that they're not really truly related to those people, then they will be separated for their own safety,' a chief border agent said of kids who are often recycled by smugglers to get adults into the United States." Pic.twitter.com/f3PBT57Q5T," @politico, Twitter, June 18, 2018, https://twitter.com/politico/status/1008736577265291264.

3. Ines Novacic, "U.S. Border Officer: 'Do You Think a Wall Is Gonna Stop Them?," CBS News, August 30, 2016. Accessed April 15, 2019, https://www .cbsnews.com/news/border-patrol-officers-us-mexico-border-wall/.

4. Department of Homeland Security, "DHS Releases End of Year Statistics," December 19, 2014, https://www.dhs.gov/news/2014/12/19/dhs-releases -end-year-statistics.

5. David Martosko, "Political journalism needs a bit of housecleaning on this child border crisis. I'll start. It was going on during the Obama years in large numbers. I never wrote about it. Was completely unaware, in large part because few reporters were interested enough to create critical mass," Twitter, @dmartosko, June 18, 2018, https://twitter.com/dmartosko/status /1008552828418363392?lang=en.

6. Department of Homeland Security, "U.S. Customs and Border Protection Border Patrol Chief Michael Fisher's Testimony on 'Securing Our Borders— Operational Control and the Path Forward,'" February 15, 2011, https:// www.dhs.gov/news/2011/02/15/us-customs-and-border-protection-border -patrol-chief-michael-fishers-testimony.

7. Tina Vasquez, "Before Jeff Sessions Separated Immigrant Families, Obama Did It," *Rewire.News,* June 26, 2018, https://rewire.news/article/2018/05/08 /jeff-sessions-separated-immigrant-families-obama/.

8. Colin Kalmbacher, "Obama's Immigration Agencies Separated Children from Their Families, Too," *Law & Crime,* June 18, 2018), https://lawand crime.com/immigration/obamas-immigration-agencies-separated-children -from-their-families-too/.

9. Rivas, "Here Are Some of the Democrats Who Paved the Way for Family Separation Crisis."

47: ILLEGAL IMMIGRATION MAY HAVE COST BLACK AMERICANS MORE THAN I MILLION JOBS

1. Ian Mason, "U.S. Civil Rights Commissioner Urges Trump to Get Better DACA Deal for Black Men's Sake," Breitbart News, September 20, 2017, https:// www.breitbart.com/politics/2017/09/19/u-s-civil-rights-commissioner -urges-trump-to-get-better-daca-deal-for-black-mens-sake/.

2. John Binder, "Civil Rights Commissioner Scolds DACA Amnesty Plan: Black Americans Will Be 'Disproportionately' Harmed," Breitbart News, Janu-

ary 11, 2018, https://www.breitbart.com/politics/2018/01/10/civil-rights
-commissioner-scolds-daca-amnesty-plan-african-americans-will-be
-disproportionately-harmed/.
3. Camarota, Richwine, and Zeigler, "There Are No Jobs Americans Won't Do."
4. Aubrey Shines, "Black America, Face the Facts on Illegal Immigtaion,"
RealClear Politics, May 4, 2018. https://www.realclearpolitics.com/articles
/2018/05/04/black_america_face_the_facts_on_illegal_immigration
_136979.html.

48: THERE HAVE BEEN MORE THAN 630 EXAMPLES OF LEFT-WING POLITICAL VIOLENCE AND THREATS AGAINST TRUMP SUPPORTERS

1. John Nolte, "Rap Sheet: ***639*** Acts of Media-Approved Violence and Harassment Against Trump Supporters," Breitbart News, November 5, 2018, https://www.breitbart.com/the-media/2018/07/05/rap-sheet-acts-of
-media-approved-violence-and-harassment-against-trump-supporters/.
2. Breitbart News, "Protesters Pepper Spray Trump Supporters, Hitting 8-Year-Old Girl," April 27, 2016, https://www.breitbart.com/local/2016/04/27
/protesters-pepper-spray-trump-supporters-hitting-8-year-old-girl/.
3. Ashley May, "Antifa Protesters Chant Outside Fox's Tucker Carlson's Home, Break Door," *USA Today*, November 8, 2018, https://www.usatoday.com
/story/news/politics/2018/11/08/mob-tucker-carlsons-home-antifa-break
-door-chant-fox-host/1927868002/.
4. Noah Berlatsky, "GOP Trend of Demonizing Dissent Comes from a Troubling Playbook," CNN, October 17, 2018, https://www.cnn.com/2018/10/16
/opinions/trump-calling-democrats-a-mob-berlatsky/index.html.
5. Katherine Rodriguez, "Nick Sandmann's Lawyers Release Video 'The Truth' About 'March for Life,'" Breitbart News, February 5, 2019, https://
www.breitbart.com/politics/2019/02/04/watch-nick-sandmanns-lawyers
-release-video-of-the-truth-about-march-for-life/.
6. Joshua Caplan, "Nick Sandmann Sues Washington Post for $250 Million," Breitbart News, February 20, 2019, https://www.breitbart.com/the
-media/2019/02/19/nick-sandmann-sues-washington-post-for-250-million
-over-defamatory-coverage/.

49: DICK'S SPORTING GOODS' ANTI-GUN POLICY RESULTED IN A $150 MILLION LOSS FOR THE COMPANY, BUT THE LEFT'S APPROVAL IS WORTH MORE

1. AwR Hawkins, "Dick's CEO Okay with $150 Million Loss over Gun Control Stance," Breitbart News, March 31, 2019, https://www.breitbart.com

/politics/2019/03/31/dicks-ceo-okay-companys-150-million-loss-gun-control-stance/.

2. Matthew Rocco, "Levi Strauss CEO Calls for Stricter Gun Laws," Fox Business, September 5, 2018, https://www.foxbusiness.com/retail/levi-strauss-ceo-calls-for-stricter-gun-laws.

3. Tiffany Hsu, "Citigroup Sets Restrictions on Gun Sales by Business Partners," *New York Times*, March 22, 2018, https://www.nytimes.com/2018/03/22/business/citigroup-gun-control-policy.html.

4. Laura J. Keller and Polly Mosendz, "BofA Will Stop Lending to Makers of Assault-Style Guns," *Bloomberg News*, April 10, 2018. Accessed April 15, 2019, https://www.bloomberg.com/news/articles/2018–04–10/bofa-will-no-longer-lend-to-some-gunmakers-vice-chairman-says.

5. Robert Spencer et al., "Southern Poverty Law Center Gets MasterCard and Visa to Stop Taking Donations for David Horowitz Freedom Center," *Jihad Watch*, August 25, 2018, https://www.jihadwatch.org/2018/08/southern-poverty-law-center-gets-mastercard-and-visa-to-stop-taking-donations-for-david-horowitz-freedom-center.

6. David Goldman, "North Carolina Loses 400 Jobs as Paypal Pulls Facility," CNN, April 5, 2016. Accessed April 15, 2019, https://money.cnn.com/2016/04/05/technology/paypal-north-carolina-lgbt/index.html.

7. "Amazon Bans Racial Identity Books Following Quartz Article Decrying Amazon Selling Nazi Books," *One Angry Gamer*, February 28, 2019, https://www.oneangrygamer.net/2019/02/amazon-bans-racial-identity-books-following-quartz-article-decrying-amazon-selling-nazi-books/78168/.

8. Ibid.

9. "Theodore J. Kaczynski," Amazon, accessed April 15, 2019, https://www.amazon.com/s?k=Theodore+J.+Kaczynski&i=digital-text&ref=nb_sb_noss.

10. Helen A. S. Popkin, "Amazon Defends 'Pedophile's Guide,'" NBCNews.com, November 10, 2010, http://www.nbcnews.com/id/40112145/ns/technology_and_science-digital_home/t/amazon-defends-pedophiles-guide/.

50: CHRISTIANITY IS THE WORLD'S MOST PERSECUTED RELIGION

1. Thomas D. Williams, "Nigerian Muslim Militants Kill 120 Christians in Three Weeks," Breitbart News, March 16, 2019, https://www.breitbart.com/africa/2019/03/16/nigerian-muslim-militants-kill-120-christians-three-weeks/.

2. "Nigerian Muslim Militants Kill 120 Christians in Three Weeks—Where Is the Outrage?" *MetroVoice*, March 17, 2019, https://metrovoicenews.com

/nigerian-muslim-militants-kill-120-christians-in-three-weeks-where-is
-the-outrage/.

3. Thomas D. Williams, "Boko Haram Launches Lethal Attack on Christian
Town in Nigeria," Breitbart News, March 20, 2019, https://www.breitbart
.com/africa/2019/03/20/boko-haram-launches-lethal-attack-christian
-town-northeast-nigeria/.

4. Robert Kraychik, "Expert: Media Downplay Islamic Slaughter of Nigerian
Christians," Breitbart News, March 19, 2019, https://www.breitbart.com
/radio/2019/03/19/human-rights-expert-islamic-persecution-of-nigerian
-christians-does-not-fit-narrative-mainstream-media/.

5. Dede Laugesen, interview by Rebecca Mansour and Joel Pollak, *Breitbart
News Tonight*, March 18, 2019, https://soundcloud.com/breitbart/breitbart
-news-tonight-dede-laugesen-march-18-2019.

6. Morning Star News India Correspondent, "Report: 57% Jump in Church
Persecution in India," *Baptist Press*, March 5, 2019, http://www.bpnews
.net/52518/report—57-jump-in-church-persecution-in-india.

7. Emily Birnbaum, "Rubio Calls Out China for 'Burning Bibles'," *The Hill*,
September 10, 2018, https://thehill.com/homenews/senate/405849-rubio
-calls-out-china-for-burning-bibles.

8. Associated Press and Kelsey Cheng, "Christianity Crackdown: China De-
molishes Churches, Confiscates Bibles," *Daily Mail Online*, August 8, 2018,
https://www.dailymail.co.uk/news/china/article-6034995/Christian
-heartland-opens-window-fight-Chinas-soul.html.

9. Thomas D. Williams, "Cardinal Zen: China Catholics Witnessing 'Sellout
of Our Church,'" Breitbart News, January 25, 2019, https://www.breitbart
.com/asia/2019/01/25/exclusive-cardinal-zen-says-chinas-catholics
-witnessing-sellout-our-church/.

10. ABC News, "Churches Condemned and Torn Down in Indonesia's Aceh
Following Religious Violence," October 19, 2015, https://www.abc.net.au
/news/2015—10—19/aceh-province-tears-down-churches-after-religious
-tension/6867036.

11. Anthony Faiola and Stephanie Kirchner, "'Allahu Akbar'-Chanting Mob
Sets Alight Germany's Oldest Church? Shocking Story, if It Were True,"
Washington Post, January 6, 2017, www.washingtonpost.com/world/europe
/allahu-akbar-chanting-mob-sets-alight-germanys-oldest-church
-shocking-story-if-it-were-true/2017/01/06/30470f58-d36a-11e6—9651
—54a0154cf5b3_story.html.

12. Raymond Ibrahim, "European Churches: Vandalized, Defecated On, and
Torched 'Every Day,'" Gatestone Institute, April 14, 2019, https://www
.gatestoneinstitute.org/14044/europe-churches-vandalized.

13. Thomas D. Williams, "Twelve French Churches Attacked, Vandalized in

One Week," Breitbart News, March 20, 2019, https://www.breitbart.com
/faith/2019/03/20/twelve-french-churches-attacked-vandalized-in-one
-week/.

14. Peter Burns and Nariman El-Mofty, "Christians Are the World's Most-Per-
    secuted Religion—Here's How They React Under Fire," *Washington
    Examiner*, September 18, 2017, https://www.washingtonexaminer.com
    /christians-are-the-worlds-most-persecuted-religion-heres-how-they
    -react-under-fire.

ABOUT THE AUTHOR

Jerome Hudson began writing for Breitbart in 2013. As the entertainment editor, he heads a team that specializes in "holding a mirror up to Hollywood." Prior to writing for Breitbart, Hudson worked at the Government Accountability Institute with author, investigative journalist, and political commentator Peter Schweizer. Hudson was heavily involved in uncovering government fraud associated with "Obama phones," and investigated big businesses such as Xerox and J. P. Morgan and how they profited from America's Supplemental Nutrition Assistance Program (SNAP), commonly referred to as food stamps, among many other projects. He is a member of the National Center for Public Policy Research's Project 21: Black Leadership Network, and he serves on the organization's national advisory council. Hudson was born and raised, by two loving parents, in Savannah, Georgia.